THE COLORS OF CHILDHOOD

THE COLORS
OF CHILDHOOD
Separation-Individuation
Across Cultural, Racial,
and Ethnic Differences

edited by
SALMAN AKHTAR, M.D.,
and SELMA KRAMER, M.D.

JASON ARONSON INC.
Northvale, New Jersey
London

This book was set in 12 point Bembo by Alpha Graphics of Pittsfield, NH and printed and bound by Book-mart Press, Inc. of North Bergen, New Jersey.

10 9 8 7 6 5 4 3 2 1

Library of Congress Cataloging-in-Publication Data
The colors of childhood : separation-individuation across cultural,
    racial, and ethnic differences / edited by Salman Akhtar and Selma
    Kramer.
        p.   cm.
    Includes bibliographical references and index.
    ISBN 0-7657-0155-3 (alk. paper)
    1. Separation-individuation—Cross-cultural studies.   2. Child
rearing—Cross-cultural studies.   3. Cultural psychiatry.
    I. Akhtar, Salman, 1946 July 31-   II. Kramer, Selma.
    RC489.S45C64   1998
    155.4—DC21   97-45188

Printed in the United States of America on acid-free paper. Jason Aronson offers books and cassettes. For information and catalog write to Jason Aronson Inc., 230 Livingston Street, Northvale, New Jersey 07647-1731. Or visit our website: http://www.aronson.com

To the memory

of

Margaret S. Mahler

teacher, friend, source of inspiration

Contents

Acknowledgment

The chapters in this book, with the exception of the last one, were originally presented as papers at the 28th Annual Margaret S. Mahler Symposium on Child Development held on April 26, 1997, in Philadelphia. First and foremost, therefore, we wish to express our gratitude to the Margaret S. Mahler Psychiatric Research Foundation. We are also grateful to Troy L. Thompson II, M.D., Chairman, at that time, of the Department of Psychiatry and Human Behavior, Jefferson Medical College, as well as to the Philadelphia Psychoanalytic Institute and Society for their shared sponsorship of the symposium. Many colleagues from the Institute and Society helped during the symposium, and we remain grateful to them. Finally, we wish to acknowledge our sincere appreciation of Maryann Nevin for her efficient organization of and assistance during the symposium, and her outstanding skills in the preparation of this book's manuscript.

Contributors

Salman Akhtar, M.D.
Professor of Psychiatry, Jefferson Medical College; Training and Supervising Analyst, Philadelphia Psychoanalytic Institute

Jennifer Bonovitz, Ph.D.
Faculty, Philadelphia Psychoanalytic Institute; Faculty, Institute of the Philadelphia Society for Clincial Social Work; Co-Chair, South Asia Forum of the Philadelphia Psychoanalytic Institute and Society

Daniel M. A. Freeman, M.D.
Adult and Child Analyst, Philadelphia Psychoanalytic Institute; Clinical Associate Professor, Allegheny University–MCP-Hahnemann School of Medicine; Clinical Associate Professor, Medical College of Pennsylvania; Chairman, Anthropology–Psychoanalysis Interdisciplinary Colloquium of the American Psychoanalytic Association

Selma Kramer, M.D.
Professor of Psychiatry, Jefferson Medical College; Training and Supervising Analyst, Philadelphia Psychoanalytic Institute

Purnima Mehta, M.D.
Faculty, Michigan Psychoanalytic Institute; Private Practice of Child/Adolescent and Adult Psychoanalysis; President-Elect, Michigan Psychoanalytic Society

Carlotta Miles, M.D.
Faculty, Extension Division, Washington Psychoanalytic Institute; Psychiatric Consultant; The Johns Hopkins School of International Studies, The National Cathedral School for Girls, and The Madeira School; Private Practice of Adult and Child Psychiatry

Henri Parens, M.D.
Professor of Psychiatry, Jefferson Medical College; Training and Supervising Analyst, Philadelphia Psychoanalytic Institute

Calvin F. Settlage, M.D.
Training and Supervising Analyst Emeritus in Adult and Child Analysis, San Francisco Psychoanalytic Institute; Clinical Professor of Psychiatry, University of California

1

SOME CULTURAL VICISSITUDES OF CHILD REARING

Selma Kramer, M.D.

A child's development depends upon the complex interplay between his constitutional givens and the facilitating and/or inhibiting attributes of his caregiving environment. Contemporary theory builders are beginning to recognize that this environment consists of not only parents but also siblings (Kernberg and Richards 1988, Leichtman 1985, Neubauer 1983, Provence and Solnit 1983) and grandparents (Cath 1982, 1997, Kramer et al. 1997, Madow 1997). They are also acknowledging the role of the culture at large in influencing the child's growth. It is to this last factor that this volume is dedicated. Three ethnic and racial groups, namely African American, Japanese, and East-Asian Indian Americans, are dealt with here. Patterns of child rearing in each are discussed and the roles of intrapsychic, interpersonal, and socioeconomic factors are highlighted. Extremely important while these issues are, a sharper focus on them might beneficially be preceded by a reminder that family life and child-rearing patterns have undergone considerable changes within the United States over the past few decades.

THE CHANGING AMERICAN FAMILY

Over the last 45 years of practicing adult and child psychoanalysis, I have noted many significant changes in the structure of the American family as well as in its child-rearing methods. When I began my practice, few mothers worked. There were also relatively few single-parent families, especially among the white population. This is no longer true, and we are seeing increasing, even alarming, numbers of single-parent families in the lower-class and lower middle-class white population. We are also seeing a rapidly diminishing number of mothers who are able to (or who choose to) stay home throughout the early formative years of their children's lives. The rise of the working mother has necessitated day-care and pre-school programs and, in more affluent circumstances, the use of nannies. All these practices have a considerable influence on childhood development. Interestingly, I do not discern any increased pathology in children of working mothers especially if the parents recognize the potential difficulties and attempt to fulfill their children's libidinal and anaclitic needs. Hiring full-time nannies, paradoxically, may lull the parents into thinking that all the child's needs are being met and thus end up depriving the child in crucial ways.

Recently, a new phenomenon has also come to light. Working mothers are tending to defer pregnancy until their careers are well established. Consequently, they do not become pregnant until they are into their late thirties or even forties. Often there is difficulty in conceiving, and the couple seeks to adopt a child. In either case, many newborns end up having older mothers and older fathers. The influence of this upon the growing child's ego needs further investigation. In my own child analytic experience, the situation tends to cause frequent problems. This is especially so since our culture is given to rapid changes, and the ego skills of older parents are much further removed from what a growing child needs to acquire to encounter his world in an efficacious way.

Two other cultural trends have affected child rearing. First, the economic pressures on the family and the demands of the job market frequently force the family to move. Thus visits to the extended family are infrequent. This precludes the possibility of the grandparents filling the voids left by parents in caring for the children. Fortunately, there is now some reversal of this trend and economic pressures are forcing couples with children to rely upon their own parents for child care, thus rekindling the grandparent–grandchild relationship of the old days in a new context.

Second, the media have influenced growing children in a profound way. Television shows such as "Sesame Street" and "Mister Rogers" are educational and teach children fairness, kindness, and love. Other programs that accentuate aggression and sexuality are unfortunately more prevalent and may have adverse affects on children. When we add the current violent and highly sexualized television scenes with the ready availability of drugs, we may conclude that children and adolescents in the United States develop against heavy odds. Drugs, I must note, are not the sole province of the underclass. I have treated a number of adolescents who took and, at times, dealt drugs. Their parents disapproved of them but not infrequently used marijuana themselves!

All in all, it seems that most of the changes in old traditions have been harmful to children. A very positive change I see is that American men are making themselves more available to their children, especially when their wives hold jobs. The development facilitating role of the father is thus becoming more central.

In sum, then, American children are (1) increasingly raised in broken and/or single-parent homes; (2) placed earlier and for longer durations in day care, owing largely to the mother's need to work and earn wages; (3) attended to by their fathers more, and, absent fathers notwithstanding, there seems to be a greater involvement of fathers in early child rearing; (4) often looked after by grandparents; and (5) affected by socioeconomic factors, including the changing ethnic and racial demography, around them.

The role of the father, the role of the grandparents, and the role of economic factors especially affect the children of ethnic minorities. On a somewhat optimistic note, certain measures might improve the situation of lower-class African-Americans and improve their child-rearing skills, as we shall see, below.

THE FATHER'S ROLE

Freud (1930) declared that he "can not think of any need in childhood as strong as the need for a father's protection" (p. 72). However, for the following two decades, psychoanalytic developmental theory did not pay adequate attention to the father's role in child development. Then, in 1951 Loewald emphasized the degree to which the father's role was a powerful force against the threat of reengulfment by the mother of a child of either sex. Mahler and Gosliner (1955) pointed out the father's role in development of the ego and of superego precursors in the child. Greenacre (1966) pointed out that the overidealization of the male analyst and of analysis frequently reflected the important role of the father in the first two years of the child's life. Mahler (1967) agreed with this and emphasized that the child reacted to the father as a "breath of fresh air," one who was different from the mother and was more playful. Benedek (1970) addressed the ego building influence of the "father's identification with his child and . . . the father's identification with his own father" (p. 173). Benedek states that "it is pertinent to recall the influence that the father's changing position within his family exerts upon the personality development of his children, especially upon his sons" (p. 176). Abelin (1971), who worked with Mahler, introduced the concept of *triangulation* as he described the role of the father during the preoedipal years of the child's development. Abelin reported child observations that revealed the ego-building, noncompetitive (in the boy), and nonerotic (in the girl) role of the father.

Akhtar (1995), who has recently summarized the multifaceted role of the father in child development, sees it as consisting of the following four tasks:

(1) By being a protective, loving, and collaborative partner to the mother, the father facilitates and enhances her ability to devote herself to the child. (2) By offering himself as a relatively neutral, ego-oriented, new object during the rapprochement subphase of separation-individuation, the father provides the child with stability, a haven from conflict, and (in the case of a boy) an important measure of "disidentification" (Greenson 1968) from the mother. (3) By appearing on the evolving psychic horizon of the child as the romantic partner of the mother, the father helps consolidate the child's capacity to experience, bear, and benefit from the triangular familial relationship and the conflicts attendant upon it. (4) By presenting himself as an admirable model for identification to his son and by reflecting the budding femininity of his daughter with restrained reciprocity, the father enriches his children's gender identity and gives direction to their later sexual object choices. [p. 77]

All this results in a powerful impact on both the ego and superego, especially in the realm of disengagement from mother, language organization, modulation of aggression, establishment of incest barrier, acceptance of generational boundaries, capacity to respect and idealize elders, entry into the temporal order, and, through it, a deeper sense of familial and ethnic affiliation. It is with such a backdrop that we can now take a close look at the cultural and subcultural variations in the father's contribution to his child's growth.

Freeman's contribution to this book (Chapter 2) begins by emphasizing the tremendous gratification afforded by the Japanese mothers to their children, especially their sons. Japanese mothers maintain physical contact with their children much longer than do their Western counterparts. Such deeply gratifying indulgence in the baby is continued, at least intermittently, for many years. Freeman describes the important consequences of such mothering in infants during the symbiotic phase and early phases of separation-individuation. He proposes that they do not experience the frustration and resultant anger seen in children of other cultures.

The mother is always physically and emotionally there for the child's needs. However, pressures by the outside world in Japan put the mother and child under great strain. Although early schooling appears mostly benevolent, the teachers' emphasis upon children's responsibilities for the cleanliness of the school and cooperation among themselves might burden the little child's ego. This strain becomes tremendous in high school when students must compete in rigorous college entrance tests. Once accepted into college, the students shed their responsibilities and spend the remainder of their time cavorting and drinking, as if to express negativism toward parentally based authority and the hitherto immense pressure to be "good."

Where does the role of the father fit into this interesting picture? Do the Japanese children not require the structure provided by the father? Could the mothers' need to indulge their children arise because they feel libidinally isolated from the children's fathers? In Japan, fathers are not at home very much as infants and children are growing up. Hard work, a long working day, and often considerable daily travel to their jobs do not permit them to spend much time at home. Even when Japanese fathers do not have to work late, they often spend evenings with their male colleagues[1] or, at times, with their mistresses. This disregard of the duties of fathering perhaps contributes to the reported rebellion in their children during late high school and early college years.

In Indian families, both here and in India itself, children are also overindulged by their mothers, but as far as I know, not to the degree encountered in Japan. Still, Roland (1996) states that "the boy never loses his mother" (p. 136). He goes on to state that "strivings for separation, autonomy, initiative, and self-direction—the hallmark of current American child rearing—are discouraged in the Indian context for dependence and interdependence." Not

---

[1]At times working men and their bosses go out together drinking. During such occasions, the usually inhibited men feel free to criticize their bosses, saying to them things they otherwise would never feel free to say (Jordan Kramer, M.D., personal communication, July 1997).

surprisingly, the marital relationship of adults thus raised does not assume the intensity that it does in the American nuclear family.

Roland (1988, 1996) describes the Indian father as an overtly distant disciplinarian who formulates and embodies the ideals of the family. Female children's ideals and self-discipline are usually generated by the mother who "(point) their finger at improper behavior of other girls and then (convey) how gossip about the other girls' behavior could damage her family's reputation" (1996, p. 139). This attitude carries over with immigration. Indian families living in the United States often equate their children's Americanization with licentious sexuality, and they therefore impose ideals and discipline that can inhibit individuation and growth.[2] Dr. Mehta's clinical material (Chapter 6) illustrates such difficulties and their technical handling well.

I have not encountered the terrible depression that Mehta described in young Indian-American people in Michigan when they felt they had disappointed their parents by failing to enter medical school. However, I have encountered three bitter, depressive men who became physicians because their parents (of my generation) insisted their sons go to medical school. In spite of success in their medical careers, they hated medical practice; now in their 40s and 50s they feel they now, as then, have no alternative!

In contrast to Japanese families and Indian families where the father, however busy with his own matters, is more or less present, the lowest-class black families, as described by Dr. Miles, consist of only the mother and her children (Chapter 4). There is no father and husband. The usual source of ego expansion and superego formation is missing. This is a great disadvantage to the children, especially the boys in the family. The ensuing structural defects can,

---

[2]The Indian-American family's imposition upon their children of limited career choices (with medicine being the most desirable) reminds me of the Jewish neighborhood in which I grew up. Children there were not encouraged to enter their parents' businesses. Successful children were expected to study hard and to attend college and professional schools. No wonder six children from our one city block became physicians!

to some extent, be mended if a lucky child of this lowest class en-
counters a benevolent male teacher or neighborhood adult. If the
child possesses some special talent that is recognized and promoted
by this man, the outcome might indeed be outstanding.

THE ROLE OF THE GRANDPARENTS

It is well known that in Japanese and Indian families there is a tradition of respect, even reverence, for elders. It is the expectation
that the eldest son and his wife will share a home with his parents
throughout their lives. While living in this fashion may be burdensome to both the son's parents and the young children in the family, the role of grandparents in facilitating the development of the
child's personality, recently recognized by psychoanalysis (Benedek
1970, Cath 1982, 1997, Kramer et al. 1997), gets magnified under
such circumstances.

Grandparenthood is often referred to as a "new lease on life"
(Benedek 1970b, p. 199) by grandparents themselves and also by
the new parents who are proud of their ability to foster this status
upon their parents.[3] Grandparents are often adored by their grandchildren since the grandparents, not having the responsibility of
rearing them, can afford to be more lenient toward them. More
important, grandparents can compensate for deficits in libidinal
supplies from parents and act as a buffer between parents and their
children. They might also play a role in letting the parents have some
child-free time and, at a deeper level, thus facilitate the mother's
letting go of her child's mind and body. Grandparents thus enhance
the separation-individuation of a growing child.

---

[3]Ernest Jones, visiting the Philadelphia Psychoanalytic Institute many years ago,
spoke of the mutual affection and respect between the second generation of analysts
and Freud. Comparing it to a grandparent–grandchild relationship, Jones said that Freud
and the second-generation analysts shared antagonism toward the in-between (parent)
generation.

Dr. Miles's description of lower class and lower middle-class black families, in which the father is not present, reminded me of a commonly encountered family picture at a well-baby psychiatric clinic that some of us, under the aegis of Calvin Settlage, established many years ago at St. Christopher's Hospital in Philadelphia. Young unmarried women, their babies, and the children's maternal grandmothers attended the clinic. An interesting configuration was often noticeable. The grandmother carried the baby while the mother carried coats, umbrellas, and the diaper bag. The grandmother asked questions and replied to our queries. When staff members attempted to involve the mother, the grandmother took over. Discussions held alone with the grandmother revealed that this pattern duplicated what had occurred in her life—her children had been raised by her own mother. At times she had been encouraged, even forced, to send her children "down South" to her mother's home.

I sometimes had the impression that the young mother felt obliged to offer her child as a gift to the child's grandmother, as if to make up for her earlier loss. Unlike Japanese and Indian joint families, where the role of grandparents was secondary even if important, the role of the grandmother in such situations became almost a primary maternal one.

AN OPTIMISTIC NOTE

Some measures might improve the situation of the lower-class and lower middle-class black families and their child-rearing skills as well. Many years ago I had the pleasure of visiting Henri Parens's project, Education for Parenting, at the Medical College of Pennsylvania. For the most part, the black parents were from the ghetto. Their family structures were typical of those described by Dr. Miles in Chapter 4, and they lived in a low-cost housing project. As I visited this ongoing study population over a number of years, I could see a steady emotional and intellectual growth on the part of these mothers. I understand from Parens (personal communication, May

1997) that the black mothers were ill at ease at first. This feeling gradually abated during the course of my later visits; they appeared active, responsible, interested, and eager to learn and to teach. They told me that when they returned to the project in which they lived, other mothers crowded around them to find out what they had learned. Parens and his staff treated these mothers with the utmost respect and kindness. It appeared to me that they were "fed" in many ways: (1) they were treated with a respect quite new to them, (2) they were taught Mahler's separation-individuation theory in terms they could readily understand, and (3) they were considered to be capable of teaching other women in their housing project. It is important to note that *all* black mothers in this study returned to school to attain high school credits, and at least two went on to the community college. Respect had strengthened them and knowledge had enlightened them.[4] What this demonstrates is that lower-class blacks, hitherto written off by much of society, could, under optimal circumstances, become much more effective mothers and citizens. I therefore hope that there will be more efforts like the Parens program. On a more humble but no less important note, I hope that clinicians and social workers dealing with lower class African-Americans on a day-to-day basis will offer them the respect and education that was given them in this study. Reading Dr. Miles's contribution to this book (Chapter 4) will enhance their empathy with this population and thus be an important first step in this optimistic direction.

CONCLUSION

There are many similarities and differences in child-rearing practices around the world. What remains impressive, therefore, is that

---

[4]A mother whose rapprochement-subphase daughter was alternately climbing all over her and then insisting on running away said to me with pride, "I'd have thrown my older kids across the room when they did that. But now I know why she does it. I understand."

except under conditions of severe deprivation or physical or sexual abuse, most children around the world do reasonably well. This raises new challenges for psychoanalytic developmental theory. Its stable postulates and its potential cultural biases begin to draw our attention. The complexity of the issues involved is as daunting as it is engaging. Paul Kay (personal communication, 1997) has summarized the situation elegantly.

> Aside from visible cultural dynamisms and the interaction between culture and the individual, I have been impressed by the idea of the intrapsychic culture. Consisting of and created by the individual's unique set of beliefs, values, and practices derived from life experience, the conflicts and tendencies that they engender and the genetic endowment with which they continuously interact, there is within each child, adolescent, and adult a unique culture, or, rather, set of cultures. They are an everchanging mixture of opposing and complementary beliefs, trends, values, and attitudes associated with admired figures, pursuits, and institutions. Each inner world (the sex and aggressive worlds, the race world, the parent world, the sibling world, the friend world, the dating world, the baseball world, the money world, and the countless other intertwined worlds) has its heroes, beliefs, rituals, and institutions. The intrapsychic world is, to begin with, one might say, multicultural.
>
> That multicultural intrapsychic world lives in an uneasy and exciting relationship with changes in the external culture and the individual's perception of those changes. If there is a cultural divide out there, there is certainly a cultural divide in there. Many, many divides, indeed, in both realms. One grows up ceaselessly juggling both realms. One grows up ceaselessly juggling both the intrapsychic and the externally imposed cultures as they continuously progress and regress in their inescapable and rambunctious encounters.

It is my hope that the contributions of Drs. Freeman, Miles, and Mehta and their respective discussions by Drs. Settlage, Akhtar, and Bonovitz will provide the opportunity for a no less stimulating encounter to the readers of this book.

REFERENCES

Abelin, E. L. (1971). The role of the father in the separation-individuation process. In *Separation-Individuation: Essays in Honor of Margaret Mahler*, ed. J. B. McDevitt and C. F. Settlage, pp. 229–253. New York: International Universities Press.

Akhtar, S. (1995). *Quest for Answers: A Primer of Understanding and Treating Severe Personality Disorders*. Northvale, NJ: Jason Aronson.

Benedek, T. (1970a). Fatherhood and parenthood. In *Parenthood: Its Psychology and Psychopathology*, ed. E. J. Anthony and T. Benedek, pp. 169–183. Boston: Little, Brown.

—— (1970b). Parenthood during the life cycle. In *Parenthood: Its Psychology and Psychopathology*, ed. E. J. Anthony and T. Benedek, pp. 184–206. Boston: Little, Brown.

Cath, S. H. (1982). Vicissitudes of grandparenthood: a miracle of revitalization. In *Father and Child*, ed. S. Cath, A. Gurwitt, and J. M. Ross, pp. 329–337. Boston: Little, Brown.

—— (1997). Loss and restitution in late life. In *The Seasons of Life: Separation-Individuation Perspectives*, ed. S. Akhtar and S. Kramer, pp. 129–156. Northvale, NJ: Jason Aronson.

Freud, S. (1930). Civilization and its discontents. *Standard Edition* 21:59–145.

Greenacre, P. (1966). Problems of overidealization of the analyst and of analysis: their manifestations in the transference and countertransference relationship. *Psychoanalytic Study of the Child* 21:193–212. New York: International Universities Press.

Greenson, R. (1968). Dis-identifying from mother: its special importance for the boy. *International Journal of Psycho-Analysis* 49:370–374.

Kernberg, P., and Richards, A. (1988). Siblings of preadolescence: their role in development. *Psychoanalytic Inquiry* 8:51–65.

Kramer, S., Byerly, L. J., and Akhtar, S. (1997). Growing together, growing apart, growing up and growing down. In *The Seasons of Life*, ed. S. Akhtar and S. Kramer, pp. 1–22. Northvale, NJ: Jason Aronson.

Leichtman, M. (1985). Influence of an older sibling on the separation-individuation process. *Psychoanalytic Study of the Child* 40:111–161. New Haven, CT: Yale University Press.

Loewald, H. (1951). Ego and reality. *International Journal of Psycho-Analysis* 32:10–18.

Madow, L. (1997). On the way to a second symbiosis. In *The Seasons of Life*, ed. S. Akhtar and S. Kramer, pp. 159–170. Northvale, NJ: Jason Aronson.

Mahler, M. S. (1967). Discussion of problems of overidealization of the analyst and analysis by P. Greenacre. Abstracted in *Psychoanalytic Quarterly* 36:637.

Mahler, M. S., and Gosliner, B. J. (1955). On symbiotic child psychosis: genetic, dynamic, and restitutive aspects. *Psychoanalytic Study of the Child* 10:195–212. New York: International Universities Press.

Neubauer, P. (1983). The importance of the sibling experience. *Psychoanalytic Study of the Child* 38:325–336. New Haven, CT: Yale University Press.

Provence, S., and Solnit, A. (1983). Sibling experience promoting development. *Psychoanalytic Study of the Child* 38:337–350. New Haven, CT: Yale University Press.

Roland, A. (1988). *In Search of Self in India and Japan: Toward a Cross-Cultural Psychology*. Princeton, NJ: Princeton University Press.

——— (1996). *Cultural Pluralism and Psychoanalysis*. New York: Routledge.

2

EMOTIONAL REFUELING IN DEVELOPMENT, MYTHOLOGY, AND COSMOLOGY: THE JAPANESE SEPARATION-INDIVIDUATION EXPERIENCE

Daniel M. A. Freeman, M.D.

Reaching outward while remaining on mother's lap. Toyohiro.

Comparative cross-cultural studies offer us an opportunity to step back from assumptions of our own culture to gain a broader view of the diversity of human experience and to gain insights concerning intrapsychic development. In studying non-Western cultures it is possible to observe child-rearing and developmental experiences that contrast with those in our own society and their effects on intrapsychic development, personality development, object relations, and the overall structure and functioning of a society. Cross-cultural applied psychoanalytic research may also provide unique opportunities for testing psychoanalytic hypotheses and for naturalistic prospective child development studies. The child-rearing traditions of cultures other than our own provide us an opportunity to observe naturally occurring variations in human development. Especially in cultures that have developed a considerable degree of homogeneity and uniformity with regard to particular child-rearing practices, it is often possible to study relatively large samples of individuals where significant variables have been controlled by that culture's way of raising children.

In Japan, we have the additional opportunity of being able to work with colleagues who are engaged in studying *our* culture from *their* perspective. The most valuable questions and comments raised by our colleagues from other cultures are those that indicate that we and they at times may see or experience phenomena from different perspectives, or that indicate that something we say, or one of our concepts, doesn't make sense in their experience. This can help us to recognize ways in which our cultural filters are organizing our understanding of emotional data within culture-bound categories.

Over the centuries the Japanese have often become interested in ideas from other cultures, analyzing and modifying them to extract their essence, synthesizing them with older Japanese traditions, and adapting them to fit usefully into the fabric of their own culture. This was the case when they assimilated and incorporated many aspects of Confucian and Buddhist philosophy into Japanese culture in a way that complemented their older traditions. They have similarly selectively assimilated many aspects of Western culture and science that they find to be of value.

Japanese simultaneously experience two contrasting viewpoints or states of awareness, which Takeo Doi (1973b, 1986) has described as a dual or twofold structure of consciousness. On the one hand, they experience a very autonomous inner world of personal thoughts, true feelings, motives, and individual opinions that are hidden from others and that are called one's "back side." At the same time, they are conscious of their "front side," the overt appearance, face, or facade of refined cooperative restraint, reserve, and deference that one must present in public. In view of this duality of experience, it is perhaps not surprising that they developed a very early interest in our introspective psychoanalytic science. Japanese psychologists, educators, and writers became interested in psychoanalysis in the early 1900s. The first papers on psychoanalysis written in Japanese appeared in 1912 and 1914. Collections of Freud's works were translated into Japanese and published by the late 1920s. Because of Japanese patients' sensitivity to feelings of shame, their reticence in expressing feelings verbally, and the impropriety of revealing troubling aspects of one's private inner world, the therapeutic use of psychoanalysis developed somewhat more slowly. In 1932 Dr. Heisaku Kosawa traveled to Vienna and studied with Richard Sterba and Paul Federn in the Vienna Psychoanalytic Institute. When he returned he established the therapeutic practice of psychoanalysis (Okonogi 1997, Taketomo 1990).

Freud and Kosawa noticed that the developmental interactions and intrapsychic complexes they were studying were vividly portrayed in their culture's mythology, and they each named the triadic familial complex in their culture after the hero of their respective culture's Oedipus and Ajase stories (Kosawa 1934). Mythology can be a valuable source of data concerning typical childhood interactions that contribute to a child's development. A culture's mythology and folklore portray memories of and fantasies concerning emotionally significant formative experiences that have been shared by those who have grown up together in that society (Freeman 1977, 1994a, 1997c). Interactions between key mythological figures are often reflections of interactions between intrapsychic self representations and object representations. Since many of these are the same interactive experiences as those that contribute to the formation of ego and superego precursors, mythology can serve as a valuable tool when one is studying the early stages of object relations and intrapsychic development (Freeman 1995).

A culture's most significant myths are those stories that a people have themselves selected as having the deepest personal and spiritual meaning. These stories are often considered to be sacred and they have often become part of the culture's religious cosmology. Over generations of retelling as the stories have been passed down through the oral tradition, each important theme and detail has been shaped and adjusted until the stories feel just right. Variations may be introduced by individual storytellers, but only those images that are collectively and consensually validated and refined become part of the core story that survives from generation to generation. The stories are shaped by processes of defense and revision, which are similar to those that contribute to the creation of dreams. Just as dreams offer access, or a "royal road," to understanding individual intrapsychic fantasies, the shared dreams or mythology of a people can offer access to the fantasy life, worldview, and interpersonal relationships in that society. Folk tales and historical fables are often associative variants on basic cultural themes developed by subgroups within the culture.

Progression through developmental stages is often depicted as a sequence of challenges, journeys, and death-and-rebirth transitions leading to metamorphoses or to the emergence of new mythological figures who have progressively more mature qualities (Freeman 1981). For the past 1,400 years, Japan has preserved its mythology in writing and has accumulated an extensive legacy of artistic portrayals of interpersonal emotional interactions that offer data about the unfolding of child development and the life cycle not only in the current generation but also during earlier eras. We will refer to illustrative examples from mythology, folklore, and art in order to consider people's own perception and portrayal of their life experiences.

Japanese analysts gained useful insights from what they learned from Freudian, Kleinian, and Winnicottian theory. Until recently, however, most had relatively little awareness of separation–individuation theory. They became interested in Mahler's work in the last few years when they discovered that separation–individuation theory could be helpful in understanding normal and abnormal development in their society, and in answering theoretical questions that continued to be puzzling. Mahler's work is relevant and can contribute to an understanding of early differentiation, the early stabilization of certain aspects of emotional self and object constancy while other aspects are delayed, the continuation of derivatives of sharing and refueling phenomena into adulthood, early stages of superego and ego ideal development and the functioning of shame and guilt, the shape of the triadic familial oedipal complex and its resolution, and later life maturation.[1]

JAPANESE SYMBIOSIS AND SEPARATION-INDIVIDUATION

A Japanese mother values intimate physical contact with her infant and seeks to be with the baby as much as possible. Her family role was traditionally structured in a way that made it possible for her to have a much closer relationship with her infant than is the case in many other societies. Caring for her infant and young children is given priority over other relationships. Nursing is leisurely, intense, and sensual. Much time is spent in direct physical intimate contact. In this sense, the Japanese child tends to experience an almost idyllic availability of mother. The mother feels herself to be at one with the baby. She tends to feel less dependent than a Western mother upon the baby's vocalizations as a source of data about his needs, as she feels that she understands the baby and knows how to soothe him (Caudill 1972).

An American mother tends to perceive her infant as a separate individual with his or her own needs and feelings, and seeks to discover the particular baby's needs in order to try to synchronize with them. She seeks to fulfill the baby's needs, and then moves on to her own needs and those of her husband and other children. A

---

[1]Since 1993, the American Psychoanalytic Association's Interdisciplinary Colloquium on Psychoanalysis and Anthropology has focused on collaborating with colleagues in Japan. In 1996 the Margaret S. Mahler Research Foundation contributed copies of the Mahler research films on separation-individuation to universities in Fukuoka, Hiroshima, Kyoto, Osaka, and Tokyo. Anni Bergman traveled to Japan to discuss the films and twenty-five year follow-up studies with analysts and therapists at these universities and at the annual meeting of the Japanese Psychoanalytic Society. Glimpses of interpersonal interactions and behavioral phenomena in Western families that are different from those that are typical of Japanese infants and mother–child interactions provoked thoughtful questions about our inferences and about how we in the West have understood these developmental phenomena in our own cultural context.

Western mother values the baby's vocalizations as a source of data in response to which she can organize her caring activities, and responds with playful back-and-forth baby-talk dialogues with the infant. She encourages her baby to play by itself and encourages its autonomy, using vocal interchange as a modality to maintain contact at a distance. A Japanese baby sleeps with its mother in the same room as the rest of the family, and would not usually be left alone to play by itself or left with a baby-sitter (Caudill 1972, Caudill and Weinstein 1969).

The intimate experience of the Japanese infant in the resonant dual unity of symbiosis fosters a sense of basic trust (Erikson 1959), optimism, and shared omnipotence. It moderates subsequent emotional lability and reactivity. It also sensitizes the infant to the pleasure of sensuous intimacy and to somatically communicated touch and movement cues and nonverbal communication.

At times, contrasting experiences and brief discontinuities interrupt the Japanese baby's otherwise intimate harmonious symbiotic relationship. For example, the mother's interactions with those around her can lead to sudden changes in the experience of the infant, interrupting the mother–child resonance. In social situations that call upon her to be deferential, she has traditionally automatically tended to bow deeply out of respect. This proper etiquette leads to a sudden postural change that is startling from the point of view of a young baby who is carried on her back or in her arms, and at first it elicits a startle response in the infant. A discontinuity in their warm relationship also tends to occur when the baby cries. Although an infant's crying may be a manifestation of need or distress, from the point of view of others the sound of crying tends to be experienced as annoyingly disruptive and intrusive. A mother becomes very embarrassed and uncomfortable if her baby is restless or crying and may be disturbing others (Caudill and Weinstein 1969, Lebra 1976).[2] Her sudden muscular tension alters her holding be-

---

[2]The pained reaction of others to the intrusive sound of a child's crying is vividly portrayed in Shinto mythology in the story of the Sun Goddess, Amaterasu, and her

havior. The mother hastens to appease, soothe, or distract the child in order to stop the crying. For reasons at first unknown to the infant (since mother is responding to people outside the symbiosis, of whom the child is as yet unaware), mother's holding behavior intermittently changes. The changes are experienced by the infant as discontinuities in mother's way of relating, and are all the more remarkable because of the usual intimacy and reliability of their relationship. Discontinuities may also occur when the Japanese mother, lovingly caring for the infant in accordance with her own conception of the infant's needs, is not synchronized with what the baby's actual state is at that moment. For example, a mother who has already given the infant a great deal of tender nurturance may at times become withdrawn into herself and her own needs or may be inattentive to the child's signals of a need that she had not anticipated. These experiences of discontinuity stimulate early ego adaptive efforts by the infant that contribute to shaping the child's subsequent development.

Early Onset of Individuation

Mahler and her colleagues observed that infants who are experiencing an otherwise intimate and stable symbiosis may respond to intermittent puzzling discontinuities such as those described above by starting to look outward beyond the boundaries of the symbiotic milieu. They begin the processes of differentiation and individuation earlier than do other children. This adaptive response could be observed in infants within a number of dissimilar family contexts. The common factor was an experience of puzzling discontinuity from the symbiotic infant's point of view. Such a step in

---

younger brother, Susano-o. After the loss of their mother who died when a younger sibling was born, Susano-o was unable to be consoled. His crying was experienced by others as so intrusive and intolerable that it is described as having been like a typhoon, withering green mountains, drying up rivers and seas, and causing the hills and mountains to groan out loud (Aston 1972, Freeman 1993a, 1994d, Philippi 1968).

the direction of an early beginning of visual and cognitive individuation and outwardly directed attentiveness is accompanied by an
early appearance of two additional readily observable affective phenomena: stranger reactions and a sensitivity to separation anxiety
(Mahler et al. 1975). Although Mahler and her colleagues were
studying infant development in Western culture, insofar as an infant's
responses are based upon fundamental intrapsychic processes it is
not surprising that similar adaptive mechanisms and organizations
of functions may be observed in other cultures. This pattern of
development, while not at all uncommon in Western culture, is
not the pattern most commonly seen in American children. However, it is a pattern that appears to have been characteristic of Japanese development for many centuries. It is portrayed, for example,
in ancient Japanese mythological stories that were collected and
compiled in written form in *Kojiki* and *Nihongi* 1,300 years ago, in
the early 700s A.D. (Freeman 1993a, 1994b,c,d).

The Japanese infant's positive experiences in a symbiotic relationship that is, for the most part, warmly and sensitively responsive and gratifying contribute to early strengths in the basic core of
the infant's personality (Weil 1970). The overall stability of the
symbiotic relationship contributes to a lifelong sense of security in
regard to trusting, relying upon, and transiently regressively merg-
ing with others without experiencing undue symbiotic anxiety or
fears of destructive engulfment. At the same time, although the
Japanese mother usually functions as a sensitively attuned protective shield and provider for the child's needs, discontinuities occur
periodically, particularly at times when the infant is flooded with
affect and is crying. Temporarily there is a decrease in auxiliary ego
support from the partner who usually assists in need satisfaction and
emotional regulation. The infant's attempts to understand and to
find ways to adapt at these times stimulate early outwardly directed
visual attentiveness and early cognitive development. The child takes
a small step back from the merged state of intimacy and starts to
differentiate in an attempt to gain a better perspective, understand
his contrasting experiences, and form a clearer image of mother.

The early onset of cognitive and perceptual interest in the world outside the symbiotic orbit (metaphorically described as "hatching") results in a precocious onset of interest in and reactions to strangers and a sensitivity to separation anxiety. Children who start to differentiate and to individuate early are precocious in recognizing the specific features of their mother's face and the difference between their mother's face and the faces of others. This leads to an early appearance of stranger reactions, including both stranger curiosity and stranger anxiety. Their puzzlement about a social surround that causes mother to tighten up and change her holding behavior also contributes to a degree of caution and sensitivity regarding things that are unfamiliar and stranger anxiety (Kitayama, personal communication). To the degree that children begin to hatch and to look beyond the symbiotic orbit, they also start to become aware of their separateness from mother when brief separations occur, and they show an early appearance of separation anxiety. The brief interruptions in the symbiotic relationship sensitize the infant to feelings of neediness for this relationship. An early awareness of separateness, before an emotionally stable internal image of mother has become securely established, confronts the infant with the possibility of losing the intimacy and gratifications of the relationship with mother. The child develops an increased focus on mother as a source of both pleasure and nurturance. Although the Japanese mother is a more than "good-enough" mother, and although a secure overall sense of safety and basic trust develops in relation to accumulating memories of her responsive care, the child's sensitivity concerning separations will subsequently contribute to a prolongation and more gradual process of separation-individuation.[3]

---

[3]The fact that the rate of progression through specific developmental stages varies from one culture to another may sometimes mislead observers from Western cultures that emphasize progress and are highly goal-oriented. A goal-oriented perspective may lead one to assume that progressing rapidly is better, which may or may not be the case. An abrupt move "forward" to a new level of organization may in some instances be defensive and disadvantageous, side-stepping a more optimal gradual process of working out and resolving a developmental issue. In other instances precocity may contrib-

Early Self-Regulatory Capacities

The infant discovers the adaptive utility of data from outer reality. He increasingly relies upon, and reorganizes his functioning around, his cognitive and visual modalities. The Japanese mother reinforces the tendency of her infant to look beyond the boundaries of the symbiosis, and encourages his or her development. She progressively seeks (in the second half of the first year) to get the infant to follow her example in attending to, and showing appropriate behavior toward, others in the social environment.

Capacities for modulating and shaping emotional reactivity begin to develop relatively early. The very earliest building blocks or primordia of affect-regulatory mechanisms were established during the symbiosis when the infant started to shape his or her responses to adjust to subtle preverbal unconsciously transmitted maternal communications. The baby began to recognize which of his behaviors would evoke positive responses and which would cause mother to tighten up or lead to her withdrawal, and attempted to comply with her need for him to modify the expression of negative affects. Many aspects of the mother's ways of handling her own feelings, her reactions to the child's impulses, and her reactions to impinging external events in the social milieu became internalized through primary identification as the child started to differentiate.

The mother's systematic teaching of restraint, orderliness, propriety, and sensitivity to other people's feelings begins in the second half of the first year, earlier than in many other cultures. As the infant is starting to become aware of others beyond the symbiotic orbit, his mother begins to gradually and progressively shape his behavior, teaching control of posture and movement, respect behaviors, control of affective expression, and cleanliness. This shapes the toddler's motoric and interpersonal behavior in the subsequent

---

ute to shaping personality characteristics that are adaptive within that particular cultural environment. We and the Japanese often need to remind ourselves that there are times when "slow and steady wins the race." Our story of "The Hare and the Tortoise" is, in fact, well known and popular in Japan.

subphases. The child's early initial development of socially conforming self-regulatory controls, *before* practicing subphase behavioral issues concerning autonomy and motoric activity become prominent, tends to decrease subsequent negation struggles (Freeman 1995, 1996a,b). The child also starts to learn how to shape his appeal behaviors, utilizing culturally sanctioned forms of nonverbal communication other than crying in order to evoke a special "sweet" (*amae*) relationship of gratifying indulgence with mother (Doi 1962, 1973a, Taketomo 1986a,b, 1993), which we will further consider below. Throughout life there will continue to be a distinction between the relaxed informality and gratification permissible in intimate circumstances and the orderly behavioral formality that is essential in social circumstances.

The pattern of mothering care developed in Japan over a period of millennia is sensitively matched to the needs of an infant who has begun to individuate early but is not yet ready to leave the security derived from the intimacy and sense of shared omnipotence with mother. Mahler and Winnicott both describe the kind of maternal response that one sees in the Japanese mother as being ideal for this kind of child. Mahler and colleagues (1975) suggest that for such children,

> in order that the awareness of separateness not be too traumatic, there is a great need for the mother to be endowed with a particularly sensitive "coenesthetic empathy" (Spitz 1965, pp. 44, 134–138). It is important that the mother furnish a particularly well-attuned external or auxiliary ego, a particularly sensitive protection shield. . . . It is also important that the mother as protective shield gradually recede, as it were, so as not to hinder the individuating ego's gradual exercise of autonomy. [p. 205]

Winnicott (1971) discusses this in terms of his concept of the "good-enough" mother helping the child to gradually let go of the illusion of omnipotent union. The Japanese mother's role has traditionally been structured so as to make it possible for her to be available as a protective shield and auxiliary ego, and then to permit the child to return to her for emotional "refueling" (Furer, quoted by Mahler 1968) through a relatively prolonged and gradual process of separation–individuation that lasts longer than in Western culture. At the same time, she gradually helps the child to develop his autonomous functions, to separate and to individuate.

Maternal Responsiveness and Basic Trust

During the first year of life, infants in every culture at times inevitably have painful frustrating experiences that can trigger primitive rage and biting impulses. On entering into a symbiotic bond with mother, babies purify good memories of self–mother interactive experiences by splitting off painful frustrating memories and hostile destructive impulses and projecting these outside (Freud 1938, Kernberg 1966, Klein 1952), beyond the boundary of the symbiotic mother–infant orbit of dual unity. These projected images and destructive impulses are often portrayed in mythology as persecutory biting figures. What characterizes Japanese child development, however, is that in the vast majority of cases infants do not experience significant or enduring levels of unmasterable frustration or of primitive aggressive biting feelings during the symbiosis or during the early stages of separation–individuation. The mother supports and helps the child to attain, maintain, and return to a state of stability even though there are brief interruptions from time to time. She protects, provides narcissistic replenishment, and stimulates development. Her closeness and support continue in their sharing of experiences during the early months of separation–individuation. The child feels safe about mother's continued presence and is helped to start to prepare for separation from her. In the course of their stable interactions, the initially idealized "good" images and split-off "bad" images start to become integrated into relatively neutralized unified images.

Biting figures in Japanese myths that derive from the earliest stages of development are easily mastered and subdued by the protagonist in each story. Fanged *oni*, or impish fabled demons who were said to have an appetite for human beings and who were somewhat fearsome for young children, are similarly readily chased away by Shoki the demon queller, and are regarded as simply mischievous rascals by older children and adults. The Chinese dragon and lion were defanged when they were imported into Japan, to become gentle, nurturant protectors. The lion and the deer are in fact referred to by the same name, *shishi*. More dangerous persecutory mythological figures derive from later stages of development.

Although a potential sensitivity to separations developed as a result of the early onset of the infant's individuation, Japanese babies normally do not experience actual significant physical separations. The brief discontinuities when mother is distracted are transient libidinal separations that puzzle the infant and lead him to start looking outward to orient himself, but after a very brief interruption the mother resumes her auxiliary ego role and relieves and soothes the infant. Ordinarily these transient interruptions do not lead to a level of frustration or anxiety that would overwhelm the child or stimulate hostile destructive impulses (Parens 1979). Similarly, the mother's teaching of self-regulatory controls during the differentiation subphase in the second half of the first year is gentle, gradual, and loving, and does not cause significant frustration or distress. The infant identifies with mother's self-restraint and guidance without an autonomy struggle.

In the early part of the second year, the separation-individuation process unfolds gradually. Japanese toddlers and young children tend to exercise autonomous functions while staying physically close to mother. As portrayed in many Ukiyo-e wood block pictures, a child tends at first to reach out visually to explore the surrounding world while maintaining a solid base on mother's lap, or to reach out while holding onto her hand. The child may then seek to get mother to come and to explore together with him, or he may explore on his own while remaining near her.

In the practicing and early rapprochement subphases, a Japanese mother often engages the child in playful visual games in which

she and the child look together at puzzling transitory visual phenomena, sharing in transitional experiences that help the child to
gradually begin to negotiate separation from her (Kitayama 1995a).
Their games with colorful visual toys serve bridging and transitional
functions, assisting the child in the process of separating and individuating. These games are somewhat different from Western peek-
a-boo or hide-and-seek games, which try to teach that *absence* is
transient, that what has disappeared will return (i.e., object perma-
nence). The Japanese mother tries, in addition, to prepare her child
to understand that the *presence* of things is also transient, that the
things that one enjoys do not necessarily last forever. In this way
she starts to prepare the child for the fact that the special relationship with her will ultimately need to be relinquished. Within a
protective milieu characterized by a joint sharing of experience, she
promotes the toddler's affective and cognitive development (Freeman 1995, 1996a,b).

The transitional states that are jointly experienced by mother
and child in their shared-looking games also lead to the child's starting to adaptively utilize illusion to creatively distort and imagina-
tively play with reality in fantasy, thereby beginning to integrate
polarized good and bad images and experiences of closeness and
distance (Byerly 1993). In the rapprochement process, images of
mother, of self, and of the self-object interaction are gradually creatively modified and integrated in this way, and then are symbolized and internalized to become intrapsychic representations (Jacobson 1964, Sandler and Rosenblatt 1962).

The first portion of the Japanese separation-individuation process unfolds in a way that is stable and peaceful. Children observed
in the differentiation and practicing subphases appear to be very
comfortable and secure in their attachment to and relationship with
their mothers. Enduring contributions to Japanese personality from
this early period of development include basic trust; minimal symbiotic anxiety; oral, tactile, and visual sensitivity and sensuous receptivity; moderation of the lability of affective reactivity; alertness
to and puzzlement concerning a social surround that causes mother

to tighten up and alters her holding behavior; sensitivity concerning separations; early consolidation of some ego precursor adaptive and self-regulatory mechanisms; and early progression along some developmental lines toward integrated self and object representations. A core of adaptive mechanisms has become established that will help the child to deal with the period of upheaval and the intrapsychic and interpersonal reorganization and realignment that lie ahead.

The young toddler receives sensitive care and internalizes maternal adaptive and coping mechanisms. The practicing and rapprochement phenomenon of periodically returning to mother for reassurance, sharing, and refueling contributes to the subsequent development of a lifelong pattern of intermittent reenactments of emotional reunion and refueling known as *amae*, in relation to grandparents, teachers, supervisors, erotic love objects, marital partners, and ultimately the spirits of departed ancestors.

In the rapprochement subphase in any culture, two concerns may start to add urgency to the toddler's need to periodically reaffirm and reestablish the relationship with mother. An increasing awareness of the toddler's own individuated identity and of mother's distinct identity can exacerbate concern that separation could lead to the child's being lost and alone. In addition, as the hitherto purified and idealized "good" aspects and the split-off "bad" aspects of the image of mother start to become integrated into a unified image and a toddler starts to realize that what had initially seemed to be separate "good" and "bad" mothers are really one, the child may become anxious that his or her aggressive impulses might destroy not only the fantasized "bad" mother but *also* the "good" mother that he or she needs and loves (Kernberg 1966, Klein 1952). Both of these concerns become greatly intensified in the Japanese child in mid-rapprochement, when intense separation anxiety and aggressive impulses are precipitated by the birth of a newborn sibling who displaces the toddler from what had been his or her unique position in a Japanese family, being mother's baby.

Gender–Related Differences in Development

By this stage, the developmental experiences of a Japanese girl and boy have already diverged in a number of ways. Since the latter half of the first year, greater and more consistent maternal emphasis has been placed on a girl's developing socially proper and polite expressive and postural controls and on an expectation that a girl should be deferential and reticent and should inhibit the expression of autonomous and assertive behavior. Japanese culture emphasizes propriety, politeness, respect, and etiquette in both genders and all social classes to a greater degree than is common in Western culture. Particularly consistent emphasis, however, is placed on a young girl's socialization in these regards, starting prior to the toddler period. A girl is granted less autonomy, but experiences greater guidance and auxiliary superego support from her mother. She identifies with maternal patterns of emotional response through primary identification, and does not go through a confusing subsequent process of dis-identifying with the feminine aspects of these maternal identifications as a boy does during separation–individuation (Greenson 1968). Her behavior is gradually, steadily, and consistently shaped in the direction of self control, reticence, and politeness. Maternal identifications contribute to the basic core of her personality organization, to a relatively early development of self-regulatory capacities, and to early precursors of idealized self images (Tyson and Tyson 1984).

During the same period of early individuation, mothers enjoy their sons' being assertively active and boyish. In the practicing subphase, mothers wish and dream that their sons will grow up to become as precocious and as powerful as the fabled superboy Kintaro (the Golden Boy), and that like him they will become able to vanquish wild beasts and fierce warriors (Freeman 1994c). A degree of assertive and aggressive behavior is tolerated and even unconsciously encouraged and erotized by mothers in their sons, while it is discouraged in their daughters. The encouragement of boyish assertiveness begins during the calm early portion of separation-individuation, before the boy's behavior becomes tumultuous in response to being displaced by a new baby. The mother's encouragement of assertiveness tends to reinforce his sense of infantile omnipotence.

A girl is given less leeway to behave in assertive and autonomous ways. She is encouraged to develop in the direction of becoming altruistically sensitive to the needs of others, and she is taught that self-centered assertive behaviors are shameful and hurtful. The girl will grow up to become more responsible than her brother. As an older sister, she later will be called upon to assume a substitute maternal nurturant role in helping her mother to care for displaced toddlers, and will be called upon to accept and forgive the demanding, clinging, and boisterous aggression of male siblings. The girl identifies with her mother and sublimates many of her own dependent needs in becoming a caregiver who serves and is cherished by others. In that role, positive interdependent and altruistic gratification will occur as she vicariously participates in their experiences of pleasure (Freeman 1994d, A. Freud 1936).

Frustration, Aggressive Impulses, and Ambivalence

The calm, supportive joint sharing of experience by the mother and the toddler starts to change during the rapprochement subphase, when the mother is often pregnant and a new baby is anticipated. Starting in the later stages of pregnancy but especially once a new baby is born, a toddler's mother undergoes a transformation that from the child's point of view is unprecedented and is experienced as cataclysmic. The exclusive nature of a Japanese mother's symbiotic involvement with her infant requires that she shift the primary focus of her attention to her new nursling. The displaced toddler, who had been sensitized from birth to expect an exquisitely attuned availability and responsivity of mother, experiences an abrupt fall from the special status of being mother's baby.[4] This is an over-

---

[4]Although the transition is most abrupt if the toddler is in fact displaced, even if a new baby does not arrive at this point the world changes for all toddlers. Cultural and

whelming disruption in terms of the child's expectations and sensitivity to separations. The toddler feels abandoned and betrayed. Particularly in the case of a boy whose feelings of omnipotence had been stimulated, there is an abrupt deflation. The child's sense of basic trust and safety is shaken. The rapprochement subphase becomes turbulent, and is flooded with clinging and hostile destructive ambivalent feelings (Parens 1979).[5]

The hitherto responsive maternal partner has been replaced by a transformed mother who is no longer able to offer the toddler unlimited unconditional indulgence. She tries to be patient, tolerant, and accepting of the displaced child's turmoil but is inevitably pulled in two directions. Boys' and girls' regressive experiences and adaptive efforts diverge during the ensuing rapprochement upheaval, but for both the rapprochement subphase will become prolonged. After a period of ambivalent regressive turbulence, the child's core of basic trust and the continuing availability of considerable support (albeit nonexclusive support) from mother and support from substitute maternal figures will enable the child to gradually restabilize through internalization of and identification with an ideal-child role. Some derivatives of the rapprochement conflict, ambitendency and refueling, will, however, persist into adulthood.

During the first year of life, both the boy and the girl had taken a number of steps toward internalization of maternal patterns and

---

maternal expectations as to what is considered to be age-appropriate start to shift in anticipation of the usual circumstance of a new infant's arrival. The loss of the mother of symbiosis is portrayed in mythology as the cataclysmic death of the mother goddess Izanami, as a result of having been severely burned when she gave birth to her new baby, the god of fire. Up until this point, the myths had told a story (from the child's point of view) of progressive differentiation, active mastery, and feelings of omnipotence as the infant's widening horizons were experienced as though the child was creating his or her own world. But now a destructive intruder has crashed in, everything comes tumbling down, and the mother of symbiosis is gone! The toddler, Susano-o (see footnote 2), is overwhelmed and he becomes inconsolable.

[5]The persecutory figures in Japanese mythology are often idealized mothers who have become transformed into hurtful animals, or people who have become enraged and vengeful as a result of injury and betrayal.

development of early self-regulatory capacities. However, in the second year, whereas the girl had experienced continuing consistent socialization and support in developing capacities for channeling affect in socially valued adaptive ways, the boy had mixed and inconsistent experiences. On the one hand, in social circumstances, his mother had expected him to be self-controlled, orderly, and proper. But in his intimate relationship with her, assertive, autonomous, and aggressive impulses had been indulged and his sense of omnipotence had been stimulated and encouraged. To the extent that his mother had not established consistent expectations and guidance, there had been a delay in the boy's developing inner controls and a persistence of unrealistically idealized maternal images and expectations for gratification. This leads to more turbulent experiences of frustration and deflation in the boy when gratification becomes limited. The boy had been flying higher, had a greater distance to fall, and falls harder as a result of his deflation. Having been reinforced in his sense of omnipotence and having been allowed leeway in regard to assertive and aggressive behavior, he experiences not only turbulent concerns about separation but also concerns about whether his rage has been responsible for harming and driving away the mother of symbiosis.

Although the boy experiences greater turmoil than the girl does, for a period of time he has the advantage of being permitted to openly express frustration and rage while a girl has much less opportunity to do so. The boy is indulged in that his rage is tolerated. He is allowed to be self-centered and demanding and to violate the rules of propriety, however disconcerting his disruptive behaviors may be for others. A period of license before he is required to reestablish proper behavioral controls softens the narcissistic blow of his deflation. It also permits a partial rekindling of his earlier sense of special entitlement and omnipotence.

A mother patiently tolerates her rapprochement son's (and to a lesser degree, her rapprochement daughter's) turmoil and ambitendent disruptive behavior, awaiting the time when he or she will start to recognize and become concerned about his wrongdoing and begin to control his own behavior. Children are perceived to be basically good, and their failings at this stage are forgiven as actions they cannot help or cannot yet control. The mother (or the older sister or grandparent, who may be assisting as an alternate parent) benevolently and gently guides the child, quietly makes her expectations clear, and adopts an expectant attitude. The child is given the responsibility to figure things out (Johnson 1993, Lebra 1976), and to self-regulate. Thus, the mother continues to offer a supportive (though less indulgent) environment and to promote the child's affective and cognitive development. The child becomes aware that what he is doing is making her uncomfortable.

Even in cases where a child is not displaced by a new nursling, there is an expectation that there should be a change in the indulgent relationship between a mother and a child and that a child at this stage should start to become more self-controlled and less demanding. A mother is in a difficult position because she is pulled in multiple directions. She feels compassion for the child's neediness but feels uncomfortable with his dyscontrol. She seeks to comply with the cultural expectation that she be patient, tolerant, and indulgent, but needs the toddler to behave more maturely so that he reflects well on her as a mother in the eyes of others. Japanese deeply feel, and respond with emotional recognition, to the well-known Japanese aphorism concerning a parent's wish for a child to grow up and to become more mature as soon as possible: "If you crawl, please stand up! And if you stand, please walk!" (Kitayama, personal communication, Lebra 1976).

To the degree that the Japanese mother tolerates disruptive behavior and leaves it up to the child to achieve self-regulation, she is temporarily decreasing her auxiliary superego role (Holder 1982) and placing greater adaptive responsibility upon the child. But she continues to be available as an auxiliary ego, as a nurturing, loving object for intermittent support and regressive indulgence, and as a model for identification. The joint sharing of experiences through the difficult period of the child's ambivalence conflicts supports the child's gradually recognizing socially acceptable ways to channel assertive and competitive feelings. Her support and availability (and, later, the support of others who intermittently function in comparable maternal ways) will continue through childhood and into early adulthood, although expectations for socially conforming achievement, and for the individual to not only receive but also give to others, will progressively increase.

A girl tends to experience a less abrupt deflation and a less intense degree of outrage, but is allowed less freedom to express the hurt and rage that she does feel.[6] She experiences steady expectations to precociously self-control, and to suppress the expression of rage and sublimate it into constructive caregiving activities. When intense separation anxiety and aggressive impulses are precipitated by her displacement by a newborn sibling, the requirement that she control the overt expression of negative emotions and frustrate herself in favor of the interests of others may contribute to a feeling of being polluted by assertive, demanding, and disruptive thoughts, and a feeling that she can never be clean enough or considerate enough to be worthy of her mother's approval (Freeman 1995, 1996a,b, Kitayama 1995b).

The young girl's internalization of maternal values and identification with mother had been syntonic in the early subphases of separation-individuation, but during the rapprochement crisis these become defensive precocious identifications in an attempt to suppress turmoil. As mentioned earlier, a defensive abrupt move forward to a new level of organization may be disadvantageous if it is premature and if it bypasses a more gradual process of working out and resolving a developmental issue. To the extent that mothers seek to encourage precocity and to hasten a child's maturation,

---

[6]In the well-known story of Princess Moonlight, the heroine was not permitted to directly express the rage and hostile destructive thoughts she was having toward her mother and younger brother (Ushijima 1994a). No one could understand when she then displaced the rage toward male peers who were her suitors. Rather than being responsive to them, as an older girl or a young woman ought to be, she withheld gratification and frustrated them by saying she would marry them only if they performed impossible feats for her. People were puzzled and could not understand such behavior.

achievement, and orientation to reality, the child may defensively attempt to integrate polarized ambivalent positive and negative feelings and images prematurely, before there has been adequate neutralization of the aggressive and libidinal sides of the child's feelings (Freeman et al. 1976). The girl attempts to deal with her feelings of neediness, abandonment, and helplessness by identifying with her mother's activity and becoming her mother's helper as a giver of the nurturance that she herself is longing to receive. In discussing this developmental crisis, Anni Bergman commented (1997) that precocious identification with mother's activity as a caregiver may lead to a premature apparent self-reliance and autonomy comparable to the development of a false self in Winnicott's sense. In being mother's helper, the young girl defensively idealizes (Kernberg 1997) and identifies with her mother, dissociatively separates her own inner feelings from the face she shows in public (Doi's "dual consciousness," 1973b), and puts on a mask of control rather than expressing negative feelings openly. The girl may, however, feel that she is polluted by turbulent, angry feelings and conclude that this is what has led to her being expelled from her intimate relationship with her mother (Ushijima 1994a).[7]

A girl's concerns about gender anatomical differences may also contribute to feelings of inadequacy and increase her rapprochement turbulence (Galenson and Roiphe 1971, Mahler et al. 1975). Unneutralized aggressive feelings may contribute a masochistic coloration to her fantasies about her caregiving activities, in which case caregiving may serve as a moral masochistic attempt to please and she may become what Kitayama (1991) has described as a masochistic caregiver. In normal circumstances, her turmoil and ambivalent feelings gradually resolve, so that ultimately her caregiving becomes altruistic rather than masochistic. The girl's presentation

---

[7]After Princess Moonlight was exiled from her parental home she found refuge and acceptance in the home of her grandparents (Ushijima 1994a). Catalyzed by their mature warmth and compassionate sensitivity (or, in other stories, the empathic warmth of other mature parental figures), she matures. In the Idaike and Ajase story (Kosawa 1934, Okonogi 1978, 1979), Buddha helps Idaike through a comparable transition.

of her self to others, which initially is in part a mask or false self that complies with an expected social role, gradually becomes digested or metabolized and introjected into her own functioning, and ultimately a part of her own authentic self or identity.

For the boy, the period of maternal tolerance of his disruptive behavior and her patient expectations that he will achieve self-regulation in the long run moderate the abruptness of his transition. They are supportive of his self-esteem and his cognitive development, but they do not offer models or a series of graded frustrations that might assist him in controlling impulsive behavior. His mother's indulgence permits a temporary partial revival of omnipotent feelings and feelings of entitlement, and a persistence of unrealistically idealized maternal images and expectations for gratification. This tends to postpone his achieving stable inner controls, meeting his own ideals, and being approved in the eyes of others. He therefore experiences a second deflation and a second period of turmoil and transition when consistent limits are ultimately established.

His second transition occurs in mid-childhood when increasingly emphatic demands start to be made that he stop expecting special indulgence, that he conform and live up to expectations. If he has ignored the subtle reactions in mother that nonverbally reflected her discomfort when he behaved inappropriately, she becomes increasingly unaccepting of his behavior, and he also starts to experience disapproval from his father[8] and from other mem-

---

[8]Hitherto, the father traditionally played a reticent, somewhat distant, and secondary role in the child's experience, as a respected member of the social milieu but not continuously or intimately involved with the child, and as one of several intermittent but relatively peripheral competitors for mother's attention (Johnson 1993, Nakakuki 1994, Taketomo 1982). He did not serve as an alternate parent at the time of the child's initial rapprochement turmoil, as is described in Western culture by Abelin (1971); that role was played by the child's older sister and/or grandparents. The father tends to be seen as an important formidable figure, both because of the deference mother and others accord to him (Johnson 1993) and because of his role in the primal scene; his disapproval and criticism of the child's dyscontrol therefore have an important impact. The boy's and girl's much more intimate relationship with their grandfather catalyzes their discovery and emotional investment of their father as a real person and an oedipal figure

bers of the family. The other family members are less reticent than the mother about conveying their negative reactions.[9]

From now on, the boy is not able to impose inappropriately upon his mother's indulgence, and both his mother and members of the social milieu assert the cultural expectations and requirements for control that he knew he was violating. His world changes from one in which he had been relatively unrestricted, indulged, and the center of unconditional maternal adulation, to a world in which he is critically evaluated by others and he is required to comply and to exert unwavering effort. Approval becomes conditional, fragile, and uncertain. The pressure of social expectations increases as a boy or girl moves into peer relationships in the outside world beyond the family (Hori 1995).

This second experience of deflation is relatively traumatic in that the mother is no longer as permissive in offering special indulgence (Hori 1995), and she no longer allows the boy to seek indulgent support and gratification from her in an aggressive demanding way. In the period of his disruptiveness and demandingness, he may not simply have been refueling but may also at times have taken advantage of his mother's indulgence manipulatively and coercively. He had been aware that he shouldn't be doing what he was doing and that his unruly disruptive behavior and intrusive violation of boundaries were regarded by others as contaminating and pollut-

---

(Ushijima 1994a), contributing to the girl developing a libidinal attachment to her father and the boy identifying with his father's role (Nakakuki 1994).

[9]After the loss of the mother of symbiosis, Susano-o's disruptiveness was intolerable (footnote 2). His older sister, Amaterasu, took over the role of being his mother, patiently tolerating and making excuses for his disruptive and destructive behavior. She was the Sun Goddess (the central figure in the family) upon whom all depended. Although the other gods were furious about his behavior, there was nothing that they could do as long as she protected him and offered him special indulgence. This continued until his disruptiveness became so overwhelming that even Amaterasu could stand it no longer. She fled and locked herself in a cave, plunging the world disastrously into darkness and winter. At this point, the other gods were free to deal with Susano-o. After getting Amaterasu to come back out of the cave, they punished him by plucking out his nails and his beard, and then they ostracized and exiled him.

ing.[10] He may conclude that the change in his world and the bursting of his illusions have been caused by harm that he has done to his mother by thoughtless, self-centered, excessive demands for gratification (Kitayama 1991).

The boy experiences a final deflation of omnipotent fantasies, a disruption of his sense of narcissistic safety and intactness, and he may become depressed feeling himself to be soiled, repulsive, and dirty.[11] Kernberg (1997) has commented on the internalization of aggression into superego functions that occurs at this point. Initially, the boy's internalization of values takes place as a defensive attempt to move forward to a new level of organization through a precocious identification with his father's role, comparable to the false-self identification in the girl. Since this final transition period, characterized by deflation and internalization, is relatively abrupt, without gradual neutralization and integration of the two sides of his feelings, both his self representation and the object representation are initially suffused with unneutralized ambivalent feelings. Ambivalent feelings that had previously been expressed in an ambitendent back-and-forth interactive oscillation between closeness and distance become symbolized and internalized in a fantasized representation of the relationship within the child's representational world. He feels guilty, often feeling that he has done irreparable harm and that he

---

[10]The change in his mother occurs at the time of the upswing of the boy's phallic impulses. This is clearly indicated in the Amaterasu and Susano-o story. Susano-o's ultimately unbearable violation was not his defecating in the Hall of the Tasting of the First Fruits, but rather his phallic aggression in making a hole penetrating into the sacred women's secret chamber and throwing a polluting, dead, and skinned corpse of a horse inside, which resulted in the genitalia of the goddess being penetrated by a shuttlecock, a device used to weave threads through a loom. Once the boy's aggression has become genital in its coloration, his mother can tolerate it no further. Kitayama (1985) has discussed this period in terms of myths and folk tales that portray the boy's violating his mother's prohibition, "Don't look!" and allowing himself to become consciously aware of the genital, animal side of his mother that he had previously not allowed himself to know.

[11]Ajase developed foul-smelling disgusting skin lesions as a result of his violent impulses toward his mother.

no longer deserves to be loved, and he is left with a deep sense of obligation (Freeman 1995, 1996a,b, Kitayama 1995b).

The boy is thrust into the nonindulgent social world beyond the family, but does have fallback support systems available to help him through the transition. Replacing the previous mother of relatively unconditional permissive acceptance and special indulgence, there is a new and seemingly different mother who responds to and supports him if he conforms to expectations. His mother does not disappear, but the child must reorganize himself to relate to her in a new kind of way. He intermittently will continue to have opportunities to regress and to receive special *amae* supportive gratification, and in fact his mother will continue to enjoy interacting indulgently with him, provided that he approaches her in a culturally acceptable, nonsexualized, nonaggressive, age-appropriate way.[12]

Because of the sensitivity to separations and the regressive turbulence of the rapprochement crisis after the toddler had been displaced, children continue to attempt to rework the intrapsychic process of attempting to rework and resolve derivatives of separation-individuation phase in symbolic fantasy. Although the developmental paths of the boy and the girl have diverged, both have experienced deflation and feelings of vulnerability and helplessness. Their stable core of basic trust and the continuing availability of mother and substitute maternal figures for support and refueling enable them to restabilize. At first they precociously identify with culturally prescribed male and female roles, developing a formal presentation of the self to others that is distinct from their inner thoughts and feelings. This creates the discontinuity of experience and dual perspective that has been described as a twofold structure of consciousness (Doi 1973b, 1986). Derivatives of rapprochement ambitendency

---

[12]Some mothers who have problems with sadomasochistic conflicts of their own may become masochistic caregivers (Kitayama 1991). However, a healthy mother communicates her expectations when the child is starting to go too far, and declines to enter into an *amae* interaction if he appeals for *amae* in a manipulative sadomasochistic way or is becoming intrusive or invasive.

and the reworking of the initial precocious role identifications and of early internalized self and object representations will continue into adulthood.

The identifications that are involved in becoming an ideal daughter or ideal son in relation to an idealized image of mother permit an initial stabilization of the rapprochement crisis and a preliminary integration of internal self and object representations. Henceforth, the experienced internal presence of an idealized mother leads to the feeling that mother is always with you and that her eye is looking down benevolently upon you wherever you are when you are performing your assigned role. This permits spatial separation without undue anxiety. The stable internal presence of a representation of an idealized mother also permits the individual to intermittently return for emotional refueling without a threat of harmful reengulfment.

By mid-childhood the Japanese boy and girl are on the way toward and achieve the beginnings of emotional self and object constancy (Mahler et al. 1975). Their sensitivity to separation anxiety has sufficiently subsided (Okimoto, personal communication 1997) to make it possible for them to separate from mother and go to school. Some maternal functions become transferred to the teacher, but the mother's availability for support and for intermittent emotional refueling continues to be important.

Once the child has stabilized initial internal representations of his or her self and the object, and the beginnings of object constancy have been achieved, the child no longer experiences the intense separation anxiety and urgency for reunion that had been experienced during the period of rapprochement crisis. The subsequent continuing peaceful emotionally gratifying pattern of periodic *amae* refueling differs from the turbulent conflict-laden ambitendent interactions of the period of upheaval. *Amae* can be considered to be a derivative or an intermittent revival and reenactment at a more mature stage of development of the quiet, calm, nonanxious mother–child interactive pattern of the early subphases of separation-individuation in which the child periodically returned to mother for reassurance, joint sharing of experience, sensuous intimacy, and emotional refueling.

In distinguishing between *amae* and the precursors from which it is derived, in the next section of this chapter it may be helpful to consider the distinction between biologically based dependency needs of infancy, primordial part-object wishes, and later abstract differentiated object-related wishes (Akhtar 1997, Freeman 1997a). Fulfillment of fundamental needs is essential to emotional integration and development, while gratification of specific wishes (which represent personal ways of fulfilling needs) is less obligatory, since other ways of fulfilling the needs can be developed or substituted. Primordial concrete sensory wishes start to develop during the symbiosis when associative links are first established between experiences of need and perceptions of the activities of the need-satisfying part object. More sophisticated abstractly conceptualized object-related wishes develop considerably later when the individuating rapprochement child develops fantasies of being gratified by a differentiated mother who has come to be recognized as distinct from his or her self, and the child internalizes symbolic representations of these fantasies as wished-for interactions between the self and the object. The lifelong interactions of *amae* are wish-fulfilling interpersonal enactments that serve to intermittently gratify nostalgic wishes for previously experienced pleasures.[13]

---

[13]Some semantic and theoretical unclarity has arisen from the fact that the word *amae* has at times been expanded to include not only intermittent gratification of these nostalgic, more sophisticated wishes in late childhood and adulthood but also (1) the underlying biological *drives* that motivate an infant's affiliative and dependency needs; (2) the sweet, affectionate, intimate maternal cherishment and gratification of the *libidinal needs* of an infant; and (3) the permissive, tolerant, but uncomfortable special indulgent support of the *ego developmental needs* of a misbehaving son during the rapprochement crisis. Although the use of the single word *amae* to describe underlying drives, libidinal needs, ego needs, and abstract wishes may be proposed to have the advantage of indicating that connections exist between these various phenomena, it has the disadvantage of potentially being misunderstood unless each distinct phenomena is specified and distinguished from the others by adding a qualifying explanatory phrase or adjective. When a single term is used in a global way to refer to phenomena at different developmental

AMAE: CREATIVE MUTUAL REGRESSION IN THE SERVICE OF THE EGO AND REFUELING

Amae is an intermittent, recurring, culturally formatted interaction in which the customary rules of formality and propriety are temporarily suspended (Taketomo 1986a,b), allowing people to seek, to regressively receive, and to give one another affectionate support and indulgence (Doi 1962, 1973a). In shared enactments that are comparable to childhood creative make-believe play, the experiences of *amae* recall and transiently symbolically re-create the reassuring intimacy of the mother–child relationship of early childhood and the experiences of reunion and refueling of separation-individuation. It involves a transient interactive mutual regression in the service of the ego, which both gratifies and serves the progressive intrapsychic growth and development of both of the participants (Freeman 1993b).[14]

The typical interaction begins when a would-be recipient of *amae* gratification appeals nonverbally to a potentially benevolent parental figure and they jointly agree to enter into an *amae* interaction (Taketomo 1986a,b). Although the symbolic interactive format is of a parental benevolent giver of special indulgence and a

---

levels, this may create a misperception that adult *amae* is equivalent to infantile gratification or indulgence. This may lead people unfamiliar with Japanese culture to erroneously conclude that *amae* indicates that Japanese adults are arrested in their development or immature, rather than understanding *amae* as a series of sophisticated culturally formatted interactions that both gratify wishes and serve an adaptive growth promoting function through shared regression in the service of the ego. (A comparable potential for misunderstanding arises from the ambiguity of the English words *dependency* and *dependent*, which will be considered below.)

[14]In each episode of *amae*, the participants may regressively reenter a transitional world, in which illusion can be adaptively utilized to creatively distort and play with reality in fantasy (Byerly 1993). Modified images of mother, of self, and of the self–object interaction, which have been shaped within the world of transitional illusion, gradually become internalized, modifying or replacing earlier self and object representations.

recipient of gratification, starting in late childhood and increasingly as one matures thereafter there are bilateral aspects to the interaction. *Amae* is a derivative of the practicing and early rapprochement phenomena of refueling and sharing. It includes both passive wishes for sensuous gratification and active wishes to nurture, to reciprocate, and to give sweet, sensuous gratification to the other participant in the interaction. The interaction provides both participants feelings of well-being, safety, and security in being able to regressively participate in transitional magical feelings of shared omnipotence. It also provides a feeling of being recharged and replenished by being esteemed and valued, which contributes to secondary narcissism. An individual's role in the periodic giving–and–receiving relationship of *amae* gradually matures and becomes increasingly compassionate as he or she moves through the life cycle, from infantile dependency to becoming a giver of nurturance and sharing in interdependent mutuality.

The experience of alternating between contrasting periods of permissive indulgence and periods of socially required self-control had its origins in the early months when the differentiating infant's mother began to teach the child to shape his or her behavior in certain specific circumstances to conform with the expectations of others. This resulted in the development of two kinds of self experiences—the relaxed experience of the inner self and the formal etiquette of the socially presented self. Correspondingly, there were two kinds of good-mother experiences—a permissive good mother of gratification and a protective, supportive, good mother of stability and order.

On the one hand, in relation to the protective good mother of stability and order, the child internalized self-regulatory capacities and developed a good self of compliant achievement, cooperative coordination with others, and responsibility. This good self enjoys perfecting and doing well what others have done traditionally, and develops secondary narcissistic feelings of self-esteem in relation to group values. On the other hand, the child enjoyed an intimate relationship with the permissive and supportive good mother of gratification, indulgence, and sensuous pleasure, who was forgiving and who gave recognition to the child for personal striving and achievement. In relation to this mother, one enjoys gratifying experiences, feels admired and specially esteemed, and gains feelings of secondary narcissism based upon personal accomplishment. One's enthusiasm concerning autonomy and personal goals subsequently becomes moderated, however, by an awareness that in the outer social milieu beyond the maternal orbit—except in group-sanctioned circumstances—a self-centered focus on personal enjoyment or striving for goals of one's own may be regarded by others as shameful and offensive.[15]

What the infant first passively experienced as two alternating contrasting experiences, of relaxed merged dual unity as opposed to expectations that he control his behavior and self-regulate, starts to be actively explored by the toddler in the second year when he initiates alternating back and forth oscillations between periods of refueling and outwardly directed practicing exploration. In the Japanese separation-individuation process, times of looking outward and moving away from mother are times of moving out into the social world of formalities, etiquette, and expectations for performance. By way of contrast, times of returning to the reassuring intimacy and safety of mother's lap and arms are times of release from the need to perform and to self-regulate, providing opportunities for permissive gratification and fulfillment of inner wishes.

These alternating experiences in separation-individuation were the beginning of the pattern of alternating between proper control and reticence in public circumstances and specially structured release from the rules of propriety in culturally approved circumstances. Intermittent experiences of suspension of the customary rules offer opportunities to relax from one's reality-oriented individuated sense of responsibility, regress into an illusory transitional experience of

---

[15]A common aphorism in Japan warns, "A nail that sticks up gets hammered down." As Susano-o painfully discovered, socially disruptive, assertive, self-centered behavior can lead to ostracism, rejection, and punishment.

sensuous pleasure, feel protected and cared for, and to perhaps express inner feelings that one would ordinarily not communicate. Throughout life, the more controlled, immaculate, public front side will be periodically suspended, allowing people to relax with their own group, let their hair down, and be more open, natural, frank, and honest. For example, "salaryman" work groups go out to relax and drink together in the evening to release some of their pent-up feelings after an exhausting day of intense compliance and formality (Allison 1994). Similar experiences of regressive release from formality occur when groups of people relax together at a hot spring or *onsen*, at a cherry blossom viewing party, or watching fireflies or fireworks, or when people relax together in a garden or in the privacy of their own home. There also are stimulating culturally approved opportunities for release from customary social restraints when they exuberantly participate in *matsuri* festival celebrations.

Expectations for the child to be considerate of and to give to others will progressively increase. Dependent *amae* gratification continues to be sanctioned only insofar as it fulfills age-appropriate developmental needs. Requests for *amae* that are perceived to be inappropriately dependent and perceived as seeking to trespass unreasonably upon the generosity of others are gradually frustrated. As Taketomo (1993, 1997) has described, until preadolescence a child is allowed to playfully regress, and to happily mimic and pretend to be reenveloped in the sensuous gratification, security, and acceptance of an infant's attachment to mother. The mother agrees to respond playfully to the child in the way she would have responded when the child was an infant. But at the same time the child is progressively reminded that he or she is no longer a baby. The reminder may range from gentle comments, such as, "You are *amaeing*. But you are much older than that. You understand, don't you?" to mild disapproval with some degree of shaming, or, if necessary, disapproval of the child's lack of expectable age-appropriate restraint and maturity and rejection of the child's inappropriate approach for *amae* (Taketomo 1993, 1997).

Recurrent *amae* enactments with parents, grandparents, teachers, companions,[16] supervisory figures, and erotic love objects contribute to a gradual reworking and modification of intrapsychic self and object representations. Identifications with mother's comforting and consoling ministrations contribute to the individual's gaining the capacity to respond to his own and others' affective signals in the same comforting and protective self-organizing ways as mother had done previously (Tyson 1988) and to the development of empathic and altruistic capacities (Blum and Blum 1990, Furer 1967). By late childhood, children feel a sense of gratitude and indebtedness (Kitayama 1991), have identified with the active nurturant *amae*-giving functions of the good parents and grandparents, and start to request not only to receive but also to give *amae* to their parents and grandparents, to repay them and to reciprocate in an increasingly shared give-and-take interaction. For example, when I was relaxing with a group of graduate students in an *onsen* or public hot bath, one of the junior students shyly asked a senior student to tell me that he would like to wash my back. After doing so, he told me how happy it made him to wash my back, just as he used to do as a child for his father. Later, other students asked if they could give us a shoulder massage. A travel companion reminisced how she had enjoyed massaging her grandmother's back ever since she was a young child. They conceived of this childhood giving of sensuous gratification to parents and grandparents as giving of *amae*. Similarly, Taketomo (1986a,b) quoted a young woman's description of how her periodic approach to her mother ostensibly requesting *amae* was actually not a wish for her own gratification but rather her way of helping her mother to feel good, by helping her mother to feel needed.

It is important to note this element of give-and-take reciprocity, which increases from childhood onward, since earlier formulations of *amae* in terms of dependency, passive receptivity, and passive love,

---

[16]Such as Okuni-nushi's dwarf helper Sukuna in the ancient sacred mythology, or Nobita's robot helper Doraemon in modern cartoon animations (Tezuka 1996).

and ambiguities of the connotations of these words, may have in-
advertently tended to create an incorrect impression that Japanese
culture is characterized by an unusual degree of unilateral passive
dependency. Although Japanese (and Americans) do interactively
rely and depend upon others, and do intermittently experience
wishes for and enjoy dependency gratification, Japanese do not
normally have dependent personalities. In *Psychoanalytic Terms and
Concepts*, Moore and Fine (1990) mention problems that arise from
the connotations of the word *dependence*. They quote Parens and
Saul (1971) concerning the normal place of dependence in psychic
development and object relations, but note that, "Though it has
normative influences on development and is experienced as a need,
dependence generally carries a pejorative meaning" (p. 51). English
words based on the root '*depend*' have unfortunately confusing connotations. The capacity to depend or rely on others and to be de-
pendable or reliable has a positive connotation and is an essential
component of mature healthy functioning in both cultures. The
DSM-IV's dependent personality, characterized by chronic age-
inappropriate dependency and an inadequate ability to function independently is regarded as inadequate and aberrant in both societies.

Although Japanese are less conflicted than Americans about
enjoying sensuous dependent gratification, active initiative, achievement, and mastery (within culturally sanctioned channels) are strongly
culturally fostered and reinforced in Japan, and dependent clinging
and seeking of excessive indulgence are discouraged and negatively
sanctioned in a way that is comparable to Western culture.[17]

In later adulthood, the erstwhile recipients of *amae* indulgence
become givers of refueling to their own children and grandchildren. Their former *amae* interaction with their own parents becomes
a periodic experience of religious reunion with the spirits of their

---

[17]Problems arising from the ambiguity and sometimes unintended connotations
of the English words *dependency*, *love*, and *passive* were the focus of several presentations
at an interdisciplinary conference on *Amae* reconsidered at the American Psychoanalytic Association meeting in San Diego, May 1997.

ancestors and their departed grandparents and parents. The departed continue to be experienced as being alive, as *kami* or spirits, and one continues to interact with them periodically. They may be consulted, and offered food, drink, and gifts, at a small shrine within one's home or at the cemetery at the Buddhist temple. In a recent article, Nicholas Kristof (1996) described the continuing relationship with the departed.

> Mr. Tsujimoto may be dead, but he is certainly not gone. As is common in Japan, he remains a respected presence in the house, regularly consulted by family members on important matters. They give him a rundown on the local news, present him daily with tea, rice, and water, and even include him in family meals. . . . What is most striking about the Japanese way of death is that there is no stark, impenetrable wall to divide the living from the dead. . . . The dead still linger, offering comfort and counsel to the living. [p. 1]

In mid-winter at the time of the New Year, and again in mid-summer at the Obon festival, the ancestral *kami* return to visit their offspring, most of whom travel to their villages of ancestral origin, if possible, for this reunion. People traditionally conceived of and anticipated their own death as a reunion with the departed. In addition, just as reunion with mother had throughout life been experienced as regenerating and had contributed to progressive intrapsychic reorganizations and metamorphoses, reunion with one's ancestors in death has traditionally been conceived to be a prelude to regeneration and rebirth. This idea was congruent with the experience of members of an agrarian rice-growing society, who experienced the seasonal cycle in which the death of plant life each autumn fertilized rebirth the following spring.

In 1896 Lafcadio Hearn, a Westerner who was an early student and insightful interpreter of Japanese culture, offered a explanation of the continuing relationship to ancestral spirits that is similar to our concepts of the enduring contribution of object relations and internalized object representations to an individual's intrapsychic functioning:

The Japanese never think of an ancestor as having become "only a memory": their dead are alive. . . . The . . . impulses and acts of men [are] explained as due to the influence of the dead. . . . This [is a] hypothesis [that] no modern thinker can declare irrational, since it can claim justification from the scientific doctrine of psychological evolution. . . . We cannot honestly deny that our impulses and feelings, and the higher capacities evolved through the feelings, have literally been shaped by the dead; and even that the general direction of our mental activities has been determined by the powers of the special tendencies bequeathed to us. . . . All our actions are truly influenced by them. [pp. 266–306]

Maternal deities have always had a preeminent role in Japanese cosmology. The supreme deity in Shinto religion is the maternal Sun Goddess, Amaterasu. In Buddhism, Kannon, the compassionate Goddess of Mercy, plays a similarly central maternal role. Just as a child might have sought to attract mother's attention when it had drifted away or when she was otherwise occupied, the *kami* spirits need to be beckoned when one seeks to communicate with them or when one seeks to invite them to join in an *amae*-like reunion. In individual worship, one does so by clapping one's hands firmly together twice. In group religious ceremonies and festivals, the *kami* are invited to participate by the sound of a drum or bells.

Major *matsuri* festivals begin with an invitation to the *kami*, followed by a formal ceremony of sharing food and drink with them and offering them gifts and prayers. However, what really pleases the spirits of the departed and what they like best of all is an exuberant joyous celebration, in which rules can be relaxed, everyone can regress, beer and sake can be enjoyed, and the *kami* can vicariously participate in their youthful descendants' vitality, exuberant activity, and vigorous competitive achievements.[18] Within the set-

---

[18]In traditional folklore, the superchild Kintaro would often cheer up his lonely widowed mother, and rouse her from her distracted periods of reverie and sadness, by performing feats of precocity and superhuman prowess. The first raucous exuberant *matsuri* was staged by the gods to appeal to the supreme mother-goddess Amaterasu to

ting of their own group, people share in a traditionally ecstatic, sensuous, sacred experience, suspending the boundaries of formality, releasing inhibitions, and competing for the favor of, and reuniting with, the mother of permissive indulgence. The ecstatic suspension of reality and joint regressive *amae*-like merger is temporary, and is structured to lead to a foreseeable denouement.

There is a letdown from the excitement, and the participants reindividuate and return to customary reality. After a period of license and indulgence, the decrescendo leads on the one hand to an experience of separation and loneliness, and on the other to an experience of "nothingness" that is felt to be very significant and very emotionally meaningful. It is a return to the lap of the good mother of stability, order, sensible structure, safety, and reason, which has a reassuring quality. One is relieved, in some ways, to return to the world of customary cultural values, and to be back in a meaningful world of secondary process after a period of having let meaning dissolve and caution go to the wind. One reintegrates with one's group and refuels with the supportive, protective good mother of structure, stability, and order.

One could regard *amae* as an intermittent temporary move from the lap of the good mother of predictable consistency and propriety into the lap of the gratifying mother of sweetness and indulgence. At the same time, one moves from one's public outer self of reticence, cooperative reasonableness, group conformity, and propriety to an interlude of rest and relaxation in which one has a chance to gratify some of one's inner wishes. Adults give *amae* gratification to their children and grandchildren, refuel with increasingly reciprocal mutuality with their spouse, and refuel spiritually with the *kami* of their parents and grandparents.

---

come back out of the cave into which she had withdrawn, and to rejoin everyone because they cherished and needed her. Since both the *kami* and the purpose of the celebrations were connected with the cycle of death and rebirth and with agricultural and human fertility, the *matsuri* often included sexual exuberance. In the first *matsuri*, for example, Amaterasu was attracted out of the cave by the roar of approval of the crowd when the goddess Uzume did a striptease.

ACKNOWLEDGMENT

The author wishes to thank Patricia A. Freeman, who contributed to the research and assisted in the preparation of this chapter.

REFERENCES

Abelin, E. L. (1971). The role of the father in the separation-individuation process. In *Separation-Individuation: Essays in Honor of Margaret S. Mahler*, ed. J. B. McDevitt and C. F. Settlage, pp. 229–253. New York: International Universities Press.

Akhtar, S. (1997). *The distinction between needs and wishes: implications for psychoanalytic theory and technique.* Presented at the Scientific Meeting of the Philadelphia Psychoanalytic Society, Philadelphia, April.

Allison, A. (1994). *Nightwork: Sexuality, Pleasure, and Corporate Masculinity in a Tokyo Hostess Club.* Chicago: University of Chicago Press.

Aston, W. G. (1972). *Nihongi, Chronicles of Japan from the Earliest Times to A.D. 697.* Tokyo and Rutland, Vermont: Charles E. Tuttle. (English translation.) (Also commonly known in Japan as "Nihon-shoki.")

Bergman, A. (1997). Formal discussion at the American Psychoanalytic Association conference on *Amae* Reconsidered, San Diego, May.

Blum, E. J., and Blum, H. P. (1990). The development of autonomy and superego precursors. *International Journal of Psycho-Analysis* 71:585–595.

Byerly, L. J. (1993). The therapeutic alliance. In *Treatment of Neurosis in the Young*, ed. M. H. Etezady, pp. 19–50. Northvale, NJ: Jason Aronson.

Caudill, W. (1972). Tiny dramas: vocal communication between mother and infant in Japanese and American families. In *Transcultural Research in Mental Health*, vol. 2, pp. 25–48, ed. W. P. Lebra. Honolulu: University Press of Hawaii.

Caudill, W., and Weinstein, H. (1969). Maternal care and infant behavior in Japan and America. *Psychiatry* 32:12–43.

Doi, T. (1962). *Amae*: a key concept for understanding Japanese personality structure. In *Japanese Culture: Its Development and Characteristics*, ed. R. J. Smith and R. K. Beardsley. Chicago: Aldine.

——— (1973a). *The Anatomy of Dependence.* Tokyo: Kodansha.

——— (1973b). Omote and Ura: concepts derived from Japanese two-fold structure of consciousness. *Journal of Nervous and Mental Disease* 157:258–261.

——— (1986). *The Anatomy of Self.* Tokyo: Kodansha.

Erikson, E. H. (1959). *Identity and the Life Cycle: Psychological Issues*, vol. 1, no. 1. New York: International Universities Press.

Freeman, D. M. A. (1977). Psychoanalysis, folklore and processes of socialization. *Journal of the American Psychoanalytic Association* 25:235–252.

——— (1981). Mythological portrayal of developmental processes and major intrapsychic

restructuralizations. In *The Psychoanalytic Study of Society*, vol. 9, ed. W. Muensterberger, L. B. Boyer, and S. Grolnick, pp. 319–340. New York: Psychohistory
Press.

———— (1993a). *Mythological portrayal of Japanese developmental experiences: the male story
line in sacred Shinto mythology.* Presented at the American Academy of Psychoanalysis, panel on Japanese Separation-Individuation, San Francisco, May.

———— (1993b). *Looking, precocious individuation and appeal behavior portrayed in Ukiyo-e
art of the 17th to 19th centuries.* Presented at the American Psychoanalytic Association, Interdisciplinary Colloquium, New York, December.

———— (1994a). *Mythology as a culturally shared developmental autobiography.* Presented at
the American Psychoanalytic Association, discussion group on mythology, Philadelphia, May.

———— (1994b). *Creation and the early generations of the gods in sacred Japanese mythology.*
Presented at the American Psychoanalytic Association, discussion group on mythology, Philadelphia, May.

———— (1994c). *Early cognitive and visual individuation in Japanese child development.* Presented at Noguchi Kinen Kaikan, Tokyo, August.

———— (1994d). *Some aspects of Japanese female development reflected in the female story line
in mythology and folklore,* parts I and II. Summary of presentations at the American
Psychoanalytic Association discussion group on mythology and interdisciplinary
colloquium, December. Also presented at Jikei University, Tokyo, September.

———— (1995). *Precursors of shame and guilt in Japanese early child development.* Presented at
the International House, Tokyo, August; at Doho University, Nagoya, September; and at the American Psychoanalytic Association, discussion group and interdisciplinary colloquium, New York, December.

———— (1996a). Nyuyoji No Hattatu To Haji No Taiken (child development and shame
experiences). In *Haji* (Shame), ed. O. Kitayama, pp. 65–102. Tokyo: Seiwa
Shoten.

———— (1996b). *Precursors of self-regulation and shame during Japanese early child development.* Presented at the Kyushu University seminar on Japanese culture and psychoanalysis, Fukuoka, October, and at the pre-congress meeting of the Japan
Psychoanalytical Association, Tokyo, October.

———— (1997a). Formal discussion of Salman Akhtar's paper, "The Distinction Between
Needs and Wishes: Implications for Psychoanalytic Theory and Technique," at
the Scientific Meeting of the Philadelphia Psychoanalytic Society, Philadelphia,
April.

———— (1997b). *Precocity, separation-individuation, refueling, and amae.* Presented at the
American Psychoanalytic Association interdisciplinary conference on "Amae
reconsidered," San Diego, May.

———— (1997c). *Japanese developmental experiences and object relations as reflected in mythology.* The Eighth Abram Kardiner Lecture on Psychoanalysis and Culture, spon-
sored by the Association for Psychoanalytic Medicine and the Columbia University Center for Psychoanalytic Training and Research, at the Academy of
Medicine, New York, June.

Freeman, D. M. A., Foulks, E. F., and Freeman, P. A. (1976). Superego development and psychopathology. In *The Psychoanalytic Study of Society*, vol. 7, ed. W. Muensterberger, L. B. Boyer, and A. H. Esman, pp. 107–122. New Haven, CT: Yale University Press.

Freud, A. (1936). *The Ego and the Mechanisms of Defense*, 2nd ed. New York: International Universities Press, 1966.

Freud, S. (1938). Splitting of the ego in the process of defense. *Standard Edition* 23: 271–278.

Furer, M. (1967). Some developmental aspects of the superego. *International Journal of Psycho-Analysis* 48:277–280.

Galenson, E., and Roiphe, H. (1971). The impact of early sexual discovery on mood, defensive organization and symbolization. *Psychoanalytic Study of the Child* 26:195–216. New Haven, CT: Yale University Press.

Greenson, R. (1968). Dis-identification. *International Journal of Psycho-Analysis* 49: 370–374.

Hearn, L. (1896). Some thoughts about ancestor worship. In *Kokoro: Hints and Echoes of Japanese Inner Life*, pp. 266–306. Rutland, VT: Charles E. Tuttle, 1972.

Holder, A. (1982). Preoedipal contributions to the formation of the superego. *Psychoanalytic Study of the Child* 37:245–272. New Haven, CT: Yale University Press.

Hori, S. (1995). *Shame in Japanese society: fear of "Mura Hachibu" and "amae" trauma.* Presented at the American Psychoanalytic Association, interdisciplinary colloquium on Japanese shame and guilt, New York, December.

Jacobson, E. (1964). *The Self and the Object World.* New York: International Universities Press.

Johnson, F. A. (1993). *Dependency and Japanese Socialization.* New York: New York University Press.

Kernberg, O. (1966). Structural derivatives of object relationships. *International Journal of Psycho-Analysis* 47:236–253.

——— (1997). Formal discussion at the American Psychoanalytic Association conference on *amae* reconsidered, San Diego, May.

Kitayama, O. (1985). Preoedipal "taboo" in Japanese folk tragedies. *International Review of Psycho-Analysis* 12:173–185.

——— (1991). The wounded caretaker and guilt. *International Review of Psycho-Analysis* 18:229–240.

——— (1994). *Japanese tragic legends and a maternal prohibition.* Presented at the American Psychoanalytic Association, discussion group on mythology, Philadelphia, May.

——— (1995a). *Symbolic transitionality and maternal disillusionment.* Presented at the International Psychoanalytic Association meeting, San Francisco, August.

——— (1995b). Formal discussion of paper by Freeman (1995) at the International House of Japan, Tokyo, August.

Klein, M. (1952). Some theoretical conclusions regarding the emotional life of the infant. In *Envy and Gratitude and Other Works*, pp. 61–93. London: Hogarth, 1975.

Kosawa, H. (1934). Two kinds of guilt feelings—the Ajase complex. *Japanese Journal of Psychoanalysis* 33:1.

Kristof, N. D. (1996). For rural Japanese, death doesn't break family ties: dead but not gone. *The New York Times*, September 29, p. 1.

Lebra, T. S. (1976). *Japanese Patterns of Behavior*. Honolulu: University of Hawaii Press.

Mahler, M. S. (1968). *On Human Symbiosis and the Vicissitudes of Individuation*. Vol. 1: *Infantile Psychosis*. New York: International Universities Press.

Mahler, M. S., Pine, F., and Bergman, A. (1975). *The Psychological Birth of the Human Infant: Symbiosis and Individuation*. New York: Basic Books.

Moore, B. E., and Fine, B. D. (1990). *Psychoanalytic Terms and Concepts*. New Haven, CT: American Psychoanalytic Association and Yale University Press.

Nakakuki, M. (1994). Normal and developmental aspects of masochism: transcultural and clinical implications. *Psychiatry* 57:244–257.

Okimoto, J. T. (1997). *A cultural comparison of the appeal cycle in American and Japanese dyads*. Presented at the American Psychoanalytic Association, interdisciplinary conference on *amae* reconsidered, San Diego, May.

Okonogi, K. (1978). The Ajase complex of the Japanese (1). *Japan Echo* 5:88–105.

——— (1979). The Ajase complex of the Japanese (2). *Japan Echo* 6:104–118.

——— (1997). A history of psychoanalysis in Japan. In *Psychoanalysis International: A Guide to Psychoanalysis Throughout the World*, vol. 2, ed. P. Kutter, pp. 123–141. Hillsdale, NJ: Analytic Press.

Parens, H. (1979). *The Development of Aggression in Early Childhood*. New York: Jason Aronson.

Parens, H., and Saul, L. J. (1971). *Dependence in Man*. New York: International Universities Press.

Philippi, D. L. (1968). *Kojiki* (Record of Ancient Matters). Tokyo: University of Tokyo Press. (English translation.)

Sandler, J., and Rosenblatt, B. (1962). The concept of the representational world. *Psychoanalytic Study of the Child* 17:128–145. New York: International Universities Press.

Settlage, C. F., Bemesderfer, S., Rosenthal, J., et al. (1991). The appeal cycle in early mother–child interaction: nature and implications of a finding from developmental research. *Journal of the American Psychoanalytic Association* 39:987–1014.

Spitz, R. A. (1965). *The First Year of Life*. New York: International Universities Press.

Taketomo, Y. (1982). The reticent father: some thoughts on Japanese culture and conflict. *Academy Forum* 26:12–14.

——— (1986a). Toward the discovery of self: a transcultural perspective. *Journal of the American Academy of Psychoanalysis* 14:69–84.

——— (1986b). *Amae* as metalanguage: a critique of Doi's theory of *amae*. *Journal of the American Academy of Psychoanalysis* 14:525–544.

——— (1990). Cultural adaptation of psychoanalysis in Japan, 1912–1952. *Social Research* 57:951–991.

——— (1993). *Amae interaction in childhood and through the life cycle*. Presented at the American Psychoanalytic Association, interdisciplinary colloquium, December.

——— (1997). The suspension of formality in interpersonal relations: a review of interactional *amae* and intrapsychic *amae*. Presented at the American Psychoanalytic Association Interdisciplinary Conference on "Amae Reconsidered," San Diego, May.

Tezuka, C. (1996). *Doraemon and Snoopy.* Presented at the American Psychoanalytic Association, interdisciplinary colloquium on shared myths and fantasies in modern folklore, December.

Tyson, P. (1988). Psychic structure formation: the complementary roles of affects, drives, object relations, and conflict. *Journal of American Psychoanalytic Association* 36(suppl): 73–98.

Tyson, P., and Tyson, R. L. (1984). Narcissism and superego development. *Journal of the American Psychoanalytic Association* 32:75–98.

Ushijima, S. (1994a). *On the anality of Princess Moonlight (Kaguya-hime).* Presented at the American Psychoanalytic Association, discussion group on mythology, December.

———— (1994b). *Female development seen in some Japanese folktales.* Presented at the American Psychoanalytic Association, interdisciplinary colloquium on Japanese mythology, December.

Weil, A. P. (1970). The basic core. *Psychoanalytic Study of the Child* 25:442–460. New York: International Universities Press.

Winnicott, D. W. (1971). *Playing and Reality.* London: Tavistock.

3

A CROSS-CULTURAL PERSPECTIVE ON SEPARATION- INDIVIDUATION THEORY

Discussion of Freeman's Chapter "Emotional Refueling in Development, Mythology, and Cosmology: The Japanese Separation- Individuation Experience"

Calvin F. Settlage, M.D.

It was in 1970 that the annual Margaret S. Mahler Symposium Series on Child Development was initiated under the leadership of Selma Kramer. These symposia have constituted the major forum for an ongoing, vigorous, scientific dialogue serving the elaboration, clinical application, and testing of separation–individuation theory. As this symposium further demonstrates, it is very clear that the studies of Margaret Mahler and her research colleagues, and the conceptualization of separation–individuation theory, have been enormously helpful in fathoming the details of preoedipal development and in extending psychoanalytic theory and treatment to preoedipal psychopathology (Akhtar et al. 1996, Settlage 1991, 1993, 1994).

As background to my discussion of Dr. Daniel Freeman's chapter, I take note of three ways in which I value his thought and work. First, at one of these symposia, some years ago, I presented a finding from separation–individuation–based research on mother–child interaction during the second year of life. The finding was the *appeal cycle*, a normal phenomenon of early mother–child interaction.

At that symposium, Freeman observed that the appeal cycle might be culture bound and seen only in Caucasian-American culture. His comment prompted a cross-cultural study, some years later, employing the same methodology with mother–child pairs of Japanese nationals living temporarily in America, Chinese-Vietnamese immigrants, and Caucasian Americans.* The study demonstrated that the appeal cycle is present in all three cultures but that its form and the nature of the mother–child interaction varied in accordance with culture-specific values and child-rearing practices. I will refer to this study later with regard to the cross-cultural perspective and to the arousal, expression, and regulation of aggression in early separation-individuation.

Second, I am now indebted to Freeman for his detailed discussion of Japanese child rearing and his insightful elaboration of the relationship between culture, child rearing, and child development in both its behavioral and its intrapsychic, structural dimensions.

Third, I want to underscore Freeman's unique contribution to the study of child development in the context of culture. Mythology has been the object of study for many years, and the oedipal myth was employed by Freud as the basis for the Oedipus complex in normal development. Freeman was the first, though, to perceive that myths regularly reflect the shared developmental experience of the members of the culture. As he has demonstrated in other articles (Freeman 1977, 1981, 1994), mythological data can complement data from direct observational research on child development. In this regard, I am particularly interested in the idea that both unremembered preverbal experience and later repressed experience can, as in dreams, gain representation in mythology. I will bring this idea to bear on the issue of aggression in early separation-individuation.

---

*The Appeal Cycle Phenomenon in Three Cultures: An Exploratory Cultural Comparison of Child Development in the Second Year of Life. This study was undertaken in Seattle, in collaboration with Joseph T. Okimoto, M.D., project director.

SEPARATION AND LOSS
IN HUMAN DEVELOPMENT

Freeman's analysis and discussion of Japanese child rearing makes it clear that separation and loss of relationship, and their management, are a central preoccupation in Japanese culture. That separation and loss are important in Caucasian-American culture is demonstrated by the derivation of separation-individuation theory from observational research on Caucasian-American subjects. A discussion of the nature of human development will help explain our sensitivity to separation and loss.

Development is a sine qua non of the human species. The largely innately provided, species-typical behavior patterns of organismic regulation and adaptive behavior in other animals are superseded in the human by generic instinctual drives and the capability of developing self-regulatory and adaptive behavior. Achieving this capability is dependent upon a developmental relationship. The mother–infant relationship, the initial developmental relationship, is the species-specific accommodation to the immaturity at birth and the prolonged dependency of the human infant. In the mammalian species generally, survival during the first weeks and months of life depends upon parental care and protection, and parental behavior provides the model for some learned behavior. Unique to the human species is the role of the mother as a developmental object (Settlage 1980, 1996). It is in interaction primarily with the mother that the child's basic personality develops during the first few years of life.

As a developmental object emotionally available for interaction with her child, the mother serves her child's development in several ways: (1) she supports and facilitates the development of the unfolding biologically predetermined capacities; (2) as the primary love object and primary caregiver, she contributes to the development of the child's sense of well-being and core sense of self; and (3) as a temporary auxiliary ego participating in the regulation of the child's internal processes and external behavior, she provides a model for self–regulatory and adaptive capacities acquired through internalization and identification. The relationship with the mother clearly is crucial for the child's development.

But the mother–infant intimacy of the symbiotic phase and the infant's near-total dependence on the mother must yield to the normal developmental thrust of individuation and therefore to separation. The intimacy and dependence of the symbiotic relationship is not only exceedingly close but insures the survival of the otherwise helpless infant. Therefore, separation poses a huge threat to the child: disruption of the security of the closeness with the mother and loss of relationship with the indispensable mother. This threat evokes anxiety and anger, and correlated defensive and expressive behaviors.

The detailed comparison that can now be made of separation-individuation experience in Caucasian-American culture, as described in Mahler's separation–individuation theory, and in Japanese culture, as sensitively and comprehensively described by Freeman, is beyond the scope of my discussion. I shall content myself with (1) a lesser comparison from the cross-cultural study of the appeal cycle, (2) comments on emotional refueling and *amae*, and (3) some thoughts about the role of preoedipal aggression and its management in the formation of psychopathology.

A CROSS-CULTURAL COMPARISON

The appeal cycle was conceived on the basis of observations made in two studies of mother–child interaction during the second year of life (Settlage et al. 1990, 1991). The experimental stimulus in both studies was separation in the form of the mother's diminished involvement with her child. When the mother–child relationship in a play situation was disrupted by a phone call to the mother and then an interview with the mother in the child's presence, the child was observed to at first adapt to the social situation. Then the child would become increasingly distressed, manifesting signs of anger and anxiety. The distress culminated in an appeal to the mother. If the mother responded empathetically to the appeal, the child's distress was temporarily relieved. The cycle would then be repeated. We regard the appeal cycle as a normal, regularly occurring phenomenon serving developmental process. Libidinal or emotional separation, while in physical presence of the mother, is paralleled by internalization in the development of the capacity for self-regulation as evidenced in the adaptive phase.

As noted, the more recent cross-cultural study, which is about to be reported, demonstrated that the appeal phenomenon is present in all three cultures, but that its form and the nature of the mother–child interaction varied in accordance with cultural values and child-rearing practices. Generalizing and condensing, the Japanese mother was very closely interactive with her child, and separation was hardly in evidence. The Chinese-Vietnamese mother was similarly closely interactive but took an overtly directive stance with her child in supervising the play. The Caucasian-American mother encouraged her child to take initiatives and to play independently at a distance from the mother. Even this epitomizing summary points to cultural differences in the separation-individuation experience. In the full report of this cross-cultural study, we discuss the hypothesis that the internal mental representations that are considered important in psychic structure formation will reflect the different cultural characteristics of the mother–child relationship.

With regard to my later discussion of aggression in preoedipal development, I take special note of the fact that even a relatively minor disruption of the relationship with the mother, as was introduced in the second year of life studies, aroused anger in the child.

EMOTIONAL REFUELING AND *AMAE*

In Mahler's separation-individuation theory, *emotional refueling* is a phenomenon of the practicing subphase. The term is applied to the toddler's periodic and unanxious return to the mother out of a need for refueling through physical contact (Mahler et al. 1975). In his study of Japanese culture, Freeman compares the concept of *amae* in Japanese child rearing to that of emotional refueling in Caucasian-American culture. Initially, *amae* referred to an intermittent, regressive, indulgent interaction between mother and child. Defined from the child's position, *amae* is the need to be responded to, taken care of, cherished, and given special significance (Johnson 1993). Freeman sees *amae* as central in Japanese child rearing. Noting that the Japanese see *amae* as going beyond early childhood, Freeman extends the concept to include the entire life course of the individual. He also broadens the concept, emphasizing that both of the participants are beneficiaries of the *amae* interaction. An adult gets as much out of giving *amae* as does the child receiving it. Freeman defines *amae* as a Japanese cultural interaction in which people intermittently seek, receive, and give one another affectionate support, intimacy, and indulgence. Freeman agrees with Taketomo (1997), who conceives the regressive, indulgent interaction of *amae* to be temporal and involve a consensual suspension of the usual rules of behavior. The adult engaging in *amae* is not to be seen as underdeveloped and fixated at an infantile level (Popp and Taketomo 1993, Taketomo 1986).

Freeman conceives further that the periodic emotional refueling of *amae* interactions promote growth and development in both of the participants, whether child and parent or adult and adult.

In his elaboration of the concept of *amae*, Freeman agrees with psychoanalytic thinking that sees human development to be an ongoing, potentially lifelong process (Settlage 1992, 1996, Settlage et al. 1988). Beginning in earliest childhood and continuing throughout later childhood and adulthood, not only the mother but other individuals can serve as developmental objects. This can be true of any two-person relationship embodying a developmental potential or gradient whereby one individual can learn and develop in the interaction with the other (Loewald 1960, Settlage 1980), for example, as between student and teacher, and professional and mentor.

In learning about *amae* in Japanese culture, I found myself reflecting on its possible relevance for Caucasian-American culture. There clearly are cultural differences in child rearing and personality development as determined by the accepted or official values of the culture as a whole. It struck me, though, that the behavioral phenomena in the two cultures are not strikingly different. The phenomenon Dr. Freeman describes as a developmental norm in Japanese culture is sometimes seen in individual mother–child pairs in Caucasian-American culture.

Cross-cultural knowledge might be helpful to clinicians who deal with deviation from our culture's developmental norm and the related psychopathology. This knowledge could extricate us from our own culture-bound perspective on the rights and wrongs of child rearing. It could help us place the clinical problem presented by a given patient in a broader developmental context.

It is in retrospect that I wonder whether the prescription of *amae* might have furthered the treatment of a young boy suffering from protracted separation anxiety.

> Beginning at age 3 years, 6 months, this boy was in analysis for intense separation anxiety. Work on his underlying, repressed anger in response to significant, separation trauma with its attendant threat of loss helped him to separate without difficulty except in one respect. Continuing into his preadolescence, he insisted that one of his parents stay in his room until he fell asleep. If he drowsed off, he alertly awakened when the parent started to leave the room. If he fell asleep but awakened during the night, he would go to his parents' bedroom and want to finish the night there. Thorough analysis of the possible oedipal determinants of this behavior did not alter it.

I came to think of this boy as making daily sorties into the outside world—where he had good friends and did extremely well as an outstanding student and athlete—and then returning to the bosom of the family where he sought comfort (refueling) through reunion with the parents of his early childhood.

Amae is not sanctioned in Caucasian-American culture, particularly for the child beyond infancy. On the contrary, the cultural values and parental attitudes disapprove of such "babyish" behavior, and pressure is exerted to give it up, grow up, and behave like a "big boy." I wonder whether explaining the concept and purpose of *amae* to the parents and encouraging them to interact with their son in this way might have ameliorated the separation trauma and enabled an earlier resolution of the boy's separation anxiety.

AGGRESSION IN EARLY SEPARATION-INDIVIDUATION

I turn now to a subject of great interest to me, namely, the role of repressed aggression in the formation of psychopathology. This subject has come increasingly to the fore because of separation-individuation theory and its focus on preoedipal development. I discuss it here because cross-cultural studies indicate that aggression is dealt with differently in the child-rearing practices of different cultures.

With regard to aggression, it is of interest that Freud's (1940) summation of the basic tenets of psychoanalysis conveys his lack of satisfaction with his understanding of the role of aggression in the genesis of neuroses. His observations had shown that repression seemed to arise invariably from the component instincts of sexual life. Yet psychoanalytic theory suggested that the demands of the aggressive instinct should occasion the same repressions and pathological consequences. He referred to this as a gap in theory that could not then be filled, and indicated that it remains to be decided whether the large part sexuality plays in the causation of neuroses is an exclusive one.

It seems safe to say that separation–individuation theory has enabled the recognition that the primary developmental confrontation with aggression takes place during preoedipal development. Aggression and its management become a definitive developmental issue in the practicing, rapprochement, and object constancy subphases of the separation–individuation process. Operating beyond the bounds of normal development and in the service of maintaining, at all costs, the all-important relationship with the parent, the defenses evoked to deal with anger, rage, and hostile aggression are central to the formation of preoedipal pathology.

In preoedipal development, repression normally is employed during the rapprochement subphase to secure an initial degree of autonomy from the aggressive drive. Normal repression of aggression has a further role in the next subphase of attainment of libidinal object constancy. In usual, expectable child–parent interaction as compared with pathological interaction, Mahler (Mahler et al. 1975), and Kernberg (1975) postulate that an important shift in the management of hostile aggression takes place toward the end of the second year of life. Repression submerges the bulk of the hostile aggression toward the love object, replacing splitting of the object into an all-good and an all-bad object. The intrapsychic conflict engendered by the confrontation between the immature ego of early psychic development and what Freud called the untamed aggression of the id is thus seen to be resolved.

However, clinical experience in Caucasian-American culture suggests that our modes of dealing with aggression in early childhood largely fail to achieve a healthy modulated—as contrasted with a pathological, rigidly controlling, or shutting off—regulation of aggression (Akhtar 1996, Settlage 1994). Instead, the combination of the external, parental suppressive mode and the child's internal defensive mode tend to result in excessive repression of aggression.

A pathologic child–parent interaction can grossly interfere with the development of regulation of aggression. Such is seen, for example, when the child experiences the parent as a malevolent *inconstant object* (Blum 1981) rather than a relatively constant love object. With an inconstant object, "the threat of betrayal and desertion is ever present" (Blum 1981, p. 108). Hostile aggression is not dealt with through its integration with predominantly loving experiences in the formation of libidinal object constancy. The psychic representation of the inconstant object is conceived to be the reciprocal of libidinal object constancy (Blum 1981).

Once repressed, aggressive urges and affects are no longer consciously felt or directly expressed. They thus are removed from the usual, social, interactive processing in the child–parent relationship. The child tends to fail to learn about their nature, their range of intensity, their monitoring function regarding the state of a relationship, and their appropriate use in a relationship.

Repressed, unconscious anger, rage, and hostile aggression lie at the heart of our most severe pathologies. Readily triggered by disruption of an important object relationship, these repressed urges and affects tend to evoke defensive splitting. The recurrent splitting of the object into good and bad representations interferes with the integration of these representations under the aegis of a predominance of loving experience. The result usually is the failure, outside of treatment, to establish object constancy as a reasonably stable psychic structure, despite loving relationships in later childhood and adulthood.

Although quite different on a manifest level than Caucasian-American child rearing, Japanese child rearing, too, does not appear to achieve optimal regulation of aggression. This seems to be the case despite the Japanese mother's sensitive attunement and empathy with her infant, despite the prolonged separation-individuation that provides time for the working through of feelings and for internalization and structuring, and despite the repeatedly available refueling and emotional support of *amae*. Freeman notes that both the Japanese girl and the Japanese boy tend to suffer the negative consequences of repressed aggression. The girl feels polluted by her aggressive feelings, and the boy fears his angry feelings and destructive impulses.

I now turn to mythology and the light it can shed on early developmental experience, particularly on aggression. Freeman states that myths vividly portray an unfolding drama of intrapsychic and interpersonal development, extending from infancy through the life cycle. Myths present a series of dangerous challenges and death-and-rebirth transitions and metamorphoses representing a sequence of developmental crises or stages, each with its concomitant personality reorganization and intrapsychic restructuralization (Freeman 1997).

With this conceptualization as background, I found myself intrigued by the series of myths about *The Age of the Gods* in sacred Shinto mythology. These myths, which are only alluded to in footnotes in Freeman's chapter, are fully presented and discussed in other papers (Freeman 1994, 1997). As one of the earliest stories in sacred Shinto mythology, written down in the 700s A.D., *The Age of the Gods* is interpreted as representing the developmental period of shared magical omnipotence of infancy and early childhood. It expresses intense rage and contains much violence. Over the course of the story, the rage and violence are moderated through the progressive development and emotional maturation of the portrayed mythological figures.

Selecting them for my purpose, I present some examples of the rage and violence. In so doing, I liberally paraphrase Freeman's (1997) account of *The Age of the Gods*. I regret that I cannot include the details of Freeman's (1997) perceptive and sensitive analysis of *The Age of the Gods* as a representation of the Japanese separation-individuation experience.

> The primal mother-figure, Izanami, suddenly is burned while giving birth to the God of Fire. After terrible suffering, she dies. Furious with the baby who has caused the mother's death, the primal father-figure, Izanagi, cuts off the baby's head.
>
> When Izanagi ignores Izanami's request that he not look at her in her deteriorated condition, she becomes enraged and sends the Thunder Gods and all of the Hideous Female Spirits of Hades to kill him. And she tried to kill him.

Her youngest surviving child, Susano-o, the Storm God, is inconsolable, and his loud and intrusive crying is described as being a typhoon. His rage and dyscontrol are intolerable. He is impetuous, violent, and destructive. His wailing withers the green mountains, and dries up rivers and seas.

When his older sister, Amaterasu, the Sun Goddess, learns that he wants to visit her in her realm of Heaven, she fears that he will wreck her Kingdom. She puts on male attire, dons a suit of armor, and comes out with weapons ready to do battle. But the sister and brother make peace.

Later Susano-o's impetuous, aggressive, and destructive side again breaks through. He starts to break down boundaries—dikes between rice fields, fences, and walls—and he defecates and urinates on the floor of Amaterasu's palace when she is about to celebrate the feast of tasting first fruits.

At the climax of his impetuous behavior, Susano-o throws the skinned corpse of a horse into Amaterasu's sacred chamber, a most extreme act of violation, pollution, and contamination. Amaterasu becomes so frightened, incensed, and enraged that she withdraws and seals herself in a cave, plunging the world into darkness and winter! This offers evil spirits and ghosts an opportunity to gain control, and all manner of calamities occur.

Giving the loving, nurturing, tolerantly patient, and "*amaeing*" nature of Japanese child rearing, what is the explanation of the rage and violence in *The Age of the Gods*?

As was noted in the foregoing discussion of aggression in early separation-individuation, anger and rage are usually defensively repressed in the interest of adaptation within the mother–child (parent–child) relationship, earlier in the Japanese girl and later in the boy. Thereby the interpersonal conflict is internalized and the repressed urges and feelings are blocked from direct access to consciousness and from direct expression. But these feelings can gain symbolic expression in mythology because, even more than is true for dreams, the lack of conscious participation in the creation of the myth allows a protective distancing from the disturbed personal implications of its content.

It also seems true that the subjectively experienced feelings of anger and rage aroused in the child by separation and its threat of loss are much greater than observation and evaluation of child behavior suggests. This likely is the case whether the observation is made in everyday life or in a research situation such as that of the appeal-cycle studies. Whether a parent or a researcher, we no doubt prefer not to fully empathize with the child's feelings and are prone to minimize and deny their intensity. This attitude may be due to our reluctance to confront and resonate with these feelings as we experienced them in our own childhoods.

In this same regard, it is of interest to note that the problem of self-regulation of aggression is generationally transmitted. The parents' discomfort with their own aggression interferes with their ability to use it effectively in setting limits on the child's aggressive behavior. A familiar pattern is to avoid or defer exerting effective control over the child's aggressive behavior, meanwhile voicing admonitions, and then to express angry, sometimes rageful, exasperation when the child does not conform to the parent's wishes. In this pattern, the parent first undershoots and then overshoots the mark. The use of the gun metaphor is intentional.

In this kind of regulatory behavior, the parent does not present a good model for identification in the development of self-regulation of aggression (Settlage 1994). Dynamically, in both parent and child, the effective use of healthy aggression is blocked by the unconscious fear that repressed rage and hostility will escape from repressive control by riding on the coattails of expressed healthy aggression. By the term *healthy aggression*, I mean the necessary employment of aggression in the service of adaptation respectful of the rights of others, and in the service of maintaining a good relationship.

CONCLUDING REMARKS

As the world has witnessed, not only in the past but currently, some cultures and subcultures sanction terroristic violence against innocents in the pursuit of what they believe to be just causes. And as the United States, which does not sanction terrorism, witnesses at the time of this writing, individuals reared in the United States can embrace the terrorist attitude.

At the opposite pole, there is the defensively determined constraint against the expression of aggression seen in individuals suffering from schizophrenia. What follows is not meant to deny or ignore the fact that some schizophrenic individuals do act violently toward themselves or others. According to Bak (1954), the inability of the ego to control and neutralize aggression makes the aggressive drive instrumental in bringing about major regression. For example, the catatonic state, with its immobility and inability to take action, defends against destructive impulses. He presents the postulate that the ego's falling to pieces, and splitting of the self, and the dissolution of the object within the ego defensively serve the dispersal of the destructive impulse toward self or others.

How are we to understand the failure of empathy for other human beings and lack of constraint on violent aggression in the terrorist, and the constraint of violence in the schizophrenic individual suffering from this most serious of mental disorders? In the case of the terrorist, do specific cultural and subcultural values offer sufficient explanation, or do specific child rearing attitudes and practices also pertain? In the case of the schizophrenic, where we believe that untoward childhood experience is an etiologic factor in the condition, alongside possible if not probable genetic factors, does the blocking of violence suggest that there is an innate inhibition against violence toward members of one's own species? Might there be such an inhibition, which, because of the paramount importance of development and therefore of environmental influence in our species, can be overridden in the case of humankind?

Perhaps, as Anna Freud (1946) observed, the problem of aggression in the human species is an unresolvable struggle between the aggressive drive and psychic structure that is developed rather than innate—between the "relative immutability of the id" (p. 153) and the ego. But the arousal and external and internal management of aggression as observed in child rearing and as conceptualized in early separation–individuation make me unwilling to settle for that view. I believe that there is the possibility of a better development of self-regulation of aggression (Settlage 1994).

It is my hope that insights derived from the combination of (1) studies of mythology, cosmology, and religions, all of which include and represent the attempts of humans to deal with aggression and the ultimate separation, death (Settlage 1973), and (2) cross-cultural studies of the nuances of regulation of aggression in child rearing may reveal avenues for better ways of dealing with aggression during early child development.

REFERENCES

Akhtar, S. (1996). Object constancy and adult psychopathology. In *The Internal Mother: Conceptual and Technical Aspects of Object Constancy*, pp. 127–156. Northvale, NJ: Jason Aronson.

Akhtar, S., Kramer, S., and Parens, H., eds. (1996). *The Internal Mother: Conceptual and Technical Aspects of Object Constancy*. Northvale, NJ: Jason Aronson.

Bak, R. C. (1954). The schizophrenic defense against aggression. *International Journal of Psycho-Analysis* 35:129–134.

Blum, H. P. (1981). Object inconstancy and paranoid conspiracy. *Journal of the American Psychoanalytic Association* 29:789–813.

Freeman, D. M. A. (1977). Psychoanalysis, folklore, and processes of socialization. *Journal of the American Psychoanalytic Association* 25:235–252.

——— (1981). Mythological portrayal of developmental processes and major intrapsychic restructuralizations. *The Psychoanalytic Study of Society*, ed. W. Muensterberger, L. B. Boyer, and S. Grolnick, 9:319–340. New York: Psychohistory Press.

——— (1994). *Some aspects of Japanese female development reflected in the female story line in mythology and folklore, parts I and II*. Presented at the American Psychoanalytic Association, discussion group and interdisciplinary colloquium.

——— (1997). *Japanese developmental experiences and object relations as reflected in mythology*. Presented as the Eighth Abram Kardiner Lecture on Psychoanalysis and Culture, the Academy of Medicine, New York, June.

Freud, A. (1946). *The Ego and The Mechanisms of Defense*. New York: International Universities Press.

Freud, S. (1940). An outline of psycho-analysis. *Standard Edition* 23:141–207.

Johnson, F. A. (1993). *Dependency and Japanese Socialization: Psychoanalytic and Anthropological Investigations into Amae*. New York: New York University Press.

Kernberg, O. (1975). *Borderline Conditions and Pathological Narcissism*. New York: Jason Aronson.

Loewald, H. (1960). On the therapeutic action of psychoanalysis. *International Journal of Psycho-Analysis* 41:16–33.

Mahler, M. S., Pine, F., and Bergman, A. (1975). *The Psychological Birth of the Human Infant*. New York: Basic Books.

Popp, C., and Taketomo, Y. (1993). The application of the core conflictual relationship theme method to Japanese psychoanalytic psychotherapy. *Journal of the American Academy of Psychoanalysis* 21:229–252.

Settlage, C. F. (1973). Panel report: On the experience of separation-individuation and its reverberations throughout the course of life: infancy and early childhood, ed. M. Winestine. *Journal of the American Psychoanalytic Association* 21:135–154.

—— (1980). Psychoanalytic developmental thinking in current and historical perspective. *Psychoanalysis and Contemporary Thought* 3:139–170.

—— (1991). On the treatment of preoedipal pathology. In *Beyond the Symbiotic Orbit: Advances in Separation-Individuation Theory: Essays in Honor of Selma Kramer, M.D.*, ed S. Akhtar and H. Parens, pp. 351–367. Hillsdale, NJ: Analytic Press.

—— (1992). Psychoanalytic observations on adult development in life and in the therapeutic relationship. *Psychoanalysis and Contemporary Thought* 15:349–375.

—— (1993). Therapeutic process and developmental process in the restructuring of object and self constancy. *Journal of the American Psychoanalytic Association* 41:473–492.

—— (1994). On the contribution of separation-individuation theory to psychoanalysis: developmental process, pathogenesis, therapeutic process, and technique. In *Mahler and Kohut: Perspectives on Development, Psychopathology, and Technique*, ed. S. Kramer and S. Akhtar, pp. 17–52. Northvale, NJ: Jason Aronson.

—— (1996). Transcending old age: creativity, development, and psychoanalysis in the life of a centarian. *International Journal of Psycho-Analysis* 77:549–564.

Settlage, C. F., Bemesderfer, S., Rosenthal, J., et al. (1991). The appeal cycle in early mother–child interaction: the nature and implications of a finding from developmental research. *Journal of the American Psychoanalytic Association* 39:987–1014.

Settlage, C. F., Curtis, J., Lozoff, M., et al. (1988). Conceptualizing adult development. *Journal of the American Psychoanalytic Association* 36:347–369.

Settlage, C. F., Rosenthal, J., Spielman, P., et al. (1990). An exploratory study of mother–child interaction during the second year of life. *Journal of the American Psychoanalytic Association* 38:705–731.

Taketomo, Y. (1986). *Amae* as a metalanguage: a critique of Doi's theory of *amae*. *Journal of the American Academy of Psychoanalysis* 14:525–544.

—— (1997). *The suspension of formality in interpersonal relations: a review of interactional amae and intrapsychic amae*. Presented at the interdisciplinary conference, *Amae* Reconsidered, meeting of the American Psychoanalytic Association, San Diego, May.

4

MOTHERS AND OTHERS: BONDING, SEPARATION-INDIVIDUATION, AND RESULTANT EGO DEVELOPMENT IN DIFFERENT AFRICAN-AMERICAN CULTURES

Carlotta Miles, M.D.

Child development among African-Americans* varies not only according to life experience, but also according to the attendant customs, values, and attitudes of economic and class status. This chapter considers the child-rearing practices of three distinct African-American cultures: the lower/underclass; the middle-middle class; and the upper-middle and upper class, or "elite blacks." Particular emphasis is placed on the mother or surrogate mother–infant relationship and the vicissitudes of caregiving in these three cultures.

"ARE YOU MY MOTHER?": PATTERNS OF CHILD CARE AND INDIVIDUATION IN THE AFRICAN-AMERICAN UNDERCLASS

This is the culture most exploited by the media, and is therefore the group that most other Americans think represents the race as a

---

*In 1994, the United States population was just under 260 million. The black population was 23 million, about 12.7 percent, or one in eight (Bennett 1993 and 1994).

whole. In fact, the group (family income below $10,000) constitutes about 25.8 percent of all married-couple African-American families. It is a culture characterized by a great deal of pathology, both sociological and psychological. There is pervasive unemployment, welfare dependency, teenage pregnancy, absent males, and poor education.

This lifestyle is not temporary, nor is it new. It is a culture in and of itself, with its own values and guidelines. For example, there is no connection at all between childbearing and marriage. It is further characterized by multiple siblings and therefore large, extended families idealizing, but not necessarily practicing, the "village" concept of child rearing. Family structure is matriarchal, with a high degree of parental helplessness. Parents have lower level or inadequate defense mechanisms (denial and projection), and no concept of psychological child development. Bonds are made and broken randomly and little attention is paid to separation anxiety. Survival concerns are uppermost. There is little penetration from the outside world and little change in the rules of living from the outside; change comes from the inside and is often even more destructive and dangerous when it does come. During the 1960s this culture became isolated from the other African-American cultures and thereby lost role models for traditional success and middle-class support, previously valued.

Constitutional factors play a great role in the degree of ego strength possible under these circumstances. Other factors might also contribute to the survival of the egos of these children. Early physical illness, surgical procedures, and witnessing family violence especially foretell an adverse outcome in this regard. Individual egos are characterized by low self-esteem, limited psychological coping mechanisms, and poor judgment and problem-solving skills. Collectively, there are limited or nonsupportive relationships with family, few friends, and no involvement in community groups. Because men are often seen as children themselves, or as liabilities, women do not look to them for protection or economic help, only emotional and sexual closeness, which are usually short-lived. In fact, an unemployed and/or alcoholic or drug-using male is seen as the same kind of liability as a child. Women know they are on their own, and with the help of the government, they try to simply survive. Children are not planned, and abortion is often viewed as "genocide." Infants can start out being valued for themselves or as evidence of love for the father, or as concrete evidence of the father's sexual prowess. However, when the relationship ends, as it typically does, the child becomes a responsibility carried solely by the mother.

Childbearing starts very early—at 14 years of age and sometimes earlier. After several cycles of love relationships, pregnancy, and abandonment, the young woman is left with several children and no mate. She may try her best to meet the demands of motherhood as she understands them, but with limited knowledge and experience, poor education, no money, and unmet emotional needs of her own, she cannot provide the consistency needed for good ego development in her children.

Infants of these mothers cry a lot; they may show little or no evidence of bonding to the mothers, but may have chosen a sibling, relative, or neighbor with whom to bond, or in the worst cases may simply be depersonalized—going with anyone and calling everyone "Mama." Breast-feeding is virtually nonexistent, as teen/young mothers are vain and involved with their own developmental agendas, and different people take turns feeding the infant. Hospitals have trouble getting premature infants picked up when they reach the discharge birth weight; postpartum depression is common, and crack-addicted babies abound. Given these conditions, many babies have the initial attachment phase interrupted; never go through subsequent phases, such as rapprochement; and at the age of 3 are anxious, and sometimes depressed and depersonalized, with no concept of who will meet their essential needs.

New siblings follow closely on the heels of first or second babies, and a mother's delight in an infant may now turn to anger at the increased responsibilities of more than one child. Her rejection of the first child coincides with the child's first individuation attempts, so the child, meeting suddenly with his or her mother's shift to an impatient, punitive way of relating, develops a negative association with separation and enforcement of age-appropriate ambivalence.

Older mothers dream of education for their children, and are very disappointed when teen pregnancy or violence overtakes the children and starts the familiar cycle again. Getting out of the underclass is not easy. There is very little concept of how to reach goals. Emotional deprivation makes postponement of gratification impossible.

Untreated depression and other mental illness, along with histories of abuse and neglect, are commonplace among parents. There is little or no basic understanding of parenting responsibilities and skills or of child development, so that discipline is almost always punitive. There is also little demonstration of affection toward the children (after infancy) or of getting any enjoyment through interaction with the children. During infancy, teen mothers identify with their babies. Everyone loves the baby and shows it affection and attention. When the baby begins to walk and to separate, everyone stops indulging it and the mother's identification ceases. She no longer has her own feelings of deprivation addressed through the identification process. Her solution is to have another baby.

Because of poor nutrition, substance abuse, and random and careless childcare, ego development is poor and often id-dominated. Adult rage is not subliminated, and so is readily available and projected outward and expressed in violent acts toward both whites and blacks.

Children are often given away, preferably to relatives, but sometimes to friends, relatives of ex-lovers, or neighbors who step in. Social services often remove children and place them in the foster care system. Because childbearing starts so early, the generations are short. If the mother is 15, her mother may only be 30 and her grandmother 47. The grandmother may still be having children herself, or may be a substance abuser, making the backup caregiver of forty years ago virtually nonexistent.

The concept of bonding is foreign. The "good" baby is one who goes anywhere with anybody; the "bad" baby is one who cries and expresses frustration or fear when separated from the familiar. Mothers prolong developmental stages far beyond their age-appropriate limits: bottles are allowed into the third and fourth years. With oral-stage emotional needs unmet, a hostile dependency is set up. "The process of individuation is burdened not only by the widening world of reality, but by the child's phase-specific psycho-sexual conflicts" (Mahler 1968, p. xii). Thereby, fixation points occur out of excessively distorted symbiotic phases. Mahler further states, "The success or failure of the symbiotic phase promotes or impedes the subsequent individuation process" (p. xii).

In adolescence we see both a fear of separation and a fear of reengulfment, leading to associated negativism. "Violence abounds, with little apparent value of the lives of others and little ability to truly mourn losses" (a therapist at Northwest Clinic in Washington, D.C., personal communication). Is this because there has been so little cathexis of early objects? In addition, I believe that this extreme acting-out behavior is a defense against the emptiness and depression that are the result of such early, traumatic, and interrupted relationships.

Another pervasive symptom that is the outgrowth of chaotic early relationship experiences is intellectual limitation. The mechanisms that lead to pathological limitation and restriction of intellectual functions of the ego have been examined by many analysts: Landauer (1929), Rado (1919), Bornstein (1930), Bergler (1932), Oberndorf (1939), Jacobson (1932), Maenchen (1936), and others.

With young children constantly experiencing disruptive and inconsistent relationships, abuse, viewing of the primal scene, and violent death and its result, there is a great probability that cognitive functioning is compromised. The causes of lowered intellectual functioning due to inhibition are also described by Freud (1926), in "Inhibitions, Symptoms, and Anxiety." He noted that erotization of the intellectual functions of the ego causes the ego to give up this function "in order to avoid a conflict with the id" (p. 90).

Such conditions as pseudostupidity and/or a feminized social stance as a symbolic display of being castrated to escape the fear of literal castration and the perceived loss of a loved object (Landauer 1929, Maenchen 1936), and exaggerated masculine behavior, as exhibited in street gangs, are easily understood accommodations to damaged egos due to early neglect and trauma (Mahler 1968).

There is constant interaction with public services—the police, the welfare system, the foster care system, the school system, and the public health medical system ("the clinic"). A large percentage of men and some women are incarcerated.

Because many lives are interrupted, before high school is completed, by pregnancy or the law, there is little chance for future employment beyond the unskilled jobs (busboy, domestic) that are disdained because they pay poorly. Currently the best job for men is selling drugs; for women, prostitution. Both pay very well, and there is minimal effort required. There is a very weak work ethic and a frustrating environment. Getting up early every day, and finding the money to pay for public transportation to the job, along with finding child care situations that are reliable, make working difficult. In addition, alcoholism and drug abuse plague both women and men. Alcohol and drugs are used to self-medicate depression and feelings of helplessness, hopelessness, inadequacy, and insecurity.

Race and Identity

Racial identity is very strong in this group, as is Afro-centricity. Alienated from America by their own failures and by institutional racism, they seek to identify with an idealized "homeland" they have never seen. In this place they would/could be whole, surrounded by black people. Little is known about the real Africa. The fantasy is that Africa is "good" because of the absence of a white majority, while America is bad.

Splitting as a defense is commonplace as are denial and projection. Because of negative experiences and circumstances, the self concept is also split into the good self and the bad self. Evil characteristics are projected outward onto whites, who are credited with running "the system," which is responsible for all the troubles and deprivations that plague them. Try as they may, therapists too are subject to this splitting. Trying to be a new and good object at war with the old and bad careless and abandoning introjects is an uphill battle that any therapist can lose despite all efforts (Altman 1995).

The Concept of "Mother"

In this culture, despite its dysfunctional patterns of mothering, the idea of "mother" is revered. The role of mother is honored, and denigrating her is not allowed, not even in jokes. Is she honored for "I brought you into this world, I can take you out"? Her own deprivation forces her to reverse roles with the child as soon as possible so that if the child achieves anything, she wants some of it. The child grows up seeing and incorporating her pain, her deprivation, her feeling of having been cheated, and her vulnerability. Regardless of how abandoning, punitive, cruel, or unhealthy their relationship has been, the child can be made to feel ashamed for not providing for her if he acquires anything as an adult. It is difficult for him to show anger toward her. As a small child, any show of aggression toward her meets with her instant rage or force. There is an incorporated paradox then, as he believes she is not strong. Ambivalence toward her is profound. There is a strong message of "go out and get it for me!" Later, men from this culture show an inability to sustain positive feelings toward females. They may revere "mother," but they may also be wife abusers. Splitting is sustained.

Children from this culture who find success through athletics or illegal means like drug dealing are expected to take care of their mothers first. One sees the houses that are bought for her with the "first check." She never had a house of her own, usually having lived in public housing complexes. Her children are her only hope.

Mental Health Care

Mental health care is often available through clinics at hospitals and at other social service agencies, but no one wants to be labeled "crazy" or "mental," so prolonged and consistent treatment is hard to provide. Usually it is a required adjunct to a social service agency's treatment plan following a crisis. As soon as mothers meet the requirements for getting their children returned to them or their food stamps reinstated, they abandon the treatment. The best treatment results have been obtained by providing therapy in the schools.

Actual clinical data are very difficult to obtain, especially since people from this culture rarely enter the private world of psychotherapy. There are a few notable exceptions where analysts volunteer in public psychiatric clinics. The following clinical material was gathered from a very experienced therapist in a social service agency. In this case and in all others to follow, names have been changed to protect confidentiality.

Case 1

Ms. Smith is a 35-year-old mother of four children. The oldest child, age 17, has always lived with his paternal grandmother. His father is currently incarcerated and has a long history of drug, assault, and weapons offenses convictions. Ms. Smith is currently living with her pre-teenage children, a boy and girl, ages 10 and 12. These children have a history of poor school attendance, and are often late when they do attend. The 12-year-old has been suspended twice this school year, after verbally assaulting her fifth grade teacher. This child is frequently disruptive in the classroom, and special education testing has been recommended to assess her learning and behavior problems. Despite the school's efforts, Ms. Smith has refused/failed to give permission for the testing, stating that her daughter can learn, but is just stubborn and "bad." The 10-year-old boy is observed to be quiet and withdrawn. Although he, too, has learning problems, testing has not been recommended for this child.

Ms. Smith smokes crack cocaine, and misuses the family AFDC income (Aid to Family with Dependent Children) to buy drugs. The children were previously removed from her care three years ago, after she left them alone on numerous occasions while out seeking and using drugs. The children lived with a maternal aunt and her family in Maryland, while their mother successfully participated in a drug treatment program. The children were returned home after one year. Reportedly, their mother relapsed about one year ago.

Ms. Smith's youngest child, age 3 months, is hospitalized due to malnutrition and dehydration. The family has again been referred to the court on behalf of the baby, who will be placed in foster care. Protective Services has offered services for the two older children, but the mother denies a need for further drug treatment services, stating that she can get off drugs by herself. She has also rejected mental health services for herself and the two children at home. She states that she is not "crazy." She has also rejected parenting education, stating, "My parents raised me, and I'm doing the same way as they did with my kids." Ms. Smith expresses a reluctance to use services, and frequently says that she does not "want people in my business."

Case 2

Ms. Jones is a 21-year-old mother of three children, ages 6, 3, and 18 months. She is five months pregnant. The children have different fathers; only the 3-year-old's father is in contact with the family. He is a 38-year-old married man who visits the family and provides financial support occasionally.

Ms. Jones is the youngest of eight children born to a mentally ill, alcohol-abusing mother. She was raised by various relatives and the foster care system until the age of 18. Ms. Jones and the children live in a cluttered one-bedroom public housing unit. The family is supported by public assistance.

The family was referred for Protective Services a year ago when the 3-year-old fell from a third floor window. The mother, who appears depressed and lethargic, was sleeping at 11 A.M. when the child fell from the unscreened window. At that time it was discovered that the 6-year-old, who was of compulsory school age, had never been enrolled in school. The children's immunizations were not up-to-date.

Ms. Jones worked well with agency social workers who offered intensive (daily) in-home services for a period of ten weeks. She seemed more energetic and motivated to learn how to care for her children more adequately.

Her pregnancy and failed relationship with the expected child's father have been a setback for her. She has dropped out of a parent support group and the 6-year-old's school attendance is becoming irregular. The child reports missing school because her mother doesn't get her up, or because she has no clean clothing to wear. She also reports cooking for herself and her siblings because her mother is always sleeping or watching television. Ms. Smith shows little attention to the children except to yell at them and threaten them with a belt when they do something that annoys her.

Therapy Guidelines

To provide therapy to these needy children, it is always necessary to find a way to deliver therapy to their mothers concurrently. Without support and attention to the mother, the child's therapy will be sabotaged because the mother is still governing her relationships at the symbiotic level. She sees the therapist's attempt to establish another relationship as an attempt at separating her child from her.

Mothers enjoy support groups and parenting classes, but sometimes it is simply the attention of the therapist and the opportunity to socialize with others in the same circumstances that really attracts their interest. If the child is in individual treatment, the mother will often attempt to speak to the doctor at the beginning of the session or request that the last ten to fifteen minutes be saved for her. With adolescents, this behavior cancels any trust that the teenager may have built up with the doctor.

At best, consistent attendance to sessions can't be expected. In public clinics there is a 40 to 50 percent dropout rate and 25 to 30 percent no-show rate. Before evaluation proceedings are concluded, the patient has disappeared. Reality-based issues like transportation and long clinic waits provide concrete excuses, and bonds with the therapist are fragile at best. So many patients have an "internal object world characterized by devaluing and traumatically abandoning relationships" (Altman 1995, p. 21); therefore, the level of expectation is low and there is little basis for trust-based object constancy, so the therapist's interest and presence are not expected by the patient either.

For those who successfully get out of the underclass, it has been shown that one experience in another culture can make a difference (Dash 1996). The experience with the therapist or a good grandmother or teacher could be that experience.

"MY CHILD IS MY LIFE": CHILD CARE, BONDING, AND SEPARATION-INDIVIDUATION PATTERNS IN THE AFRICAN-AMERICAN MIDDLE-MIDDLE CLASS

While the number of intact nuclear families increases as we go up the socioeconomic scale, there are still high numbers of single mothers due to divorce and separation. In 1994, 46.5 percent of the black families had a single female householder; 47.9 percent had married couples as the householders. Thirteen percent of blacks had bachelor's degrees or more. Middle income as used here refers to families with incomes of between $35,000 and $50,000. Thirteen percent of married-couple black families were in this middle-class category.

This is a group that does not typically live in the urban inner city, but is as likely to live in the new suburbs, edge cities, or in more protected communities in the city, where homes are owned. Mothers are much more likely to be college educated and many have graduate degrees, but they are not high-profile professionals. The partnership model of marriage is present. That is, both parents work to provide the economic base on which to define the family as middle class. In many cases the family is economically overextended. If one parent is unable to work, the family is unable to maintain its lifestyle.

There is a dramatic difference here in superego development, with typical, traditional, middle-class concern for reputation, reliability and accountability, and appropriate behavior and respect for authority figures, especially parents and grandparents. When possible, the extended family is very closely involved. Boys and girls are valued equally.

Children are very important, and the number of children is purposely limited because of economic constraints, and there are very high expectations for educational achievement placed on them. Education is seen as the key to security in a racist society. Children are overprotected and discipline is stiff, though not often punitive. There is no approval for the permissive approach to child rearing. The church and its teachings are an integral part of the lifestyle. There is still little knowledge of child development, and child-care decisions are made on tradition and expediency with little consciousness of the child's psychosexual needs.

Separation from the mother begins early in this social class. Day care is used until around the age of 2, if the child is lucky. It is then replaced with a formal preschool placement. There is always some anxiety on the parents' part to get the educational process going; that is, the preschool should be teaching early academics rather than just focusing on socialization and caring for the child. Separation anxiety is not noticed or honored; instead, the "good" baby is the one who will go to anyone and the "difficult" baby is the one who insists on choosing.

If there is no available family member, child care outside the home is typical. The old model was the community day care, where the infant was taken to a mature black woman in the neighborhood who cared for infants and young children in her home. Bottles are preferred to nursing, as time off from work is limited for the mothers. There is a gradual changeover taking place today as many middle-class families are moving or have moved to predominantly white suburbs. The child-care patterns remain the same, but now the caregivers are as likely to be white Americans or from an immigrant ethnic group, such as Spanish, Caribbean, or Puerto Rican. These women care for children in their homes and meet the infant and child/caregiver ratio requirement set down by day-care standardization guidelines.

Since these children are with the caregiver all day, five days a week, the separation-individuation phases take place with her. Unfortunately, some are removed to the preschool setting while still in the phase of rapprochement (Mahler 1968). The neighborhood or family day-care situation is usually small, with a limited number of infants and toddlers, simulating a natural family. The "mother" usually has a good working knowledge of child development and so she honors the young child's attachment to her. After the child leaves her care, she remains an important figure in the child's memory, especially if separation didn't take place until the third or fourth year.

During infancy and during the bonding stage, all infants incorporate skin color into the bonding process. I think of this as "color tagging." Infants who are cared for by surrogates who have the same skin color and features of their mothers have a stronger emotional bond with their own mothers. If the caregiver is radically different in color and features from the natural mother, and the majority of the infant's time is spent with the surrogate, one sees a diluted attachment to the mother. These children, whether black or white, first assume themselves to be the color (race) of the surrogate and often do not notice that they are racially different until age 3. Language is of significance here also, since many surrogates talk and sing to the infants in a different language or accent, which is incorporated along with the "color tag." For African-American children in particular, I have found that self-esteem issues evidenced by self-hatred can sometimes be traced to having incorporated a color-tagged surrogate whom they do not resemble.

The oral stage of development is prolonged by the use of the bottle sometimes into the third year, although pediatricians regularly advise against it. I have noticed that the bottle regularly becomes a transitional object and it is permitted and accepted over objects like blankets and stuffed animals because it is a source of food and is considered necessary for that purpose. (In most ethnic cultures food is love, and taking the bottle away is seen as a deprivation.) Many of these toddlers and preschoolers in church-run day-care programs, run around with an empty bottle hanging from their mouths by the nipple. The bottle has become the transitional object. (Pacifiers are not encouraged in the same way.) Sucking is still encouraged as a way of going to sleep at nap time or bedtime well into the second and third years despite pediatric advice to the contrary.

Because separation anxiety is evidenced more toward the caregiver than the mother, one often hears of a smooth transition from the day-care environment to the preschool environment because the child is taken there by the mother. Already accustomed to living in a group, if the preschool setting is interesting, the routine is stimulating, and a specific caregiver is available to them, these children seem to thrive. If the caregivers rotate or are not consistently emotionally available, the children are at risk for faulty development of libidinal object constancy (Mahler 1968). While their parents may be very reliable, their attachments to their natural parents are often shallow in comparison to children who have spent more time in a dyadic relationship. This pattern of child rearing is spreading as a standard for rearing all middle-class American children.

Ego strength is, as always, dependent on constitutional factors as well as absence of trauma, and on the teaching and reflective experience of oneself at the hands of the mothering one. These children seem to have adequate ego strength as evidenced by their ability to cope and to learn and to be confident. They are highly valued as a part of the family and as evidence that the family is doing well. Family pride is expressed through their achievements and accomplishments. Physical affection is shown with ease and is rarely withheld as punishment. One observes these families coalescing around the child's needs in the evenings and on weekends when they are the parents' first priority. They are disciplined strictly from a very early age and required to respect the authority of the parents. Socialization takes place within a close nuclear family, church, and extended family, if they are present.

Interestingly, the importance of the natural mother grows and a deeper bond seems to form in the second and third years with children showing obvious delight at the appearance of their mothers at the end of the day care or preschool day. The pickup is preceded by a period of obvious anxiety and apprehension as others are collected. I wonder if the joyous affect at reunion is based more on relief at again avoiding loss of the object than at reclaiming the lost precious object.

The role of the father is large in this group. Parents often interchange roles within the family, with fathers doing the cooking, picking up children, or taking charge of their physical care. There is no fear of feminization associated with child care in the African-American cultures. Macho behavior is exhibited in other areas of family life.

Because there is a healthy suspiciousness about the outside world, these families do not encourage separation-individuation from the family. Camp experiences are limited to summer day camps or camps run by the church. Sleep-away camps are rarely considered, both for economic reasons and because parents don't trust people of other races to look after their children's interests in their absence.

Mental Health Care

The therapeutic situation reflects many of these attitudes. When treatment is sought for these children, parents insist on a black therapist and are more likely to listen if the recommendation for treatment has been made by a black teacher, pediatrician, or other professional. Treatment with an unknown therapist is rarely sought. The therapy is not resisted if the black therapist first makes friends with the parent or parents and begins with a positive comment about the child and then follows with comments on what a good job the hard-working parents have done in some area of the child's life.

It is important to make an assessment as to whether the family is solidly middle class or in transition from a working-class background, as attitudes about therapy and the therapist are strongly influenced by background.

Case 3

Sharma, a 9-year-old African-American girl, was recommended for therapy because, although very bright, she had stopped doing her homework and was on the verge of failing in her predominantly white public school. Her teacher felt that she was depressed. Sharma's parents came for the first session and were obviously angry and resistant to the idea of therapy and especially resistant to paying for it even though, as two grade-eleven government workers, they had very adequate health insurance. Her father felt that therapy was an indulgent, child-oriented solution to a problem that could be better handled with harsher discipline. He stated that he would never have disappointed his parents like Sharma was doing; his father was a mechanic and worked double shifts so that his mother could stay home and raise eight children. He felt that Sharma was spoiled and that her problems emanated from associating with white children who didn't respect their parents and who had it "too easy."

Though Sharma was regularly isolated from her peers and not allowed to attend birthday parties, her father wanted to increase the isolation and add additional household chores to "teach" Sharma that going to school was a privilege, not a right.

Case 4

Calvin, the 12-year-old son of a fifth-grade public school teacher and a Caribbean grocery store owner, was referred for treatment because he was found to have repeatedly skipped school for several days at a time and then lied about his whereabouts.

Calvin's life was and had always been tightly supervised. His parents had decided to have only one child because they wanted to be able to ensure Calvin's educational future. Both his grandmothers had been teachers, and one grandmother had been his caregiver for the first four years of his life. His parents drove twenty-two miles round-trip daily to get him to and from her house. Once in school, he went to his other grandmother's house right after school to do homework under her supervision. His parents picked him up on their way home in the evening. Their new suburban home was in a neighborhood with several children Calvin's age, but his parents had him work in the city at the grocery store all day on Saturdays and they went to church and visited family and friends on Sundays. He was required to do homework when they returned. Calvin was at the top of his class.

Calvin had heard about his classmates and friends going to malls together on the weekends. On the days he truanted, he waited until his parents drove away and he took the bus to the mall and spent the day indulging himself by eating junk food and going to the movies. He got back to school just in time to be picked up. Asked whether he could tell his parents that he needed time with his peers, he said, "No, my life is already planned, and there's not much I can do to change it. I'm supposed to become a lawyer."

Depression and hopelessness were easy to hear. So was the defeat. No amount of interpretation could make Calvin's parents accept his need to individuate. They saw it as their duty to keep him on the "straight and narrow" and wanted me to use therapy to reinforce their authority. Calvin began a "secret method" of getting back at them. Every time his parents restricted him when he wanted to go to a party or game, he took something of theirs (jewelry, tools, books) and put it out in the garbage.

When all else failed, they attacked me: "You've been on Connecticut Avenue too long," implying that I'd lost my connection with the black culture. They wanted to seek another psychiatrist who would tell them what they wanted to hear. I gave them three referrals. I also told them that if they didn't listen, Calvin might find his way into trouble with the law later. They left, only to return three years later when Calvin had been arrested.

Case 5

Karen was referred for treatment by a psychiatrist and family friend in another city. At 28, she had finished professional school and lived in a different city than her parents. She is the fourth of four children, the other three siblings being male. The father, a college-educated, small-business owner, worked hard to educate all four children, each of whom has professional degrees. The mother, although educated at a historically black college, had worked intermittently at sales jobs or in the family business.

Karen presented with depression, which she had attempted to treat in many ways, including group therapy, women's retreats, and, most recently, therapy with a white male social worker. As the depression deepened and the need for medication increased, she finally sought treatment with me at the suggestion of the family friend.

Karen's symptoms began when her lover, a black male professional twenty years her senior, failed to marry her despite her having had his child. Her decision to maintain her relationship with him and to have the baby had caused a great deal of trouble with her family, who had objected both to the relationship and to the out-of-wedlock pregnancy. Although the child's father had promised to marry her again and again, he never did, and when the child was 2 years old, Karen left him. She expected her family to rescue her and to embrace her responsibilities as if they were their own. When they didn't and instead made it clear that she had made this decision against parental advice and now must live with it, she developed a severe depression, which ultimately required hospitalization.

Finding herself in a situation where she felt abandoned in her efforts to act out and individuate from her parents, feeling ostracized by society as just another unwed black mother despite her academic achievements, left Karen feeling bereft. Never having developed problem-solving skills as a child and never having acted out as a teenager, she had no experience with conflict resolution within her family. Her strong sense of entitlement together with her lowered self-esteem made her a frustrating patient.

She immediately transferred to me, a black female therapist, as a gratifying mother, and whenever I was seen to step outside that role, she threatened to stop treatment, as if she would be hurting me and not herself. I wasn't sure that I could continue to treat her, as there were many demands and manipulations, ranging from trying to avoid paying for canceled sessions to paging me three and four times in twenty-four hours rather than waiting to have her calls returned.

Her fears of separation and individuation were masked by extreme efforts to be treated in a special way by everyone she encountered. She didn't want to accept the responsibility of being an adult. Her depression and anger were closely intertwined but infantile in nature. For example, her love for her child alternated with preconscious wishes to kill her and the conscious wish to put her up for adoption. The defense of undoing was interpreted to her and was met with anger.

Karen's parents described her as a good child who never disagreed with them and who did well in school. They didn't understand her criticism of their child-rearing practice of allowing their sons total freedom, including sharing a room with girlfriends when they were home on college vacations, while admonishing her to adhere to the strict middle-class rules (for girls)—no suggestive clothes, no premarital sex, no boyfriends overnight at home on vacations, no living with "significant others." They could not understand how her anger about gender differences in behavior could have led her to rebel so much. They thought she seemed to want to prove at all costs that she could have the same freedoms as men.

Having concerned herself in an irreversible individuation plan that backfired, Karen found herself now in need of support by her parents, who finally acknowledged her severed relationship and withdrew their support. She experienced this acknowledgment as a punishment.

"POWER, AFFLUENCE, AND PRECIOUS CHILDREN": BONDING AND SEPARATION-INDIVIDUATION IN THE AFRICAN-AMERICAN UPPER-MIDDLE AND UPPER CLASS

This group is the smallest of all the African-American cultures (less than 1 percent), and while it shares many characteristics with parallel Caucasian-American groups, there are significant differences, some of which relate to child rearing. For this class of African-Americans, economics is not a problem. They live the American dream, and in many cases have done so for several generations. Because America does not recognize black success as readily as it aggrandizes the failures of the race, this group constantly fights anonymity. Referred to as "the talented tenth" by W. E. B. DuBois, members of this class have provided leadership and scholarship for two hundred years. Class identity is not governed solely by current economic status, but by lifestyle, inherited wealth, education and achievement, family affiliation, and cultural depth. Religion is less of a marker than in the other classes, but is respected in others.

Once again, children are seen as very valuable. There is much more intellectual awareness of child development, and the economic base exists to allow mothers the time to launch their infants if they choose to do so. However, since achievement is the cornerstone of the identity of this class, surrogates may enter very early. Child care is typically done in the home, with the current trend being six months with the mother and then a nanny. Breast-feeding is popular, though vanity may intrude upon the decision to do so.

There are rarely more than two or three children, and the partnership model of marriage is most typical, with two-profession couples being commonplace. Fathers maintain high interest in their children, but their care is managed by their mothers. Two generations ago, the ideal was a professional father and a highly educated, teacher mother, thereby fostering maximum time spent together by mothers and children, with mothers using their expertise to promote the children's excellence in school. The stay-at-home mother has never been the norm for this class, as female achievement is as valued as male achievement, although there have always been a few stay-at-home mothers, especially in the child's first three to five years. (This pattern continues today.) Children are expected to be smart.

While surrogates are important, the mother is absolutely the primary maternal figure to whom the child is firmly bonded. In observing today's children from this class, one disturbing issue is entitlement. Latina and Filipina nannies are most typical and the children exploit their gentle natures, pushing, in the absence of their mothers, for liberties unacceptable in their mothers' presence. Families fortunate enough to have black Caribbean caregivers or strong, American black caregivers are not as bothered with this problem.

In infancy and early childhood, bonding to both parents is very strong and particularly to the mother if she has been the infant caregiver. Transitional objects are tolerated. The first separation is at age 3 when the child leaves for nursery school and both parents make themselves available to help the child through the separation-anxiety stage.

Once again, these are highly valued children, and neither parent is able to tolerate criticism of the child easily. Material indulgence is very common and often seems determined to bond the child or children to the mother (particularly) through infantile indulgence, another avenue that fosters the development of entitlement. Familial indulgence and acceptance of out-of-bounds behavior is most common in families with only one child. But in general, children are seen as extensions of the parents' egos as evidenced in the following series of names—Roland III, Rolanda, and Roland IV; Michael Sr., Caroline, "Little" Michael, and "Little" Caroline. Parents are unaware of reliving their lives through their children and simply push for what has worked for them or what they wish their parents had done with them. Just as it is not politically correct to make jokes in the black cultures about mothers or parents in general, it is also never funny to joke about being rid of one's children.

The joke that "He can be anything he wants as long as it's a doctor or a lawyer" is really true in this class. Children do not come first in the intact family, the parents do, but children know they're important and if they perform well in school, there are no limits to the indulgence. The work ethic is very strong and "play" is seen as a legitimate reward. It is not unusual to meet 7-year-olds and 10-year-olds who have been to Europe, Africa, Hawaii, and/or the Orient on vacation trips with their parents and/or grandparents.

Because success is a large part of the identity of this group, survival skills are incorporated in the child rearing. There is no premium on talking about feelings or understanding the psyche. The premium is on performance. Similarly, race is not allowed to be used as a defense, since most have succeeded against the odds.

Parents find it very hard to hear about or recognize their children's failures, and they therefore have trouble resolving their children's emotional difficulties.

Individuation problems can begin (1) when the child doesn't do well in school; (2) when the child wants to work in a nonprofessional career; (3) when the child chooses a mate from another race or class; (4) when the child exhibits habits or styles that are not success oriented, such as dreadlocks, braids, beards, and ghetto language; and (5) when the child is critical of the parents or their value system.

Strong families are seen as those in which the children achieve, marry within the group, and choose careers similar to, equivalent to, or better than their parents', and in which parents and children remain close. They are expected to "go and do" and geographic distance is not resisted. Like all affluent people, parents run interference for their children and use all their professional and social contacts to further their children's success.

Tenets of success practiced by elite blacks include the following: (1) Never use race as a defense. (2) Promote confidence in children early and often. A strong ego will defend against racism and adversity. (3) Idealize family and ancestors and their achievements. Use them as role models when the models in school or social environments aren't satisfactory or plentiful. (4) Promote identification with the greater world, not just the United States. (5) "Family uber alles" (family first). (6) Encourage strict superego development. (7) Teach self-discipline. (8) Promote accomplishment, achievement, and excellence in all things. Never do less than your best. (9) Class tags must be cathected: speech patterns, cultural appreciation, beauty in nature, belief in a higher power, self-presentation, and conservative lifestyle. (10) Discourage risk-taking behaviors. (11) Keep survival techniques in the forefront. (12) Don't socialize or identify with underclass blacks. (13) Never back away from a hard task. (14) Support and initiate efforts to help less fortunate blacks.

Histories are not particularly remarkable except in cases of extreme dysfunction or mental illness. What brings children to therapy from this group is school failure, depression or obsessive-compulsive disorder, situational problems, lack of motivation, conflict with parents, and identity issues.

Case 6

Brad is the oldest of three sons. When he was in elementary school, he was discovered to have a genius I.Q. His father was very proud of his intelligence and constantly bragged about his son's academic abilities. He became overly invested in Brad and unconsciously overidentified with him, all but ignoring the other two boys despite their superior abilities and athletic prowess. Brad's father and mother both held challenging high-profile positions in major corporations, and in fact it was his mother whom he most resembled in every way. She, too, was very intelligent but not as ambitious as his father.

Brad was a thoughtful and very cooperative child throughout his childhood and adolescence. Often placed in situations where he had to meet important people and converse with them, he was always well dressed and a willing participant. At his predominantly white private school, he was respected but not as popular as his extremely handsome and athletic brothers. As he approached his junior year, and his father became more and more involved in his college admission process, Brad became more quiet and passive. It wasn't that he didn't have definite ideas about where he wanted to go and what he wanted to study, but he couldn't make himself heard. His father was symbiotically attached to him and seemingly determined to relive his life through Brad. He could not have gotten into Yale, but Brad could, and that was his father's choice.

The resistance Brad showed was not to fill out any college applications. As retaliation, his father locked him in a hotel room while on Christmas vacation, and wrote the applications with him and then mailed them himself. Brad became depressed. His mother comforted him. When his acceptance to Yale arrived, he locked himself in his room. His father opened the letter.

Brad graduated from high school first in his class and received several prizes. He described his father as "strutting about like a Puffer pigeon," which enraged Brad. His freshman year at Yale was a series of academic disasters punctuated by events that produced power struggles with his father. Brad essentially did no work. His father kept tabs on him by ingratiating himself with the university by donating large gifts. He wrote many of Brad's papers and turned them in.

In addition, for the first time in his life, Brad encountered black students from the ghetto. They instantly disliked him, accusing him of being "too white." Because they constituted the largest part of the black university community, Brad had little support. Every part of his character and his socialization were attacked by these students. He realized that allying himself with these students drove his father into a rage. Soon, Brad wore dreadlocks and baggy clothes, and was dating an inner-city girl with multiple braids in her hair.

Brad was seen as an embarrassment to his family. His father didn't want to take him to any social events with him, and if he couldn't avoid having him along he required that Brad wear a hat or pull his hair back in a ponytail. Brad was very happy and some-what euphoric at times. For the first time he had the upper hand. His father tried bribery, but more often had screaming matches with him in which he called him worthless and ungrateful. Brad felt depressed after these scenes, which often left his mother in tears, but he refused to change his hair or his dress. His distress had not yet reached the level of a transient borderline condition secondary to frustrated individuation attempts, but was moving in that direction.

To avoid these scenes, Brad didn't go home for two years and accepted no money from his parents. He became lonely and de-pressed, but triumphant. At the urging of his friends and relatives he entered therapy with me, which was paid for by an aunt. He was a delightful, intelligent, and hard-working patient who was relieved to have the opportunity to explore the conflicts that had plagued him for so long.

Analysis uncovered a deep-seated ambivalence toward his fa-ther for "being someone no one in his right mind would want to be like." Side by side with this ambivalence toward his father was a different kind of ambivalence toward his mother. While he felt a deep, quiet love for her based on a childhood in which she was the star of his life—reading to him, and exposing him to cultural expe-riences that shaped his musical and literary awareness and awakened his intellect—he also blamed her for allowing his father to emascu-late him. He worried that he had too strong an identification with his mother to be an effective male.

His dreadlocks served three purposes: (1) to experience the racism that was outside his experience as a privileged black male, and thereby identify with the ghetto males he had encountered in college and whose aggressive anger appealed to him; (2) to profoundly anger his father, and thereby break the bond with him; and (3) to express with a feminized appearance his deep identification with his mother. He had no plans to cut his hair.

During the two years of little contact with his parents, Brad arranged to spend a semester at a historically black college. Again, he experienced ridicule at the hands of some of the students. He was not popular with the college women because he didn't seem to know where he belonged. The semester there seemed to settle something for Brad. He returned to Yale and began working. Since his father was greatly relieved that Brad was back in school, he readily agreed to stay out of his academic life, but his campaign to get rid of the dreadlocks was as alive as ever.

In analysis Brad tested the bond he had with me; he arrived early and would chat with other patients, who became confused as to whose hour it was. He never told them he was an hour early. I saw him drive by my house once. He had me paged once, telling the operator he was my son. I repeatedly invited him to deal with these issues within the sessions. It was clear that he was tightly bonded to me and had fantasies of being my child.

After six months, Brad increased the acting-out behavior, skipped sessions, and tried to advise his aunt not to pay for them. He was trying to shake me loose. I told him he didn't have to shake me, he could leave whenever he wished, but that I didn't think he really wanted to stop.

Brad stayed in analysis for three years. When he began the termination process, he was much calmer. He was applying to law schools out West. He appeared on the last day having cut his hair and wearing a shirt and tie. He brought me two dozen roses.

Race, Identity, and the Individuation Process

This culture lives at the interface between the black and white worlds (Gatewood 1990) and is the group that constitutes "society." It is

Eurocentric rather than Afrocentric. Its history is racially mixed, and while there may not have been an interracial marriage in recent generations, the historical relationships have contributed to phenotypes that are not typically African-American. Native-American ancestry is also common and looked upon with pride. There is a color range, and a range of hair textures and facial features more common in this group than in the previous two. However, racial pride is strong, without denying the blood ties to whites. (There is intraracial prejudice, although interracial prejudice is less prevalent than in the other cultures.) In many families there are documented connections to famous white Americans of history, and the African-American descendants have forced historical organizations like the Daughters of the American Revolution to recognize and admit them as members.

White ancestors are not denied, nor are they idealized. The economic head start received by many families in this culture is often traced to early emancipation (sometimes before the Civil War) and/or property left to an ancestor by a white father or grandfather. Many people enjoyed a privileged status during slavery bestowed upon them by their white slavemaster fathers (Gatewood 1990). While some white-appearing members of the culture are adamantly African-American at all times, others may practice a form of "optional blackness." That is, they pass for white when it is convenient or expedient. Still others quietly cross the color line and completely sever their ties with their families or come home only for important family events.

Families in this culture vary in the value they place on physical appearance. It is very important that white psychotherapists not assume knowledge about this very individual racial value system. It is best to pay close attention to the individual's history and to find out if there is a "tagged" pattern that might have adversely affected the individual. Some families value white-appearing skin and the opportunity it affords them to move back and forth between the races, thereby avoiding some experiences of racism. Other families value hair texture and length, but embrace browner skin tones, wishing to avoid the problems attendant to being too light skinned. Still others place a high value on facial features, eschewing the typical African features of thick lips and flat noses. There is an acceptable range of skin colors ranging from brown to white and hair textures ranging from straight to tightly curly and a wide range of facial features, but ebony skin and short, kinky hair are universally rejected in this culture (Gatewood 1990).

Any one of these physical distinctions isn't enough to gain entrance or acceptance into the group. "Ancestry and family background, as well as evidences of education and gentility, were (are) virtually always seen as important" (Gatewood 1990, p. 169). Various regions have their own preferences and combinations of requirements, but in no region is there just a single attribute that suffices. Insiders describe the rigid requirements necessary for social acceptance as family, color, and money, and two of the three must be present in any candidate. Many people with aspirations fail to understand, for example, that skin color or money is not seen as enough.

Psychopathology

The aforementioned values about appearance can contribute negatively to the bonding and separation–individuation process for children in this culture. A very white-skinned child in a family of browner-skinned people may be rejected by his or her mother for a number of reasons, such as resemblance to a hostile grandparent, or simply because the child doesn't look like the mother. A very dark-skinned child may feel distanced from its light-skinned mother, who may feel disappointed that the child does not look like her or her family. Similarly, kinky-haired or short-haired light-skinned children may feel alienated in their straight-haired families. Children who are in these kinds of family situations are particularly at risk for self-hatred and for a good self/bad self ego split.

In some families these issues become so complex that the adolescent children cannot separate from their families because home is the only place that they feel acceptable and comfortable, and they despair that they will ever find a love object who will understand the complexities of their feelings or meet the complex requirements for entrance into the family. This leads to a prolonged adolescence with some issues that may not be resolvable.

THE AFRICAN-AMERICAN WORKING CLASS

In 1993, 32.3 percent of married-couple black families had incomes between $15,000 (the poverty level for a family of four) and $35,000. This is the African-American working class. While this forms the largest group of statistically represented African-Americans, this is also the hardest group to track for purposes of psychological observation and treatment potential. One can speculate about some of the reasons for this. Members of this socioeconomic or sociocultural class are in transition, both upward and downward. They have geographical mobility. While public housing is one option, property ownership is always a goal, and families (all variations) may move more frequently depending on the stability of employment. Also, unlike members of the underclass, they are not the subject of constant attention from various public agencies. Generally they are extremely hard-working, both men and women often having two or three jobs just to meet minimal economic survival standards. Children pick up values not necessarily shared by their parents, and ego strength has to be great to withstand the exigencies of daily life. Many succeed in moving up the ladder to success through businesses or education if their parents are strong and manage to stay close to their children through adolescence, but there is a typical unevenness regarding success among siblings in this class, with some getting stuck or moving down the social scale and others (sometimes only one) moving up rather rapidly because of opportunity or talent. Mundane jobs such as security guards, sanitation workers, waiters, maintenance men or women, food workers, and hotel maids, are all subject to administrative whim or business budget downturns. Children and parents in this group are inordinately vulnerable to fantasies about success in the entertainment industry or through professional athletics.

CONCLUSION

There are several distinct African-American cultures, three of which have been considered at length here, with special emphasis on bonding, child care, and separation–individuation. As one goes up the socioeconomic scale, the impact of institutional racism on ego development lessens. Self-sufficiency dramatically increases and cognitive abilities escape destruction. The use of psychotherapy and psychoanalysis also increase as we move up the scale. In order for African-Americans to benefit from these therapeutic opportunities, it is absolutely necessary for members of our profession to educate themselves about these cultural differences and to confront their own tendency to utilize racial stereotypes.

The African-American class system has its roots in the slavery system. Distinctions between field hands and house servants remain today in the minds of many. The dependency issues still being worked out in the lower sociocultural classes can be easily traced to the helplessness felt by freed field hands following emancipation. Ill-equipped to take care of themselves after more than a century of institutional dependency, a culture had been established. Conversely, racially mixed house servants often faced life before or after emancipation with skills, trades, and education, which allowed them to support themselves independent of the slavery system. While working "in the house" African-Americans were indoctrinated into the Christian religions of the household and became Baptists, Catholics, and Episcopalians, field hands celebrated remnants of African ritualistic services and established camp meetings, which later became African Methodist Episcopal and Pentecostal as well as other fundamentalist forms of Christianity with a survival-religion orientation.

Mistrust of white America remains today as healthy suspicious-ness in an American culture that continually seeks to categorize all African-Americans as secondary in status to whites. This entrenched system has a profound impact on the development of all African-Americans regardless of class status, and any attempt at psychotherapy or psychoanalysis must use a larger perspective than is included even in the two-person model (where the analyst's subjectivity is in-cluded). This is a "larger perspective, called a 'three-person model,' the third 'person' representing the social context . . . in the sense that I emphasize the analytic significance of the racial, cultural, and social class of patient and analyst" (Altman 1995, p. 56).

Each class resists or incorporates the stereotypical imagery of the outer world into its character structure, how each copes (or doesn't) with the standard issues of bonding and individuation, and develops healthy or unhealthy class-specific defenses that enable them to succeed or fail in this country. To quote from Philip Roth's *Portnoy's Complaint*, "Now we may perhaps to begin."

REFERENCES

Altman, N. (1995). *The Analyst in the Inner City*. Hillsdale, NJ: Analytic Press.
Bennett, C. E. (1993 and 1994). *The Black Population in the United States*. Washington, DC: The U.S. Department of Commerce, Economics and Statistics Administration, Bureau of the Census.
Bergler, E. (1932). Zur problematic der pseudo-debilitat [The problem of pseudo-debility]. *International Zeitschrift fur Psychoanalyse* 18:528–538.
Bornstein, B. (1930). Zur psychogenese der pseudodebilitat [Psychogenesis of pseudo-debility]. *International Zeitschrift fur Psychoanalyse* 16:378–399.
Dash, L. (1994). Rosalee. *The Washington Post*, September 18.
Freud, S. (1926). Inhibitions, symptoms, and anxiety. *Standard Edition* 20:77–174.
Gatewood, W. B. (1990). *Aristrocrats of Color*. Bloomington, IN: Indiana University Press.
Jacobson, E. (1932). Lernstorungen beim Schulkinde durch masochistiche mechanismen [Learning difficulties of the school-child through masochistic mechanisms]. *International Zeitschrift fur Psychoanalyse* 18:242–251.
Landauer, K. (1929). Zur Psychosexuellen Genese Der Dummheit [On the psycho-sexual genesis of stupidity]. *Zeitschrift fur Sexual-Wissenschaft und Sexualpolitik* 161:12–22.

Maenchen, A. (1936). Denkhemmung und Aggression aus kastrationangst [Thought inhibition and aggression caused by castration anxiety]. *Zeitschrift fur Psychoanalyse Padagogik* 10:276–299.

Mahler, M. (1968). *On Human Symbiosis and the Vicissitudes of Individuation, vol. 1, Infantile Psychosis.* New York: International Universities Press.

———— (1979). *Selected Papers of Margaret S. Mahler, vol. 1. Infantile Psychosis and Early Contributions.* New York: Jason Aronson.

Oberndorf, C. (1939). The feeling of stupidity. *International Journal of Psycho-Analysis* 20:443–451.

Rado, S. (1919). Eine besondere Ausserungsform der Kastration-sangst [A specific manifestation of castration anxiety]. *International Zeitschrift fur Psychoanalyse* 5:206.

5

PSYCHOANALYSIS AND THE RAINBOW OF CULTURAL AUTHENTICITY

Discussion of Miles' Chapter "Mothers and Others: Bonding, Separation-Individuation, and Resultant Ego Development in Different African-American Cultures"

Salman Akhtar, M.D.

In a dramatic return to Freud's (1921, 1927, 1930) deep and abiding interest in the dialectical relationship between the individual psyche and social institutions, psychoanalysis is undergoing a cultural rejuvenation. The cultural relativism of its developmental and structural postulates is being acknowledged. It is also being recognized that the ethnic, racial, socioeconomic, religious, and linguistic difference between the analyst and the analysand can affect their dialogue in profound ways. Such recognition is a belated, though salutory, accompaniment to the emerging theoretical pluralism in psychoanalysis and a response to the shifting population patterns throughout the world and more specifically the changing demographic makeup of the United States, which is becoming a truly multiethnic and multiracial nation.

THE CULTURAL REJUVENATION
OF PSYCHOANALYSIS

Enthusiasm regarding such cultural rejuvenation of psychoanalysis[1] is evident in many ways. First, there is a burgeoning psychoanalytic literature on the interface between the individual psyche and its social context. Prominent here are the investigations of the effects of the intergenerational transmission of the acute and devastating trauma of the Holocaust (Bergman and Jucovy 1982, Blum 1995, Kestenberg 1980, 1985, Kestenberg and Brenner 1996) and of the insidiously malignant collective soul murder resulting from years of African-American slavery (Apprey 1993). The applicability of psychoanalytic theory and technique to diverse ethnic, racial, and cultural populations has also become a focus of serious psychoanalytic attention. Articles and monographs regarding the impact of immigration (Akhtar 1995, Grinberg and Grinberg 1989), polylingualism and polyglottism (Amati-Mehler et al. 1993, Potamianou 1993), ethnic and racial difference between the analyst and the analysand (Fischer 1971, Goldberg et al. 1974, Holmes 1992, Perez Foster et al. 1996), and the psychoanalytically relevant distinctions between the Eastern and the Western mind (Freeman 1977, 1981, Kakar 1985, Roland 1996, Taketomo 1989) have begun to appear in a steady flow. The resurgence of interest in Erikson's (1950, 1959) sociocultural extensions of the Freudian developmental theory, as evidenced in a day-long panel on this topic at a recent meeting of the American Psychoanalytic Association, is yet another manifestation of this trend. Noticeable in the same vein is that a plethora of socioculturally inclined discussion groups (e.g., those pertaining to prejudice, multilingualism, immigration, and racial and ethnic diversity in psychoanalytic practice) have become a regular feature of the American Psychoanalytic Association meetings over the last few years.

---

[1]The current openness of psychoanalysis to sociocultural matters stands in sharp contrast to the skepticism with which the early post-Freudian forays in this realm (Fromm 1950, Horney 1937, 1950, Roheim 1943, 1952) were met by the profession.

Second, a concerted effort is being made by psychoanalytic organizations to be culturally and demographically more inclusive than before. This is evident at both the American and the International Psychoanalytic Associations. The American Psychoanalytic Association established an Ad-Hoc Committee on Racial and Ethnic Diversity in 1994, a task-oriented group that is on its way to becoming a standing committee of the organization. This committee has been assigned the task to encourage greater minority representation on the various programs of the American, prepare model bibliographies and curricula regarding psychoanalysis and cultural diversity, organize scientific programs at local and national levels, explore ways and means of encouraging minority candidate recruitment, and bring together the various community outreach programs already in existence at the various institutes and societies of the American Psychoanalytic Association. The International Psychoanalytic Association has also undertaken a similar sort of mission on a worldwide scale. Its newly formed Committee for Development of Psychoanalysis in Asia, for instance, has been assigned the task of assessing the status of the few existing (and often moribund) psychoanalytic societies in Asian countries and seeking ways to propogate psychoanalytic knowledge in these nations, especially by supporting the interest groups that have newly arisen there.

Finally, the movement toward cultural pluralism and communal inclusiveness is also discernible at a grass-roots level in the component societies and institutes of the American Psychoanalytic Association. While some centers, for example Michigan (Mehta 1994), are much more active than others, most societies and institutes of the American are beginning to undertake some form of community outreach programs. Efforts are under way to establish liaison between psychoanalytic societies and local schools, universities, day care centers, art museums, and ethnic organizations. Psychoanalysts are beginning to go out in the community and hold workshops and discussion groups with lay people on topics ranging from day care to divorce, movies to motherhood, and prejudice to poetry!

THE AFRICAN-AMERICAN SCENARIO

A refreshing addition to this new cultural movement in psycho-analysis is the chapter by Dr. Carlotta Miles. Her important contri-bution joins the small but growing body of psychoanalytic litera-ture (Fischer 1971, Goldberg et al. 1974, Holmes 1992, Jones 1985, Thompson 1996) dealing with the African-American subcultures and the way their unique features affect the psychoanalytic under-standing of development, psychopathology, and therapeutic tech-nique. Before underscoring the strengths of Dr. Miles's contribu-tion and indicating the areas that have not received optimal attention in her chapter, I will summarize its main points.

1. The historical and socioeconomic realities of the Cauca-sian and the African-American populations in the United States differ considerably. These differences have an impact upon the child-rearing patterns and the resulting mother-infant bonding as well as the subsequent ego development in the two respective cultures.

2. Race, however, is not the only variable here. Indeed, the issue of race is closely tied to minority status as well as the socioeconomic class. Thus, within the African-American population, there are three distinct subgroups: the poor and socially disenfranchised, the hard-working and occasion-ally suburban middle class, and the highly affluent, wealthy group.

3. The first of the groups has to contend with poverty and all its attendant ills: overcrowded and unhygienic living cir-cumstances, lack of means of transportation, dependence on welfare and food stamps, malnutrition, and so on. Not surprisingly, this group is characterized by pervasive psycho-social pathology. The social dimension of such pathology involves broken families, lack of education, absence of community role models, rampant substance abuse, violence, crime, and prostitution, and the group as a whole being the

target of racial stereotyping and prejudice. The psychological dimension involves overwhelmed and half-hearted mothering, weak mother–infant attachment, much unneutralized aggression, cognitive lag, and a promiscuous and impulse-ridden overvaluation of sensual pleasure in order to compensate for the chronic emotional deprivation. In a psychoanalytic investigation of such multifaceted developmental arrest, Burland (1986) has described the syndrome of the autistic character disorder comprising social unrelatedness, pathological narcissism, cognitive delay, and much destructive aggression. This population might or might not be an "inescapable community of fate" (Glazer 1996, p. 99), but it certainly is a "subculture of maternal deprivation" (Burland 1984, p. 161).

4. The second group is constituted by intact families that live in better, often suburban, neighborhoods, and where both parents hold reasonable jobs. In this group, the number of children is purposely limited and education is seen as the key to survival and success. Children are overprotected. Physical affection toward them is shown. Discipline, however, is stiff, though not punitive. There is still little knowledge of child development and child care decisions are based upon tradition and expedience. When household help is recruited, the ethnic groups preferred are Caribbean or American blacks.[2] The child often gets more attached to the caregiver than the mother, in a psychic step toward group socialization that often smooths the transition to school. The family has a strong relationship to the church

---

[2]Some deeper aspects of such a choice became evident in a personal conversation with an especially candid, African-American junior colleague. She revealed that she did not feel comfortable receiving a pedicure from an African-American for she might come across as demeaning her own people. However, she also did not feel comfortable having a white person perform this service, since she feared that she might "sadistically" (said tongue in cheek) enjoy herself too much. Her compromise was to go to salons run by Korean immigrants!

and carries the typical middle-class concern for reputation, reliability, and respect for authority figures. As a result, the superego development is more consonant with average, expectable norms of the society.

5. The last group discussed by Dr. Miles is highly affluent African-Americans. Some of these individuals have acquired wealth themselves. Others come from a lineage of affluence (for a history of African American aristocracy, see Gatewood [1990]). The lives of individuals in this group are largely indistinct from their Causasian counterparts. Their sense of identity is not governed by racial belonging, and religion seems to be of less importance to them than it is to the group mentioned above. Their families subscribe to a strong work ethic and put a heavy premium on children's excellence and achievements. Concerns regarding skin color are minimal. There is frequent and quiet crossing of the intrapsychic as well as social demarcations between races.

6. The three groups also vary in their attitudes and responses to seeking psychotherapeutic help. The first group readily displaces its justifiable mistrust of the society at large to the mental health profession. Help is sought only during crises, attendance for treatment sessions is irregular, and the capacity as well as motivation for self observation is minimal (see also Lager and Zwerling 1980). The second group more often seeks formal therapy, not infrequently expressing a preference for African-American therapists. The third group, the most psychologically minded, seeks psychotherapy in a truly appropriate manner and contributes to the bulk of African-American individuals undergoing psychoanalysis proper.

7. In sum, as one moves up the socioeconomic scale, the chances of a child having an intact, functioning family increase and the impact of institutional racism on the psychic development decreases. Ego strength improves, superego

is better organized, and cognitive abilities escape destruction. The seeking of psychotherapy and psychoanalysis also increases.

REFLECTIONS AND QUESTIONS

The contribution made by Dr. Miles is indeed impressive. This is psychoanalytically informed ethnography at its best. The virtuosity of her conceptualization emanates from the fact that she successfully avoids the temptation of sentimentality, polemics, and cynicism while dealing with a subject that is rife with pain, prejudice, and historical as well as continuing social injustice. Throughout her discourse, which does not ignore the existence of racism, her voice remains firm, steady, and fact-based. Moreover, by highlighting the broad spectrum of psychosocial backgrounds and the consequently variable ego and superego developments in the African-American population, Dr. Miles masterfully puts to rest the unflattering stereotypes of this group at large. At the same time, she does not deny the existence of subcultural profiles and characteristically ethnic concerns. Dr. Miles also expands the study of race to include the dimensions of family structure, constitution, socioeconomic class, and the historical context of the group.[3] Her approach is biopsychosocial. She mentions constitutional factors and malnutrition, emotional deprivation and its vicissitudes, and the role of economic status as well as religion in the lives of the people she is describing. Far from narrow, unifactorial explanations of this group's psychology and psychopathology, Dr. Miles's thought is in the best tradition of the "principle of multiple function" (Waelder 1936, p. 45).

Such enthusiasm for her contribution, however, does not prevent one from noticing its inoptimal attention to certain important

---

[3]The heuristically disastrous effects of not paying attention to the economic class while studying the culture of a particular people are painfully evident in Kurtz's (1994) treatise on the mothering practices in India (Akhtar 1997).

matters. First, in commenting upon the father's absence in the ghetto population, Dr. Miles focuses only upon the impact this lacuna has upon the mother. To be sure, this brings attention to the compromise in maternal libidinal supplies and thus a secondary, deleterious impact upon the child. However, such emphasis overlooks the direct effect of the father's absence on the child. Such impact is most evident in the gender identity of the male child, the sexual object choice of the female child, and the superego of children of both sexes (Abelin 1975, Burgner 1985, Prall 1978). The intrapsychic vicissitudes of father's absence upon the oedipal conflict and their subsequent role in the adult sexuality of both sexes thus go largely unnoticed in Dr. Miles's chapter.

Second, the mention of childhood transitional objects appears only in relation to the second and the third African–American groups outlined by Dr. Miles. Children in the ghetto are not described as having transitional objects. The reasons for this omission remain unclear. Do these children really not have transitional objects? Does the overcrowding and/or constant availability of one or the other caregiver (however young themselves!) obviate the need for such objects?[4] Or do the mothers who discourage the child's bonding with them also proscribe the child's attachment to physical possessions? Yet another possibility is that transitional objects do exist in this group but are qualitatively different from the usual ones in this regard. Small, hard, metallic objects (e.g., bottle caps, keys, paper clips) firmly pressed to the skin of the palm while being carried inside a fist might serve to somatically anchor an endangered psychic self (Tustin 1980) as well as symbolically control a "hard" mother. Such unusual and small transitional objects can easily go unnoticed.

Third, Dr. Miles seems to pay less than adequate attention to the effects of transgenerational transmission of the trauma of forced

---

[4]The idea that the transitional object might be an artifact of the modal Western child-rearing practice with its emphasis on the child's separateness and autonomy finds support in the observation that such objects are infrequently witnessed in cultures where the child is offered a longer phase of dependency and much skin-to-skin contact with mother or mother substitutes (Grolnick and Barkin 1978).

immigration from Africa and slavery in the United States upon the African-American population as a whole. In this connection, Abraham's (1988) poignant reminder is especially apt. He stated, "All the departed may return, but some are predestined to haunt the dead who have been shamed during their lifetime or those who took unspeakable secrets to the grave" (p. 75). Extending Abraham's conceptualization, Apprey (1993) pointedly deals with the phantoms of a tragic past that haunt the African-American population, outlining the dire consequences of such transgenerational transmission of trauma.

Fourth, Dr. Miles's attribution of the compromised intellectual abilities in the children of the African-American underclass to a defensive inhibition of ego functions does not take into account the possibility of other etiological explanations. Burland (1986), for instance, suggests that the impairment of cognitive functioning in this group is because the ego's perceptual and cognitive apparatuses are not adequately cathected to begin with. He attributes the resulting disregard for diacritical data about the surrounding world to the inadequate "hatching" (Mahler et al. 1975)—the progression from an early infantile solipsism to being attentive to sensations emanating from perceptual equipment—during early infancy. Yet another explanation of the cognitive impairment might come from the neurological concept of disuse atrophy (see also Pettigrew 1964). After all, it is the repeated and reinforced exercise of a psychological function that facilitates its structuralization.

Fifth, Dr. Miles does not highlight the problematic effects of the absence of good, extrafamilial role models and group heroes upon this population. Coupled with an absent father, especially in the underprivileged African-American group, such lack impedes the "forward projection" (Chasseguet-Smirgel 1984) of the child's narcissism. This, in turn, results in an irreverent bravado on the one hand and a gauzy, weak ego ideal and defective superego on the other. The recent emergence (as well as the belated recognition) of national and international heroes from within the African-American population (Akhtar 1995) is thus an extremely welcome psychological development.

Finally, there remains some lack of clarity in Dr. Miles's contribution about the matter of skin color. Is the "skin color anxiety" (McDonald 1970) an important factor in the normal formation of identity? Or are the child's feelings, upon being emotionally deprived by the mother, displaced onto others ("They don't like me because I have a different skin color") and/or turned against the self ("I am not good enough because of my skin color"), with the skin color becoming a convenient vehicle for such defensive shifts of aggression (Jenkins 1994)? Also, does the skin color difference play a similar role in a less racist society? What is literal and what is metaphorical here? Does the skin stand for the actual skin à la "anatomy is destiny" (Freud 1924, p. 178) or is the skin a containing metaphor (Bick 1968) for unmanageable and internally menacing affects? Clearly, more investigation is needed here.

CONCLUSION

Questions such as the ones raised above notwithstanding, Dr. Miles's contribution remains comprehensive, balanced, and enlightening. It gently but firmly holds our hand and takes us on a highly instructive guided tour of the psychosocial terrain of our African-American counterparts. Each step of this journey mobilizes thought and emotion in us: sadness at one place, intrigue at another, and at varying other moments, pleasure, remorse, shame, horror, guilt, pride, amusement, and so on. For facilitating such a powerful encounter with the essential otherness of a distinct group of people, we remain grateful to Dr. Miles.

REFERENCES

Abelin, E. L. (1975). Earliest role of the father. *International Journal of Psycho-Analysis* 56:293–302.

Abraham, M. (1988). Notes on a phantom. In *The Trials of Psychoanalysis*, ed, F. Meltzer. Chicago: University of Chicago Press.

Akhtar, S. (1995). A third individuation: immigration, identity, and the psychoanalytic process. *Journal of the American Psychoanalytic Association* 43:1051–1084.

—— (1997). Review of Stanley Kurtz's *All the Mothers are One: Hindu India and the Cultural Reshaping of Psychoanalysis. Journal of the American Psychoanalytic Association* 45:1014–1019.

Amati-Mehler, J., Argentieri, S., and Canestri, J. (1993). *The Babel of the Unconscious: Mother Tongue and Foreign Languages in the Psychoanalytic Dimension*, trans. J. Whitelaw-Cucco. Madison, CT: International Universities Press.

Apprey, M. (1993). The African-American experience: forced immigration and the transgenerational trauma. *Mind and Human Interaction* 4:70–75.

Bergman, A., and Jucovy, M. E. (1982). *Generations of the Holocaust.* New York: Basic Books.

Bick, E. (1968). The experience of the skin in early object relations. *International Journal of Psycho-Analysis* 49:484–486.

Blum, H. P. (1995). Sanctified aggression, hate, and the alteration of standards and values. In *The Birth of Hatred: Developmental, Clinical, and Technical Aspects of Intense Aggression*, ed. S. Akhtar, S. Kramer, and S. Parens, pp. 15–38. Northvale, NJ: Jason Aronson.

Burgner, M. (1985). Oedipal experience: effects on development of an absent father. *International Journal of Psycho-Analysis* 66:311–320.

Burland, J. A. (1984). Dysfunctional parenthood in a deprived population. In *Parenthood: A Psychodynamic Perspective*, ed. B. J. Cohler, R. S. Cohen, and S. H. Weissman, pp. 148–163. New York: Guilford.

—— (1986). The vicissitudes of maternal deprivation. In *Self and Object Constancy*, ed. R. F. Lax, S. Bach, and J. A. Burland, pp. 324–347. New York: Guilford.

Chasseguet-Smirgel, J. (1984). *Creativity and Perversion.* New York: W. W. Norton.

Erikson, E. (1950). *Childhood and Society.* New York: W. W. Norton.

—— (1959). *Identity and the Life Cycle.* New York: International Universities Press.

Fischer, N. (1971). An interracial analysis: transference and countertransference significance. *Journal of the American Psychoanalytic Association* 19:736–745.

Freeman, D. M. A. (1977). Psychoanalysis, folklore, and processes of socialization. *Journal of the American Psychoanalytic Association* 25:235–252.

—— (1981). Mythological portrayal of developmental processes and major intrapsychic restructuralizations. *The Psychoanalytic Study of Society*, vol. 9, ed. W. Muensterberger, L B. Boyer, and A. H. Esman, pp. 319–340. New York: Psychohistory Press.

Freud, S. (1921). Group psychology and the analysis of the ego. *Standard Edition* 18: 65–143.

—— (1924). The dissolution of the Oedipus complex. *Standard Edition* 19:171–188.

—— (1927). The future of illusion. *Standard Edition* 21:1–56.

—— (1930). Civilization and its discontents. *Standard Edition* 21:57–145.

Fromm, E. (1950). *Psychoanalysis and Religion.* New Haven, CT: Yale University Press.

Gatewood, W. B. (1990). *Aristrocrats of Color: The Black Elite—1880–1920.* Bloomington, IN: Indiana University Press.

Glazer, N. (1996). *We Are All Multiculturalists Now*. Cambridge, MA: Harvard University Press.

Goldberg, E. L., Myers, W. A., and Zeifman, I. (1974). Some observations on three interracial analyses. *International Journal of Psycho-Analysis* 55:495–500.

Grinberg, L., and Grinberg, R. (1989). *Psychoanalytic Perspectives on Migration and Exile*, trans. N. Festinger. New Haven, CT: Yale University Press.

Grolnick, S. A., and Barkin, L. (1978). *Between Fantasy and Reality: Transitional Objects and Phenomena*. New York: Jason Aronson.

Holmes, D. E. (1992). Race and transference in psychoanalysis and psychotherapy. *International Journal of Psycho-Analysis* 73:1–11.

Horney, K. (1937). *The Neurotic Personality of Our Time*. New York: W. W. Norton.

——— (1950). *Neurosis and Human Growth*. New York: W. W. Norton.

Jenkins, L. (1994). African American identity and its social context. In *Race, Ethnicity and Self: Identity in Multicultural Perspective*, ed. E. P. Salett and D. R. Koslow, pp. 63–88. Washington, DC: National Multicultural Institute.

Jones, E. (1985). Psychotherapy and counseling with black clients. In *Handbook for Cross-cultural Counseling and Therapy*, ed. P. Pedersen, pp. 173–179. Westport, CT: Greenwood.

Kakar, S. (1985). Psychoanalysis and non-Western cultures. *International Review of Psycho-Analysis* 12:441–448.

Kestenberg, J. (1980). Psychoanalyses of children of Holocaust survivors. *Journal of the American Psychoanalytic Association* 28:775–804.

——— (1985). Editorial: child survivors of the Holocaust 40 years later. *Journal of the American Academy of Child Psychiatry* 24:408–412.

Kestenberg, J. S., and Brenner, I. (1996). *The Last Witness: The Child Survivor of the Holocaust*. Washington, DC: American Psychiatric Press.

Lager, E., and Zwerling, I. (1980). Time orientation and psychotherapy in the ghetto. *American Journal of Psychiatry* 137:306–309.

Mahler, M. S., Pine, F., and Bergman, A. (1975). *The Psychological Birth of the Human Infant*. New York: Basic Books.

McDonald, M. (1970). *Not by the Color of Their Skin*. New York: International Universities Press.

Mehta, P. (1994). Michigan analysts engage the Indo-Pakistani Community. *American Psychoanalyst* 29:6–7.

Perez Foster, R., Moskowitz, M., and Javier, R. A. (1996). *Reaching Across Boundaries of Culture and Class: Widening the Scope of Psychotherapy*. Northvale, NJ: Jason Aronson.

Pettigrew, T. F. (1964). *A Profile of the Negro American*. Princeton, NJ: Van Nostrand.

Potamianou, A. (1993). In exile from the mother tongue. *Canadian Journal of Psycho-analysis* 1:47–59.

Prall, R. C. (1978). Panel: The role of the father in the preoedipal years. *Journal of the American Psychoanalytic Association* 26:143–151.

Roheim, G. (1943). *The Origin and Function of Culture*. New York: International Universities Press.

———— (1952). *The Gates of the Dream*. New York: International Universities Press.

Roland, A. (1996). *Cultural Pluralism and Psychoanalysis: The Asian and North American Experience*. New York: Routledge.

Taketomo, Y. (1989). An American-Japanese transcultural psychoanalysis and the issue of teacher transference. *Journal of the American Academy of Psychoanalysis* 17:427–450.

Thompson, C. L. (1996). The African-American patient in psychodynamic treatment. In *Reaching Across Boundaries of Culture and Class: Widening the Scope of Psychotherapy*, ed. R. Perez Foster, M. Moskowitz, and R. A. Javier, pp. 115–142. Northvale, NJ: Jason Aronson.

Tustin, F. (1980). Autistic objects. *International Review of Psycho-Analysis* 7:27–35.

Waelder, R. (1936). The principle of multiple function: observations on multiple determination. *Psychoanalytic Quarterly* 5:45–62.

6

THE EMERGENCE, CONFLICTS, AND INTEGRATION OF THE BICULTURAL SELF: PSYCHOANALYSIS OF AN ADOLESCENT DAUGHTER OF SOUTH-ASIAN IMMIGRANT PARENTS

Purnima Mehta, M.D.

In July 1996, the Indian community of a large North American metropolitan area was dumbfounded and shattered. The members had to bury a child of theirs, a 20-year-old, second-generation Indian young adult, who committed suicide by hanging himself. This suicide has been followed by *five* other suicides by older adolescents and young adults (three males and two females) of South-Asian background, belonging to the upper middle class, and having parents with professional backgrounds. This phenomenon of cluster suicides is virtually unknown in the South-Asian community of the United States. One of the children shot himself, another used carbon monoxide poisoning, two overdosed on drugs, and one was found dead on the railway tracks. The methods were violent. A common denominator in three cases was found in their suicide notes: shame for having disappointed their immigrant parents for not getting into medical school. This tragic incident underscores the increasing difficulties of second-generation immigrant children of South-Asian background—from India, Pakistan, Sri Lanka, and Bangladesh.

FACTUAL AND CONCEPTUAL BACKDROP

A brief profile of the Indian immigration to the United States will highlight the origins of a specific group of second-generation immigrants with identity conflicts. This chapter also proposes a model for bicultural identity, presents clinical material from an analysis to demonstrate these conflicts and their integration, and discusses the developmental conflicts that face these children in five areas: (1) immigrant parenting, (2) skin-color differences, (3) separation-individuation issues, (4) sexual conflicts, and (5) career conflicts.

Immigration from India to the United States

Migration from the South-Asian Indian subcontinent to the United States is a relatively recent phenomenon. Before 1964, only 17,000 people immigrated from India. Seventy-five percent of Indian immigrants arrived between 1975 and 1990. In 1977 alone, 32,000 people arrived (the majority of them were physicians).

While South Asia/India itself is a poverty-stricken area/nation, its residents have prospered in the United States. Indians play many roles in American society, with 40 percent of them owning motels. Their prosperity is related to their higher level of education and occupation—66 percent of all employed Indians are college graduates. The average family income of Indians increased faster than that of native-born Americans despite the fact that they had only recently immigrated. Engineering and medicine are their main occupations. In the Silicon Valley in California there are 5,000 Indian engineers. In some pockets of professional people there are 20,000 engineers and 28,000 physicians. Given the fact that immigration from India has largely been restricted to the educated groups, this immigrant population in the United States, unlike other immigrant groups, has achieved remarkable economic prosperity.

The immigrants usually keep a low political profile. Politics is not associated with the rise to affluence. They hold themselves sepa-

rate and aloof from surrounding populations. Despite this clannish-
ness, they have not provoked hostility from others. The Indian community is spread out in pockets in major cities in the United States.

There is great diversity within the Indian community itself. In
greater Detroit, there are thirty-six linguistically and regionally diverse professional and cultural organizations of Indians. As a result,
a community of second-generation immigrants, with parents who
recently emigrated from a poor country, living in rapidly rising
prosperity, some reaching affluent levels, has formed. Most importantly, the second generation has been exposed to distinctly different language, goals, food, rituals, dress, music, landscapes, and values than their parents. There is a strong urge to retain ethnic identity
while rapidly acquiring awareness of American values, partially due
to rapid financial gains. This phenomenon has resulted in a split
(which shall be the focus of my chapter) between these children
and their parents. Many children refer to themselves in a colloquial
manner: ABCD (American-Born Confused Desis), that is, people
from the homeland, FOB (Fresh Off the Boat), and 9–5; 5–9 (9 to
5 o'clock represents American life, and 5 to 9 o'clock represents
Indian life). Hence, the child's ego is stressed and the consolidation
of identity has some features unique to this community.

Bicultural Identity

The second-generation Indian child chooses a multilevel identity
based on acceptance of what I call the third space, a transitional space
between Indianness and Americanization. There is a specific coping
strategy I note in these children called situational identity, in which
children learn to negotiate between the contrasting American and
Indian worlds by calling upon different models of behavior in different settings. This does not necessarily lead to a false-identity process as much as it does to becoming "culture wise," the way street-
wise children adapt to poverty. They become experts in negotiating
the social world. Four outcomes are possible:

1. *Compromised identity:* This is the most problematic outcome. There is a sense of cultural alienation, not feeling bonded to or comfortable in either culture. Parents might also be deeply conflicted about their identity upon immigration, seeking neither a strong Indian nor an American affiliation. These children are at high risk for emotional disturbance.

2. *Ethnocentric identity:* Children retain strong Indian values, are probably more comfortable in the home surrounding, and might feel isolated in the larger school community unless they can find one or two Indian friends to hang out with. Parents absorb this anxiety by placing the children in affluent schools with a larger number of South-Asian children, thereby passively resisting Americanization. The children also remain well grounded in the smaller community and academically strong, but are more likely to be conflicted about dating and separation in adolescence, when they might become more symptomatic and seek treatment.

3. *Amerocentric identity:* This occurs in a small percentage of children with strong American values and little contact with their ethnic background. Sometimes they resist ethnic connections or show indifference. They function well in the larger communities, are more likely to intermarry, and can retain stability. But sometimes they display symptoms when they go to college, where the ties to Indian parents become conflictual.

4. *Bicultural identity:* A larger percentage of children are beginning to move toward bicultural identity. An integration of the third space is less conflictual. There is the flexibility to adapt to both cultures, to their music, food, and language. The children's sense of responsibility and loyalty is great, their bicultural pride is strong, and neither culture becomes regressively constricting. These children readily identify themselves as Indian–American and remain steadily loyal in their affiliations. The parents seem more advanced in psychologically coping with their own immigration.

A deeper appreciation of these different types of bicultural identities is not possible without first taking a closer look at the concept of identity itself.

Identity: A Reconsideration

Identity formation is a crucial normative task of adolescence. It involves a dynamic time of loss and a time of gain. Erikson (1968) has provided us with a rich and evocative theory of identity formation and related this process to other aspects of ego development. He noted (Erikson 1950a) that he had focused on ego identity and its anchoring in cultural identity. Ego identity referred to that aspect of the ego which, at the end of adolescence, integrates the disparate infantile ego states and neutralizes the autocracy of the infantile superego. For Erikson (1968) ego identity is an enduring psychological structure that is subjectively experienced as a sense of psychological well-being. Erikson, though, is only speaking of a positive ego identity. Many child analysts believe that adolescents may emerge from this phase with a negative ego identity. The most obvious concomitants of a healthy identity are a feeling of being at home in one's body, a sense of knowing where one is going, and an inner assuredness of anticipated recognition from others. Time and again Erikson makes the point that identity is established through an active and reciprocal exchange between the individual and the psychosocial matrix in which he/she lives. The multiple exchanges between the adolescent and his/her peer group, family, and community allow for an inner organization of needs, abilities, and self-perceptions as well as a social-political stance for integration at three levels: (1) structurally, identity involves reorganization, mostly of unconscious needs and past identifications; (2) socially, identity marks a new assimilation of social expectations and values, and a more personal integration into one's society and culture; and (3) phenomenologically, identity manifests in a new way of experiencing oneself, characterized by a sense of unity and individuality, and by a feeling of purposefulness and self-confidence.

What do we mean by cultural identity? Rakoff (1981) proposes a model of the role of custom and history in personal psychological development analogous to Winnicott's (1953) transitional objects. Rakoff feels that without an understanding of a contextual issue called "continuing history," the individual may not know where he or she is coming from or going to. Rakoff (1981) has suggested that the child's identity might get compromised rather than liberated as a result of this phenomenon. While Rakoff's model proposes an important dimension, one can apply Winnicott's (1953) concept of transitional objects in space to the experience of the culture and the life of the child. Winnicott (1959) called the third "area of existing" (p. 57) important because it complements the previous areas he has mentioned, the individual psychic or inner reality and external reality. Winnicott (1960) provided a framework for the concept of the holding environment, a kind of transitional space that can be extended beyond the mother–infant relationship into the therapeutic dyad that can include the cultural context as well. The sameness of customs, language, dress, and other sociological phenomena allows the individual to identify, develop, and enhance his or her identity formation. As long as cultural issues remain the same, an individual has a period of relative quiet to develop his or her identity. If changes occur, there is a potential disruption in identity equilibrium. The adolescent's cultural environment complicates an already difficult period of disequilibrium related to identity development. Cultural stability allows identity formation to proceed (provided the relationship with important objects is nontraumatic). However, with cultural upheaval there is a potentially increased difficulty in adolescent identity formation.

The focus of this chapter is on the adolescent children of immigrant parents (i.e., first generation). Born in the United States, the second-generation child is not an immigrant. While psychoanalytic literature on adolescents has provided us with much understanding of the adolescent's upsurge of sexuality, rebellion against parental ego ideals, and eventual "second individuation" (Blos 1967), there has been little psychoanalytic literature on the complex task that faces an adolescent growing up in two cultures simultaneously. In a way the second-generation child has to create, like Winnicott's third space, a "third reality," neither of his or her parents' homeland nor of the adopted land, but uniquely and historically different. The cultural identity refers to the ego finding an expression within a particular role provided by the social environment. This third space spans the inner and outer reality. Social role is affected by events within the social cultural context to which the ego must adapt, such as the conflicting reality a second-generation adolescent is faced with, and the rapidly shifting cultures, ethnic and nonethnic, within the home and outside. Many second-generation immigrants say they have to live an American life from 9 to 5 and an Indian life from 5 to 9. This, I think, represents a very important feeling of split identity in the second-generation immigrant from South Asia. On the one hand, constantly changing and diffusely defined roles place a certain stress on the ego and could decisively compromise its identifications. On the other hand, identity formation is probably enriched by having diverse objects for identification. These issues arise in all adolescents but have special vicissitudes in a bicultural setting, as illustrated by the following case.

CLINICAL CASE

Working with the Patient

Nina, the oldest of three children of two physician immigrant parents from India, sought treatment just after her fifteenth birthday when she attempted suicide by swallowing a handful of pills that belonged to her mother. This followed an argument with her mother, whom she obviously wanted to hurt. The first contact with me was initiated on an emergency basis when she was referred to me by her aunt, herself a psychiatrist. Nina had refused to continue seeing a male day-hospital psychiatrist to whom she had been referred following a school consultation. She also refused to continue treatment with antidepressant medication. While the parents were overtly quite pleased at having an Indian psychiatrist evaluate their daughter, they immediately proceeded to take me into their confidence in a quasi-manipulative manner. The mother attached herself quickly to me, saw me as an immediate ally, sharing similar backgrounds and values, and made several attempts to derogate the American psychiatrist (who had seen Nina briefly), in turn idealizing me. Her agenda was clear: Nina was becoming too rebellious and pouty. Alternatively, she was passive, and would not do the tasks that her parents felt were appropriate for her age. The parents thought this was probably the "influence of America" and that my being Indian would instill the time-honored virtues of respect, compliance, and virtuosity in their now uncooperative, rebellious daughter.

The initial evaluation consisted of helping disentangle Nina's symptoms as a troubled, unhappy youngster from any significant cultural determinants. This led to both a disappointment and diluted respect for me from her parents, related to either my firmness around time and money (I was too American and strict, not permitting a casual friendliness between two immigrants), or a fear that I would hold them in contempt for their perceived failures as parents. They might also have wished to shift their inadequacy as Indian parents onto me. My consistency in limit setting both for them and their daughter was "Americanized," according to the parents, an aspect that they overtly admired and covertly despised. Hence, the two cultures took on a variety of meanings for both parents from the start, who experienced deep disappointment that their oldest child, born three years after immigrating, had run into difficulties and needed psychiatric help. They bemoaned the fact that she did not appreciate them. "She gets everything she wants—CD player, telephone, clothes, television, and private schooling. We work so hard to provide this and often tell her that a teenager in India would not have 10 percent of what she has, but she doesn't realize it. What does she want?"

What did Nina want and what did she need? Therein lay the difficulty. Nina was an attractive, well-developed teenager with body-image problems; she initially complained of feeling fat, ugly, depressed, and unloved. While she was slightly overweight, her preoccupation with her body image revealed significant masochistic trends in order to deal with a narcissistically preoccupied mother and an invested, but busy father. Interestingly, the referral also coincided with Nina's maternal grandmother's immigrating and joining the family. Thus, the early deprivation and neglect Nina experienced with the mother were revived and intensified by the grandmother's presence. Nina felt the mother's attention was further diluted because of the grandmother's presence. In reaction she attached herself rapidly to me with an object hunger suggestive of preoedipal disruption. With the onset of puberty her relationship with her now much bewildered father was minimal, resulting in Nina's resentment of, anger toward, and devaluation of him. The situation had its roots in oedipal conflict. Nina began to lose interest in friends and feared going to parties, thinking she would not have the right outfit. She desperately wanted a slim body. She had difficulty concentrating on her schoolwork, and her grades had slowly dropped. She reported a hopeless crush on a boy in school (possibly a paternal displacement), who would not even acknowledge her. Her slow deterioration in functioning dated back to puberty with increasing sadomasochistic struggles with her mother around food, weight, clothes, and fluency in the Hindi language.

Nina related her concerns with tearfulness and anger toward her mother. She felt "lost" and "useless" and "a loser" with her friends. She felt like she was the "extra person," who would easily be "dropped," with nothing to offer her friends. In trying to deal with the extra-person issue, she was eating, neglecting herself, and trying to hurt herself, hoping that the pain would go away forever. All the preoedipal and oedipal conflicts were interwoven, and oedipal problems seemed particularly significant in her wish to feel like a victim and to be the extra person. Nina seemed eager to pursue analysis.

The parents' ambivalence about analysis, on the other hand, was intense. The father minimized Nina's complaints as age-specific and thought that she would soon grow out of "wanting to kill herself." The mother, while very concerned about her daughter's misery, felt very threatened by another Indian woman becoming an important part of Nina's life. This manifested itself in the mother's numerous questions about my background and family, and she gave me pleading looks to make the treatment into a friendly, family affair. This became equally burdensome on my psyche and analytic neutrality, as I began to interpret the resistance to analytic work by empathizing and reflecting on the mother's fear of losing her daughter to me, so that the mother would feel like the extra person. The mother found my attempts to maintain time and money parameters to be different from that of other Indian physicians, such as the Indian woman gynecologist, the Indian pediatrician, and the Indian male psychiatrist the father had consulted, who was willing to do family consultations and family therapy at their home. It was because of Nina's continued misery and insistence that the parents allowed her to be in analysis in spite of much skepticism.

While Nina's analysis had complex, interwoven themes, my discussion will focus on those relevant to the topic of cultural identity and the effect on cultural identity. Once the analytic situation was secured, the intensity and pace of the work progressed. The recognition of the seriousness of her suicidal gesture and a growing trust and confidence in the privacy of our communication, despite mother's anxiety-ridden intrusiveness in the session, solidified the therapeutic alliance. Nina appeared highly motivated, very verbal, and delighted to have someone listen to her. She had no difficulty filling the sessions with numerous associations, mainly that of her distorted body image, poor self-esteem, and somatic complaints, all with an underlying agenda: When would I wave my magic wand and make all her painful feelings disappear? Interestingly, at this time she regarded my perceived incompetence in the face of continued painful affect as related to my being Indian, just like her mother.

The bad-mother transference began to emerge. Nina felt that an American woman might have been more capable of spontaneously relieving her distress. Additionally, she projected fears of not being adequate because she is not a real American and she was then able to clarify it. This led to elaboration of important themes of idealization, omnipotence versus devaluation, and contemptuous representations of me and herself. From this emerged valuable information about how Nina used her bicultural experiences to communicate split-off aspects of herself. However, the crucial question was, What contributed to this particular form of resistance and defensive maneuvering? She feared deeply that I, being an immigrant like her parents, would not understand what it was like for her to be an Indian girl growing up in America. When I invited her to tell me about it, she experienced both relief and irritation. She felt that if I had been born and raised here, I would have complete harmony with her without having to work with a variety of shifting images of herself.

As she felt free to complain about her family, it began to clearly emerge that while splitting was a common family defense, the cultural split was even further reinforced by her parents in a variety of contexts. The parents, while being quite ethnocentric, would devalue and gossip about other Indian families "as being overly connected or dependent on each other." Hence the family's dependency needs resurfaced uniquely, both as a result of immigration and otherwise, and were then denied and managed by messages to Nina to be precociously independent, which in turn was rationalized as the American way. As Nina's positive transference intensified, a revival of libidinal and dependent feelings was dealt with by an increased somatic preoccupation through disguised wishes to be cared for and nurtured. Once again my analytic neutrality in the face of her strong, dependent longings was viewed as too American and cold by both the patient and her parents. Yet Nina feared that my being gratifying and indulging would cause her to view me as soft, weak, and Indian. Her conscience, corruptible versus honest, took on a cultural significance.

Nina described frequent fights, both with her mother and her father. With her mother she was loud and critical, mainly about her mother's perceived and real unavailability, focusing on Indian and

American food, Indian and American clothes, and Indian and American music. Neither Indian nor American clothes made her instantly look perfect and desirable. Her father, whom she coldly and nonverbally (rolling her eyes) deprecated (defending against incestuous feelings), withdrew further from her, feeling hurt and betrayed. This encouraged the mother and daughter to enter into a more intense and pathological sadomasochistic relationship.

As Nina's positive transference feelings increased, she began to relate feelings about her pubertal body: feelings of shame and disgust regarding her menstruation and fears that there was something wrong and deficient about her body. Once again she began to view the pretty American girls (other patients of mine) as having phallic powers to attract my attention. She flaunted her ability to trick her mother and began sadistic attacks against me by skipping school. Maintaining my analytic neutrality was critical, as she both tested and feared my taking on a parental role. Her masochistic aspects and passivity were deeply connected by her with her Indianness. This self representation seemed to keep her close to her mother as she began to experience frightening libidinal and dependent longings in the transference. Her resistance once again found cultural paths, in that I, too, was free and wild in my view that her feared libidinal longings might have some connection with me. What seemed culturally conflictual served to defend against oedipal and preoedipal conflicts with a defensive displacement. Early memories of separation began to emerge having to do with day-care facilities and feelings of neglect and abandonment. She then launched into major acting out, as she decided to see a Salem witch for love potions. She traveled to Boston with a girlfriend, skipped a session, and tricked her parents into believing that she was away for a sleep-over. This emphasized the parents' lack of supervision and was rationalized as being like American parents, too permissive and free.

Nina quickly found an Indian boyfriend, emphasizing that an American boy would only be interested in sex. Again she had projected her forbidden wishes onto others as though this were a cultural conflict. Dating is not something that most Indian parents will easily undertake to supervise and manage. This resistance was short-lived as Nina became charged with instinctual drives and fled back to analytic work. She gradually became aware that what she feared most was her own sexuality, a feeling of foreignness in her now grown-up body, and she longed for what she felt was the "Indian prepubertal body." The real question was, How many of these cultural problems or internal conflicts (especially the forbidden aspects) was she externalizing by projecting them onto culture?

While there might be problems arising from having each foot in a different culture, one must distinguish this from defensive uses of cultural issues. This idea was deeply tied with the mother's primitive rationalization that sexuality had visited Nina in the form of an "American devil." At many levels Nina's boyfriend was used in a developmental way to avoid feelings for me, but he also served as an important developmental object to separate from the mother in the face of a hurt, frightened, and withdrawn father. Nina renewed her passive, masochistic attachment to her boyfriend through intense feeling, unprotected sex, and fantasies of pregnancy to finally capture her mother's attention, and mine in the transference to avoid feelings of intense loss and rejection precipitated by my going on vacation. As she gradually recognized her need to shift her conflict from her mother to her boyfriend, she realized that her only way out would be to examine her ambivalence about being analyzed, her fear about dependency, and most of all images of herself and her sexuality, which she feared as devouring and uncontrollable.

Nina found her sexual activity barely pleasurable; in fact, she felt nothing during intercourse but derived comfort from being held before and after. Her actual pleasure lay in mocking her mother, feeling she had one-upped her by having sex behind her back. She also felt that she had been totally left to her devices, having received no explanation about sex or birth control from her mother. With some interpretation on my part regarding the use of her body to take revenge against her mother and the passivity in the behavioral passivity in the counter phobic maneuvers that she took pride in,

Nina felt motivated to courageously ask her mother for a referral to a gynecologist. Interestingly, the mother prompted Nina to go to her own gynecologist, an Indian female friend of hers. Nina correctly feared this arrangement (once again a diffusion of boundaries) and her well-founded concerns that Mom would get information about her sexuality from her gynecologist friend. In fact, the mother saw me as quite unprotective and deviant from the traditional, collective, Indian womanhood role of protecting an adolescent girl from her sexuality. Nina was able to exercise her sense of newfound autonomy by asking her mother to refer her to an alternate gynecologist, an American woman.

As the analysis became central, Nina was able to deal more directly with homosexual transference and emerging positive oedipal aspects. Once again she deflected the powerful, positive transference onto her boyfriend, becoming competitive with other girls, now secure in her relationship with them. She became aware of her intense attachment to her father in her early years, up until 3 or 4 years of age. In fact, her father was involved in her early caregiving while the mother was busy with her residency. Nina began to lose weight, feeling a sense of confidence as she felt that her femininity integrated some form of activity and autonomy, but she was once again fearful that her father would be threatened or prefer her to adopt the mother's passive stance. This defended against her renewed awareness of her dependence on her father, who began to feel loved and accepted by his daughter. This dependence also caused her to think about her career choice, which she felt would please her father, who in his protective manner suggested that she pursue medical schooling in India. While he was offering an easy solution, he also undermined her sense of competency and interestingly used his child as a sacrifice to India to alleviate the guilt of immigrating. This emerged as Nina talked with her father (a new development), who began to reminisce about India and to consider his success in America with some guilt feelings. Nina was able to stand firm in the face of this overly appealing offer to make things easy for her and continue her dependence on him, which both hid and expressed subtle incestuous wishes. He secretly admired her independence and she began to feel that he looked at her with curiosity and was intrigued: "You're different now and I like it."

Nina progressed in her work and began thinking of college. This reactivated her parents' fear about separation and triggered mixed feelings, particularly in the mother, who began to get depressed. Although this depression stirred up guilt feelings in Nina, she was able to understand them in the context of her mother's envy and competitiveness toward her now-confident daughter. In the transference she wondered about my reaction as she began to face the prospect of leaving. She felt that she could exercise judgment in her decision, most importantly to protect her needs, whereas her previously indiscriminate decisions were geared to pleasing objects for fear of abandonment and rejection. A period of anger and loss related to her parents' shortcomings and limitations followed. She decided to undertake a year of college experience in town to permit one more year of analysis before leaving home. The parents seemed beside themselves, for their daughter was not following the time-honored American tradition of leaving home (contrary to their own college years in India, when they did not leave home). Interestingly, after discussion, the parents' response revealed their defensive reasons for wanting Nina to leave on their timetable: they feared a loss of prestige with their friends, as Nina's remaining home would reflect a lack of success on their part. They often exchanged notes with other parents about their children. In fact, for the first time the parents' defensive entreaties toward me softened as the father remarked, "It is like we stopped listening to our children. Now she makes me listen to her."

Nina finished analysis six months later (four years and three months after she had begun). She commented in the last week, "I feel beautiful inside and fortunate for this experience. It's unique. I don't have to be constantly conscious of Indian or American dress, food, and boys. Well somewhat, but pleasantly, not painfully." She no longer needed the "cultural shield."

Working with the Parents

I met with Nina's parents throughout the course of her analysis on an as-needed basis, which was mainly crisis oriented. Additionally, I had seen them for approximately ten sessions before the analysis to deal with their resistance to accepting recommendations for analysis. The father remained aloof and distant, often abdicating the responsibility of consultation to the mother. Nina resented this bitterly, viewing her father's withdrawal as a sign of his lack of interest. Initially the father also delayed payments, which resulted in my having to call him directly. He associated this to my having become "money hungry" in America, a projection probably of his own guilt and success connected to immigration. Often he used this guilt to control Nina's behavior. On further exploring this with him, it became clear that he felt it a failure in the midst of "American success" that his daughter was dissatisfied with life, especially when he had worked so hard to make their move to America successful. This revealed his guilt over his siblings' living a poorer life in India while he could afford top dollar for his daughter's emotional health, which he viewed as a luxury. The father felt that such material comfort should have led Nina to inner satisfaction and a sense of confidence, leading to solid decision-making capabilities. Much of my work was educative, helping the father (who came from an impoverished home) become aware of Nina's emotional needs, which he felt were secondary and could not compare to his own patients' bleeding to death due to ulcer hemorrhage. On one occasion the father announced that Nina was fortunate to have been born here and have a first-class status while he had to arrive here as a second-class immigrant. While he was shocked by his own revelation to himself, it led to a more meaningful understanding of his envy of his American-born daughter.

While the father's parenting issues revolved mainly around money, the mother felt at a loss in dealing with Nina's wishes to date and party. The mother linked sexuality to America, and felt at a loss in handling Nina's growing interest in boys. She wished to be viewed as progressive and permissive in her parenting, for she feared that I would view her as backward for applying traditional Indian views that there should be no dating and no interaction with boys. I emphatically communicated to her that she was on new territory with her first daughter, and that she was being too harsh on herself for not knowing the ins and outs of the American dating scene.

At many times the mother projected her own self-image onto me. She also feared that asking questions would come across as her being inadequate. She also feared that her Indian friends would view her as too Americanized. She feared what her reactions would have been if her parents had encouraged more sexual freedom for her (which would have been seen as loss of control and going to extremes), and projected this fear onto her own daughter.

The mother's dilemma of feeling caught between two cultures was understandably enormous. However, it was also clear that she used her Indian background to neurotically support her passivity and difficulty in setting limits with the daughter. This fueled a pathological closeness that warded off Nina's real need to discuss sexual issues and birth control with her mother. The mother, fearful of her own repressed sexuality, would often look in Nina's bedroom for any hints of Nina's having a boyfriend and a sexual relationship. She would then use this to attack Nina in the face of her own intimidation by Nina's temper tantrums. This intrusiveness was born out of a fantasy that her knowing would stop Nina, rather than that her discussing sexual matters with Nina would lend her an auxiliary ego to support and modulate her sexual decisions.

The mother, in her deeply embedded ambivalence toward me, which I believe was a powerful maternal transference intensified by my being an Indian, indirectly devalued me by speaking in the community about my being too Americanized and useless for her daughter. In fact, she became, I believe, envious of her daughter's receiving support from me that was not available to her. After some thought I decided to call this to her attention, to yield, I hoped, a better alliance with her and to deal with her resistances to parenting her daughter. She felt embarrassed about her gossiping. However, she also became aware that she wished to attack me where it hurt most—as an Indian professional woman in my tightly knit community—and seek revenge on me for standing as a reality between her daughter and her, which propelled a separation-individuation she overtly desired and covertly despised.

DISCUSSION

Children of second-generation immigrant South-Asian origin, like my patient, often develop both developmental and neurotic conflicts. It is important in the treatment of such patients to identify and empathize with both these types of conflicts. On the one hand, to mistake one for the other is detrimental to treatment. On the other hand, failure to interpret the use of "culture" for supporting neurotic defenses impedes the progress of treatment. The area is riddled with complexity, and the issues involved include (1) immigrant parents, (2) skin-color differences, (3) separation-individuation, (4) sexual conflicts, and (5) career conflicts. In this discussion I will interweave the material from the case described about with observations I have made in conducting workshops with Indian immigrant parents and their American-born children.

Immigrant Parents

Parenting is a unique and complex task. Winnicott (1969) said there is no such thing as a baby, only a mother and baby. Parenting, on the whole, is itself a fairly new topic in child analysis, and work with immigrant parents is an additional dimension. The literature highlights unique anxieties. Grinberg and Grinberg (1989) look at the phenomenon of immigration in terms of the different types of anxieties that it can awaken: (1) persecution anxiety in the face of change, the new, and the unknown; (2) depressive anxiety, which leads to grieving for the objective left behind and the lost part of the self; and (3) disorienting anxiety, or the failure to distinguish between the old and the new. These anxieties, together with resultant symptoms and defense mechanisms, are part of the psychopathology of immigration.

Akhtar (1995) provides detailed organizations of factors affecting the immigrant's identity in the context of separation individuation. He elucidates a variety of factors that affect immigrants' adaptation to their new environment, commenting in passing on their role as immigrant parents. What is overlooked is that these parents' children are in the midst of their own immigration process. The crucial question to ask is: Are the immigrant parents more vulnerable? Do immigrant parents, such as those from the South-Asian culture, have specific conflict issues? If so, how can clinicians recognize these difficulties unique to the immigration process? What fantasies and realities of immigrants affect the parenting process? These questions are particularly important because the psychoanalysis of the child depends upon the parents' ability to be supportive, especially in subcultures in which psychoanalysis is not readily sought.

Adolescents revive their parents' images of their own adolescence, which, for immigrants, was experienced in a different cultural setting. The adolescent's awkward attempts at integrating two cultures in dress, manner, food, and language revive parental conflicts of loyalty between two cultures. The sexually maturing adolescent body might then be utilized to express these conflicts and struggles.

Narcissistic defenses of parents are sometimes heightened by an unresolved or partially resolved sense of loss owing to immigration. This occurred in Nina's parents' reactions to my being an immigrant analyst. While consciously relieved to find somebody who would understand their culture, they also projected their self-perceived devalued "Indianness" onto me. Alternatively, to defend against guilt (universal for parents with children in treatment), they rationalized it as either belonging to the Indian culture or the American culture. This dilemma, while real in terms of values, became a resistance in exploring their own guilt about immigrating. So again, cultural factors are primarily assigned a defensive role.

What must be determined as treatment progresses is what role, if any, does culture have as a cause of conflict or symptom formation. Further, the guilt over immigration may be the primary factor, unique to those subcultural groups, such as Asian Indians, that have rapid and remarkable success in their adapted country.

A common rescue fantasy is elicited based on a pseudo-bond of one immigrant helping another in a foreign country. Thus, immigrant Indian parents seek Indian therapists for their children. However, there is also a rapid fantasy formation of parents' having control over the Indian therapist, and fear that an American therapist will be intimidating and will not comply with their wishes. Nina's parents' immediate overt comfort with me as a fantasy family member and physician for their daughter gave way later to subtle derogation of the psychoanalytic framework of time and money. This began with a sense of disappointment in me for being too "Americanized" in order to defend against their own personal difficulties with limit setting.

Limit setting becomes embedded in culture values instead of understood as a legitimate developmental need for the child's growth. The immigrant parent is particularly vulnerable to this parenting task as he or she vacillates between two cultures. In the works of Anna Freud (1958), Blos (1967), and Jacobson (1964), there is increasing emphasis on rebellion against parental values and eventual physical separation from the parents as measures of the accomplishment of the internal structural changes.

The Anglo-American social and cultural values of self-sufficiency, autonomy, and personal responsibility are often misinterpreted by immigrant parents as selfish, and the parents place excessive restrictions on their children. The parents within the cultural peer groups often become sensitive to nuances of being looked upon as too Americanized if they begin to adopt such guidelines as curfews and punitive consequences. They fear being "odd" and are particularly vulnerable to adolescents' parental introjects of them.

This reluctance to set limits generates a sense of omnipotent control in the adolescent over the vulnerable, confused, immigrant parent. This does not mean that children necessarily deprecate their parents as old fashioned and behind the times. A cultural difference does not always create this conflict, but may intensify it and be a displacement for other issues. The parent who is seen as confused might react to more intensified narcissistic injury with excessive and harsh restrictions and measures. The adolescent rebellion is perceived by the parents as a real threat to their parenting skills. The parents' real vulnerability around longings for their old country's music, food, culture, and language (things especially cherished) often becomes the very issue that the adolescent rebels about. Often the parents experience this rebellion as a deep wounding of their core selves and they will not tolerate it, hence creating a sadomasochistic struggle over cultural identity or generational identity.

Rosenbaum (1994) discusses the ability of parents to see their child individually and separately, which can allow them to support therapy. To achieve this goal, one has to keep in mind that parents who seek help often feel they are not good parents, and they have had to overcome powerful resistances against this narcissistic injury. For Nina's parents, having me as therapist for their daughter created very painful feelings of shame and failure. It painfully ruptured their fantasy that America was the land of opportunity. Although parents generally feel like failures if their child needs help, in the South–Asian culture, in which problems are kept within the family, seeking help becomes a source of shame. Consulting someone from their own background might help preserve the fantasy of a "family affair." A neutral, analytic attitude, however, might cause further narcissistic injury, so this issue needs to be handled with empathy.

Often parents provide their child with material goods in a desperate attempt to prove to themselves and people back home that they are successful. Blos (1979) describes the overappreciated child as impaired developmentally because of parents' inordinately praising and admiring their child while ignoring shortcomings and inadequacies. Blos makes a crucial point with respect to the up-bringing of these children. Not only were they overvalued by their parents, but from an early age they were allowed to make independent decisions. The problem of affluence in a financially successful immigrant community might be susceptible to what Blos (1979) calls premature overexpectation. This then leads to an identity foreclosure (Burch 1985). It becomes a precursor to a crystallized, narcissistically based identity that develops when children are allowed to make independent decisions as if they were adequately equipped to do so. Nina experienced feelings of entitlement with respect to adult prerogatives, while her parents felt increasingly chagrined and frustrated that she expected to be treated as a peer. She dealt with adolescence by not dealing with it, but by becoming a caricature of an adult. As Blos (1979) reports, these adolescents suffer a "desolate, empty, dark and frightening experience" (p. 307). Nina was a victim of these frightening feelings.

In my discussions with Nina's parents and other immigrant parents, it becomes clear that they view immigration as a huge step, with a conscious expectation that they would be held in awe and considered with pride by their family members. There may well be reality here, and indeed they may have been more daring and independent than those who remained home. However, to communicate the value of independent decision making to children leads to thwarting their dependency needs and promoting foreclosure of development with consequent narcissistic disturbances. These parents may insist that these overvalued traits were inherited by their children as genetic traits. What seem to be behaviorally autonomous, courageous, and independent immigrant qualities can harm a child's self representation because children are not equipped to live out parents' accomplishments. This can lead to developmental impairments, which become evident in the early adolescent period, when the demands for progressive development in the midst of concurrent regressive pulls are high.

Skin–Color Differences

Early childhood is a time when the child steps from the immediate home environment to a larger world. The child begins to become aware of people of different skin color, which I believe is a crucial developmental step in becoming aware of one's minority status. Yet, the physical integration of being with other children in a multicultural setting does not automatically guarantee psychological integration. Conflict arises out of skin-color differences. Parents' difficulty in handling their child's questions about the world at large (especially "Why do I look different?" or "Why does he look different?") can lead to a self-prejudiced view of one's identity. Thus the child confronts feelings about his or her skin color, and develops a sense of pride or shame about it, which will depend to a very large extent on the adult world around him.

Researchers have observed preschoolers as young as 3 years of age notice and react to skin-color differences. When the adult world denies these differences, either consciously or unconsciously, the child's perceptions and feelings about skin color differences are prone to similar denial and avoidant responses. Subsequently, children become incapable of perceiving differences in a healthy manner. Meanwhile, the adult communicates his own observation of differences as a prejudice; thus to make healthy observations about differences becomes misinterpreted as prejudicial. This does not allow the child to integrate the most basic sense of identity, that is, the skin color identity.

The discovery of one's different skin color is a most profound discovery at whatever age it is made. The skin is an organ that establishes body identity. Most parents are not psychologically prepared to handle the questions that arise as a result of this issue. Young children of South-Asian origin ask, "What is that?" "What does it have to do with me, or with him?" "Can the colors be washed off?" Mastery of this skin-color anxiety becomes an important developmental task in the multiracial community of the United States.

Common parental reactions to the issue of skin color include a wish not to talk about it. Parents often fear that questions about differences suggest difficulties, but do not realize that their reluctance to answer questions represses the child's normative efforts to integrate. It is important that attempts be made to understand what we observe in a child's behavior, so that we do not overlook what we see and hear as being linked to race and color.

> A mother of a 4-year-old Asian boy, Ravi, reported that he wanted to wash off his brown skin so that he would be like his white-skinned friend Ken. The mother had defensively ignored her child's anxiety, hoping he would grow out of it. Two weeks later Ravi developed mixed feelings about eating chocolate cookies and refused to color his picture brown. With intervention the mother was able to talk to him more empathically about the skin's color being linked with being Indian. She talked about being a minority in this country and feeling self-conscious of her skin color. Six months later Ravi proudly took to school a Ramayan comic book, with characters colored brown, to display his own people and his Indian heritage.

> A 5-year-old Asian child with brown skin regarded himself as dirty and attempted to deal with this anxiety about his skin color by informing his mother that she too should wash her skin. The mother experienced this as narcissistic injury, feeling blamed because of her own insecurity. With help she was able to feel less blameworthy and more available to her child's evaluation of her skin color.

Skin-color anxiety is often unrecognized as a part of normal developmental anxiety about body differences, which can, if not dealt with, be detrimental to self-esteem. Psychoanalysis can help explain skin-color anxiety as a normal and necessary internal response to confronting skin-color differences. To know that it is a normal response is fundamental to the healthy resolution of its accompanying conflicts. It is important to recognize that second-generation immigrants with a skin color different from the dominant white American culture might have split-off responses. The parents' increased awareness of this issue can promote a more integrated response to their skin color and a healthy integration in their bicultural identity. This is especially important since being American is often equated with being white.

Separation–Individuation Issues

The traditional concept of the developmental stage of adolescence rests largely on the oedipal resolution, which, in turn, is based on the dynamic of drive-dominated paradigms. Anna Freud (1958) and Jacobson (1964) have emphasized the drive-dominated perspective as a specific extension of Freud's drive theory, with the idea that during adolescence strong drives confront a relatively weak ego. Moreover, adolescence has been viewed largely in terms of pathology. Unfortunately, this theoretical position left little room for normal, progressive development. But adolescence is not a disease (Steinwald 1984). It is essential that any coherent developmental theory account for development not only in those aspects that are deviant and pathological but also in adaptive aspects of human functioning.

Psychoanalytic ego psychology deals with object constancy, self–object differentiation, and consolidated self and object representations. Giovacchini (1973) notes that adolescence is a particularly fascinating period because it represents a point in development in which there is a significant increase in involvement with the sociocultural milieu and in objects beyond the family boundary. This period, marked by the ego perspective, becomes increasingly important as the adolescent consolidates a character structure that can effect more varied and sophisticated interaction with the external world. The child uses the parents as an auxiliary ego. A slow relinquishment of ego dependencies must occur. Mahler and colleagues (1963) have noted that adolescence is the only period in life (other than infantile separation–individuation) with such a rich abundance of developmental energies.

Akhtar (1992) summarizes Chasseguet-Smirgel's views on ego ideal formation and on what she calls perverse character organization. He states that her views have special relevance to the experience of temporality, filiation, authenticity, and generational continuity that others have found central to a solid identity. Most importantly, her views have placed the issues of filial legacy and thus ethnic and historical continuity squarely within psychoanalytic developmental psychology. This challenges the tendency to view these identity aspects as merely social epiphenomena, not worthy of metapsychological attention. In a bicultural setting, recognizing the social dimension as being integral to the intrapsychic dimension of identity helps in elucidating the specific conflicts around individuation. One can also begin to better conceptualize the normal–pathological, progressive–regressive pulls within the bicultural setting.

While Nina was distinctly aware of our similarities, with both of us being from the Indian subcontinent, a subtle and meaningful difference was enacted at another level, which put me in the category of being an immigrant just like her parents. This axis reveals important experiences of her being a second-generation immigrant born in America. The psychic meaning and significance of this experience rested on the fact that I was not born in America; I had arrived here. This simple and yet psychically striking reality came up in the form of a birth dream and fantasies of having a baby in India. More meaningful were her wishes to have a birth identity like that of her parents and me, to obliterate the difference of the "third space," that imperfect cultural space. The wish to obliterate the third space is where the anxiety of second-generation children and first-generation immigrant parents rests. Children become aware of the difference in their birth place from that of their parents despite their same skin color.

As the case presentation made clear, however much Nina or I wanted to recognize ourselves as having Indian heritage in common, our identities were not the same. As an immigrant, my core identity remains Indian. My acquired identity is American. By contrast, Nina's core identity is American, and her acquired identity Indian. Within this realization was a variety of interactions that became analytically rich and complex.

Developmental theory recognizes envy as an important component of parent–child interactions. Envy is rooted in preoedipal omniscient fantasies and oedipal-based fantasies. The bicultural situation can become an important vehicle for expression of fantasies linked to culture. These fantasies are used defensively, and a unique and heightened envy arises in relation to parent–child interactions based on my earlier model, which states that there is a basic difference between immigrants and their second-generation children that distinguishes both at the most manifest and latent level: their birth countries are different. The birth country both betrays and legitimizes an individual in a powerful way.

The immigrant parent, like an adopted child, has to grapple with the question, "Where did I come from?" "From mommy's womb, but not this mommy, another one." The narcissistic injury is profound when parents experience rivalry with their children, who are the children of America while they are adopted. They cannot look like Americans no matter how hard they try. While Grinberg and Grinberg (1989) emphasized the adoption aspects of immigration in terms of immigrants' anxieties about being in an adopted land, my emphasis is on the parent–child interaction around powerful affects connected with birth and with core and acquired identity. I feel that this is primarily a culturally derived parent–child developmental conflict, which can, depending on the parent's responses to the child's birth in America, become neurotic if not addressed.

In Nina's analysis, the transference and countertransference, especially about authenticity, became important issues. While earlier identifications of American and Indian were linked with symbolic fusion, a slow realization of a deep difference emerged. This came up around the time Nina began to talk about college. My college days became alive for me, but they were in a country different from Nina's. Thus, I felt I was in new territory. I found myself asking for details and explanations. This revealed my unfamiliarity (experiential or cognitive) with my adopted land. She, too, wished that I could understand without relying on my acquired identity to experience it with her. Meanwhile Nina would experience Indian movies and songs in a different way than I did. Her acquired Indian identity could only partially resonate with my spontaneous sparkle, which we picked up on when she sang a Hindi song during one session, and the pride of immigrant parents hearing their child sing fluently in their native language. My suspended analytical attention had fallen prey to this interchange, but out of it grew an awareness, on both of our parts, of the third space.

This awareness is akin to role responsiveness as described by Sandler (1976). The third space, imperfect and evocative, is partially empathized with by both parties, while both long for complete empathy in the name of love. But love and respect found their place in the third space. This became meaningful as Nina began to write a biographical sketch for her college applications. As she talked about it, she began to realize that she had never quite identified herself clearly, that is, she separated her Indian friends and dress from her American friends and dress. She described attending an ethnic event where both the American and Indian national anthems were sung, a common practice. She described feeling tearful, and the tears reflected the conflicted identity, not unalloyed joy and patriotism. As the American anthem was sung, she could see herself clearly and identified with it in a deep, unknowable way. Her tears during the Indian anthem were those of empathy with her parents, which was somewhat familiar. She would like to call herself an American Indian, but native Americans have co-opted that term. She could call herself an Indian-American, but American is her core. She asked me about my United States citizenship, and one thing became clear: she was a natural United States citizen whereas I have an acquired naturalization. Ultimately this brought her closer to her immigrant parents and analyst. A third space, like an analytic space, can never be obliterated and can be only partially shared.

The third space is the true ego identity of both the immigrant and the child. Ambivalence is at the center of most conflicts in adolescence. Cultural differences might heighten ambivalence, and integration of this ambivalence might become particularly significant for second-generation immigrants because of their struggle to resolve it. Ultimately, they may be able to accept and even admire the contribution from the two cultures. Just as we learn to blend what our self representations have become by combining our identities with those of our parents and our own ego developmental experiences, the second-generation child has to accept a normal, mature ambivalence that can live with opposing rules and forces.

Because of adolescents' heightened progressive and regressive experiences of themselves and their incorporation of bicultural upbringing, psychoanalysis demands a particular kind of neutrality. My supervisor told me, "Sometimes the most neutral attitude in the face of an adolescent storm is to hold onto your chair." Nina's "cultural storms" in the analytic setting were fought in a cultural field including mother–daughter conflicts around oedipal and preoedipal issues, and Indian and American ideas about dress, language, and food, which became meaningful metaphors for communicating aggressive or sexual fantasies. The revival of preoedipal longings and the ambivalence of loved and hated images commonly occur in cross-cultural analytic dyads. However, what was crucial to this analysis was development along the continuum of regression and progression, and the use of culturally loaded material.

The theories on individuation as drive based arose in Nina's analysis when her parents decided to visit India. They stated that they were planning to "go back to India." To Nina's perceptive and adolescent mind, this became troublesome. She questioned the word *back*. She had made many strides and began to consider attending an out-of-town college. The parents' trip was coinciding with Nina's preparation to leave for college. "Back home" began to gain new meaning. Its connection with India became doubly important. The emergence of formal operational thought within the sphere of the ego apparatus of primary autonomy is an important aspect of adolescent individuation. I was pleased to note Nina's attempt to grapple with the concept of "back home" linked to her anticipated college–home rapprochement. However, what seemed more troubling to her was her parents' attempt, unbeknownst to her, to leave India with a regressive gesture, and their own images of their core Indian identities as linked to hidden regressive and shameful revelations of their longing to visit India. This was Nina's understanding of what the parents might have felt, which was later confirmed in my sessions with the parents. They did see going back to India as a more regressive move for refueling purposes.

An important issue in dealing with adolescents with bicultural identities is that parents, analysts, and patients are apt to apply concrete operational thinking to identities and to consider some cultural self representations as regressive and others as progressive. A more ego-oriented approach to adolescent development can guard against such interferences and help the adolescent integrate the two identities along a developmental continuum. This is a goal of working with the third space. Immigrant parents' attitudes about their own core (Indian) and acquired (American) self representations are regressive or progressive rather than expansive or limited. The unfortunate projections of these self representations onto the adolescent increase the internal conflict between the core American and acquired Indian self representations. Occasionally, this conflict is accompanied by a defensive hypocathexis of the American self representation in order to hide self-prejudicial use. In contrast is the healthier out come which acknowledges the continued presence of conflict between the American and the Indian self representations.

Many parents try to integrate identities with the idea of having the best of both worlds. This is dangerous because it implies that each culture has unlikable attributes. Developmentally, though, children learn to accept imperfections in their parents. Thus cultures can be imperfect and still not be devalued. This attitude allows cultural self representations to be more acceptable than split-off parts. The parents see their Indian selves as being linked to regression and their American selves to progression (or vice versa), rather than as respected core selves and admirable acquired selves. This linkage has many implications in parenting children with bicultural backgrounds and in the adolescents' attempts to view their parents as having core identities that differ because of their country of birth. The parents might have a counterdefensive response, a wish to overidentify with their American-born children by denying their own core Indian selves. Or the children might overidentify with their Indian parents to deny their core American identity. Indian parents can mirror their children's acquired Indian identity; the mirroring of American aspects is subject to an unfamiliarity in themselves, but a growing familiarity may help them reflect it sufficiently or even optimally for their children.

Sexual Conflicts

There are several conflicts around dating and emerging sexuality in South Asian teenagers, as adolescence is a time of tremendous upheaval, with internal structural reworking and sexual maturation. Developmental needs arise in the arena of opposite-sex relationships. These were major concerns Nina had in establishing her adolescent female identity, and numerous conflicts arose regarding dating. For the adolescent, dating is a means of beginning to separate from home.

To have a meaningful discussion of the conflict that occurs in the lives of second-generation immigrants, the parents' own adolescence in a different culture needs to be understood. The Indian cinema portrays Indian attitudes and expectations about sexuality. If movies aim to reveal real life, sex should be an ideal subject for movies, but it is not so in Indian cinema. There is much denial. Bad people have sex while good people fall in love. Kissing is virtually absent in Indian movies. In 1978 the famous Indian filmmaker Raj Kapoor, in his movie *Satyam, Shivam, Sundaram*, sparked a scandal in India and engendered a national debate over censorship for depicting several kisses between a man and his wife. The extinction of kissing in movies began in the early 1940s, when India's fight for independence had reached its peak. Indian filmmakers exercised restraint, doing away with kissing on the screen as an effort to promote a feeling of solidarity among the Indians. The kiss was viewed by the Indian native as a Western import. Showing an Indian character kissing on the screen meant that he or she succumbed to the evil culture and influences of the West. Further all "evil" traits like smoking, drinking, and sex were portrayed by villains and vamps with Western names, not characters with Hindu or Muslim names. These characters wore shark-skin suits and low-neck dresses. The Indian film hero and heroine were virgins and embodiments of virtuous mythical gods and goddesses.

With the split displacements and the culture's attitudes toward the emerging sexuality of adolescents, conflicts occur that interfere with an adolescent's healthy incorporation of sexual identity. Parental attitudes cause the child to feel that sexuality is a Western, intrusive, and foreign aspect of themselves. Dating is often viewed as having sex versus an attempt to interact and define themselves with the opposite sex. Major concerns that are raised by South-Asian immigrant parents include that a daughter will become pregnant or a child will be emotionally hurt.

While Nina's intense relationship with her boyfriend had a variety of internal reasons, she also found herself disappointed in her parents, who seemed to be at a loss in handling her emerging sexuality in a meaningful way (there were no curfews or supervision, and no discussion about sex, boyfriends, or birth control). What seemed to be a neurotic denial emerged as confusion on the parents' part regarding Nina's developmental need to establish a female identity in this cultural setting. The situation arose out of their own lack of experience with dating in their adolescence in India.

Traditionally, in Indian culture marriages are arranged. Girls are passive and socially withdrawn. Thus, Indian parents in America feel bewildered and worried, and their daughters feel restrained and misunderstood, resulting in increased lying and secretive dating. While I believe that Nina's fears of her sexuality arose because of the neurotic way in which her parents dealt with this issue, there were also significant cultural factors that affected her as a second-generation immigrant. For instance, proms and homecoming dances (American institutions that support a growing sense of masculinity and femininity in a supervised environment) are viewed by immigrant parents as dangerous traps and hence forbidden.

Many second-generation teenagers want to have a friendship without sex and the desire to deal with narcissistic injuries related to oedipal conflict by a series of trials and recoveries. Many parents feel that intense relationships in adolescence will lead to preoccupations that would interfere with academics. But adolescents need the dual experiences of love and work to develop a sense of competency for the future. Otherwise they might permanently regress rather than develop and progress in an effort to master the separation from parents. To the immigrant parents, who have already viewed American culture as regressive at times, the experimental forces within the adolescent in a given social context are regressive, leaving the child puzzled, confused, and guilty about his or her healthy sexual identity. This often leads to false ideas of their sexuality being American, hence leading to difficulty in linking sexuality to their Indian bodies.

Cultures have traditionally found solutions to the increased narcissistic vulnerability of girls. Additionally, the typical female role of motherhood becomes available once the child is a teenager. However, education has given women more choices, both for career and spouses. While psychoanalytic treatment has over the years found ways to address the narcissistic vulnerability of this phase, American culture probably began to adapt to it by providing a dating culture as a developmental need and a way to experiment with relationships.

Analysts of adolescents are well aware that early adolescent heterosexual relationships sometimes or often disguise homosexual relationships, and later heterosexual relationships can usefully serve to master the revived oedipal conflicts and individuation for the adolescent girl, who has to make active choices in her future relationships. In the Indian culture, adolescent developmental tasks are partially resolved by protecting the girl from the trials and tribulations of resolving the positive oedipal conflict, by providing a spouse via an arranged marriage. Additionally, the fear that the girl will get hurt comes from an extension of the inherent narcissistic developmental vulnerabilities of the girl coupled with her biological vulnerability during puberty, especially fears of pregnancy. These narcissistic vulnerabilities are protected against by wishing that the mother will bear sons. The Indian adolescent who skips the opportunity for oedipal resolution has an intensified oedipal reaction at the time of the birth of his or her children.

The adolescent girl in India might not seek active heterosexual relations, staying safely in the realm of same-sex relationships through late adolescence. Mothers who fear that their daughter will get hurt experience a revival of their own oedipal conflicts, which are well contained in arranged marriages and by having sons. Kakar (1990) notes that adolescence is the most painful period of an Indian girl's life in that many renunciations are expected of her. Also, her training as an imminent daughter-in-law must bring credit to her family. The adolescent girl is conflicted both about her wish to be nurtured and a little girl and to be treated as a young woman with emerging womanhood and potential motherhood.

There is a universal fantasy among women arising from the fact that a father tends to withdraw from his daughter at the onset of puberty, feeling that he should no longer exhibit physical closeness because of the sexual feeling the daughter arouses in him. The daughter, yearning to be at home in a woman's body, is insecure in a womanly role and may interpret the father's withdrawal as proof of feminine unattractiveness. The wished-for father–daughter intimacy becomes a major fantasy in India because the father's withdrawal from his daughter is quite precipitate once she reaches puberty. This tradition might continue in some second-generation immigrant families. I believe it might be even more burdensome for the father who has to deal with unfamiliar aspects of his daughter's sexuality, such as American teenagers' style of dressing. The daughter is given over to the world of the older women, who choose precisely this period of inner turmoil to become increasingly disciplinary and harsh. The Indian adolescent has no way to deal with incestuous longings in the form of peer relationships and dating. This is not a major difficulty in the traditional Indian setting, where daughters are prepared for a definite role. However, it does shape their character even if it does not produce symptoms. This issue can become symptomatic with immigration.

For the second-generation child of Indian immigrant parents, developmental tasks of dealing with positive oedipal feelings can be thwarted in the face of the traditional culture. For a less painful and more meaningful transition of second-generation Indian adolescents in the United States, attention to the mother's dilemma is also crucial. Additionally, girls' participation in early group dates, proms, and dances, and later in individual dating (including sexual interactions and birth control) is an experience that powerfully revives the mother's oedipal frustrations, envy, and injuries, which then causes them to cling to their Indian–American teenage daughters even more ferociously. The second-generation adolescent girl might be vulnerable to increased conflicts around her individuation from an immigrant mother:

> The sense of oneness with mother must be maintained for female gender identity to flower into an individuated feminine self. The sense of oneness must be also disrupted for the girl to develop an individuated femininity or womanhood. This contradiction underlies and effects developmental conflicts pervasively for girls. [Bernstein 1993, p. 128]

Career Conflicts

Adolescence is the time of leaving home for college and making career choices. While the idealization of a medical career is widespread in the population at large, it is even more marked in the South-Asian immigrant population. This can, at times, pose serious problems. Developmentally the older adolescent and young adult begins the task of establishing a work identity, diminishing his omnipotence, making reality-oriented decisions dealing with identity and disidentifying with parental values. Many parents feel that medical careers would allow their children to continue the lifestyle they provided them. While this may seem reasonable, children express a sense of failure in not being able to achieve these academic goals. These parents foster achievement rather than individuation. The child functions well but feels shattered.

Careers other than medicine are subtly or overtly devalued, causing children to feel inadequate in their choices. Many times being a doctor becomes a pseudo-vocation, or a vocation that has not been motivated by internal desires as much as the wish to please a parent. Grinberg and Grinberg (1984) suggest that there are other unconscious motivations for children becoming doctors, including ready availability of a trained person to take charge and control of the immigrant family's hypochondriacal anxieties. This pseudo-vocation can lead to much dissatisfaction and difficulty in separating from the family of origin. In Nina's case, the family's insistence on career forced her to break loose and to tolerate and work through feelings of guilt and failure in order to make an authentic career choice.

CONCLUSION

The adolescent crisis in second-generation children of immigrants has both normative and pathological characteristics. Increased sensitivity to and awareness of these characteristics can enrich our psychoanalytic availability to our patients, whether parents or adolescents. Working across cultural divisions is a painful and frightening process that inevitably puts at risk our self-protective strategies. Every analysis, whether child or adult, adds to our psychoanalytic identity in different ways. Nina's analysis provided a unique forum in which many psychic spaces collided. It is such tiny struggles of individuals that allow an immigrant psychoanalyst to begin to integrate his or her own many self representations, and I owed Nina the benefit of that experience. In describing our work together, I have attempted to capture an elusive process with many ebbs and flows. Such fluid movements are typical not only of analytic work but also of adolescence, as well as of being a citizen of this interesting nation of ours. In Erikson's (1950a) words,

> It is almost impossible (except in the form of fiction) to write *in* America *about* America *for* Americans. You can as an American go to the South Sea Islands and write upon taking leave; you can, as an immigrant, write as you get settled; you can move from one section of this country to another, and write while you still have one foot in each place, but in the end you always write about the way it feels to arrive or leave, to change or to get settled. You write about the process. [p. 283, italics original]

ACKNOWLEDGMENTS

The author wishes to thank Drs. Salman Akhtar, Peter Blos, Jr., Carlo Coppola, and Nathan Segel for helpful suggestions on an earlier version of this chapter.

REFERENCES

Akhtar, S. (1992). *Broken Structures: Severe Personality Disorders and Their Treatment.* Northvale, NJ: Jason Aronson.
—— (1995). A third individuation: immigration, identity and the psychoanalytic process. *Journal of the American Psychoanalytic Association* 43:1051–1084.
Bernstein, D. (1993). *Female Identity Conflict in Clinical Practice.* Northvale, NJ: Jason Aronson.
Blos, P. (1967). The second individuation process of adolescence. *Psychoanalytic Study of the Child* 22:162–168. New York: International Universities Press.
Blos, P., Sr. (1979). The overappreciated child. In *The Adolescent Passage*, pp. 289–316. New York: International Universities Press.
Burch, C. (1985). Identity foreclosure in early adolescence: a problem of narcissistic equilibrium. *Adolescent Psychiatry: Developmental and Clinical Studies* 121:145–161.
Erikson, E. H. (1950a). *Childhood and Society.* New York: W. W. Norton.
—— (1950b). The problem of ego identity. *Journal of the American Psychoanalytic Association* 9:50–121.
——(1968). *Identity, Youth and Crisis.* New York: W.W. Norton.

Freud, A. (1958). Adolescence. *Psychoanalytic Study of the Child* 13:1–3. New York: International Universities Press.

Giovacchini, P. L. (1973). Character development and the adolescent process. In *Adolescent Psychiatry*, vol. 2, ed. S. C. Feinstein and P. L. Giovacchini, pp. 47–69. New York: Basic Books.

Grinberg, L., and Grinberg, R. (1989). *Psychoanalytic Perspectives on Migration and Exile.* New Haven, CT: Yale University Press.

Jacobson, E. (1964). *The Self and the Object World.* New York: International Universities Press.

Kakar, S. (1990). *Intimate Relations: Exploring Indian Sexuality.* Chicago: University of Chicago Press.

Mahler, M., Pine, F., and Bergman, A. (1963). *The Psychological Birth of the Human Infant.* New York: Basic Books.

Rakoff, V. (1981). A reconsideration of identity. *Adolescent Psychiatry* 9:22–32.

Rosenbaum, A. (1994). The assessment of parental functioning: a critical process in the evaluation of children for psychoanalysis. *Psychoanalytic Quarterly* 63:466–490.

Sandler, J. (1976). Countertransference and role responsiveness. *International Review of Psycho-Analysis* 3:43–47.

Sowell, T. (1996). *Migrations and Cultures—The Overseas Indians.* New York: Basic Books.

Steinwald, G. M. (1984). Adolescent individuation: the culmination of a developmental line. *Journal of the American Academy of Psychoanalysis* 12:43–57.

Winnicott, D. W. (1949). *The Ordinary Devoted Mother and Her Baby.* London: Brock.

——(1953). Transitional objects and transitional phenomena. *International Journal of Psycho-Analysis* 34:89–91.

——(1959). The fate of the transitional object. In *Psychoanalytic Explorations*, ed. C. Winnicott, R. Shepherd, and M. Davis, pp. 53–58. Cambridge, MA: Harvard University Press, 1989.

——(1960). The theory of the parent–infant relationship. In *The Maturational Processes and the Facilitating Environment*, pp. 37–55. London: Hogarth, 1985.

7

REFLECTIONS OF THE SELF IN THE CULTURAL LOOKING GLASS

Discussion of Mehta's Chapter "The Emergence, Conflicts, and Integration of the Bicultural Self: Psychoanalysis of an Adolescent Daughter of South-Asian Immigrant Parents"

Jennifer Bonovitz, Ph.D.

Issues of culture and ethnicity and their derivative values are often unobtrusive in the analytic situation. When these components are ego syntonic for both analyst and patient, they form a quiet backdrop and may never become a focus of the analytic work. Sometimes, however, differences are striking and immediately come to the foreground. For example, a new patient entered my office. She was tall, very dark skinned, and wore a brightly colored sari and sandals. I was surprised to find myself acutely and uncharacteristically aware of my smaller stature, pale skin, pastel-colored clothing, and feet encased in high-heeled shoes. Looking at my patient, who was so different in appearance from me, it was as though she had held up a looking glass. For an instant I caught a glimpse not only of my outward appearance, but of aspects of my cultural and ethnic self that rarely enter my consciousness. The patient had alerted me to culturally derived differences in our outward selves, as well as bringing to my awareness the possibility that there were culturally derived differences in our psychic structures. Such cultural differences, and their derivative psychic representations in both analyst and patient, contribute to the development of transferences, countertransferences, resistances, and the therapeutic alliance. Dr. Purnima Mehta's chapter makes a significant contribution to our understanding of these cultural complexities. She joins a small but growing number of analysts who bring a cultural looking glass not only to the practice of psychoanalysis but to the theory-building endeavor.

Dr. Mehta explores the emergence, conflicts, and integration of the bicultural self, looking at identity issues in adolescence and their precursors in early childhood. She outlines the complexities facing an adolescent girl growing up in two cultures and the conflicts immigrant parents face as they raise their children in a new land. Support from either extended family or the immediate community is often missing. Absence of external supports, combined with the ravages of multiple losses inherent in the immigration experience, contributes to the sometimes desperate plight of second-generation immigrant children.

Dr. Mehta's extensive clinical material gives a valuable developmental perspective on cultural and ethnic aspects of her patient's intrapsychic life. These include the emergence of conflicts in cultural identity and the ego ideal, use of defensive splitting, sexual fantasies linked to culture, and heightened ambivalences arising from cultural disparity between generations. She discusses nuances of analytic technique. These include discriminating developmental vicissitudes from the ego-defensive aspects of cultural and ethnic issues, the matter of neutrality, and the need for culturally informed sensitivity in work with immigrant parents.

To address some of the broad issues raised by Dr. Mehta's chapter, I begin by identifying values implicit in separation-individuation theory as it has evolved in North America. If not recognized as derivatives of Western culture, these values may obscure our understanding of the separation-individuation process in other cultures. I then review psychoanalytically informed studies of Hindu families in India, where values, traditions, kinship systems, and child-rearing patterns are substantially different from those of Northern European or Northern American families. The data thus far suggest that psychic structures, processes, and compromise formations also vary. Dr. Mehta's account of the vicissitudes of separation-individuation in an adolescent patient provides data about the added complexity of psychic development when an immigrant child faces the task of integrating two sharply divergent sets of cultural and ethnic characteristics. I conclude my discussion with data from the analyses of two adult patients. Failure to integrate disparate aspects of ethnic and cultural backgrounds contributed to an ongoing confusion about identity, problems with self-esteem, and an abiding feeling of not belonging. A third clinical vignette from the analysis of a 6-year-old boy illustrates the complexity of the separation-individuation process when the child faces the task of integrating disparate cultural and ethnic aspects of self and object. Issues of multiple losses, failure to mourn, and disruption of the process of internalization are discussed. As Dr. Mehta's chapter so beautifully details, in certain situations cultural and ethnic aspects of the self do become a source of intrapsychic conflict, pain, developmental derailment, and sometimes even suicide.

VALUES EMBEDDED IN MAHLER'S SEPARATION-INDIVIDUATION THEORY

Mahler's (1975) study of the psychological birth of the human infant led to a richly detailed description of the separation-individuation process whereby the essentially normal adult comes to experience both a consciousness of self and an awareness of the world outside of the self. The development of a sense of self and of other is fundamental, universal, and multifaceted. As we look at the separation-individuation process in diverse cultural and ethnic groups we have the opportunity to identify those values implicit in Mahler's formulations that are useful in understanding the psyche that emerged in Western culture, but may mislead us if we try to apply them to our understanding of intrapsychic structures in non-Western cultures. As Mahler noted,

One becomes aware that such research, while objective in its conduct, is subjective in its implications. That is, it is the rare study—
at least on problems that are likely to be relevant to the kinds of
issues which psychoanalysis confronts—in which results are not
ultimately filtered through the mind of the experimenter in his attempts to make sense of an essentially open-ended set of findings.
[p. 247]

Her meticulous description of both the research method and of the
characteristics of the sample studied are seldom recognized. Her
sample consisted of thirty-eight children and their twenty-two
mothers living in a nuclear family structure in a white, middle-class
community. Approximately half the families were Protestant, and
the others were evenly divided between Catholic and Jewish, or a
mixture of the two.

Kirschner (1996), a psychoanalytic anthropologist, argues that
Mahler's emphasis on autonomy, separation, and individuation
strongly reflects Western religious and cultural values. Kirschner
seeks to show how "over the course of nearly two thousand years,
an originally religious story about the soul's fall away from God and
reunion with Him was transformed into a modern secular theory
about the life and growth of the self" (p. 1). Her thesis and critical
appraisal of Mahler are provocative. At the very least she confronts
us with dilemmas inherent in any scientific endeavor—to what
extent do the values of the researcher contaminate the data, and to
what extent can we universalize our findings? As Hartmann and
colleagues (1951) remind us, "The question in what respect groups
of human beings—races, nations, classes, etc.—differ from each
other, in what respect they are linked to each other by the fact of
their being human, is age old" (p. 31). To address this question from
a psychoanalytic perspective requires the researcher's ability to experience both immersion in, and distance from, the culture being studied. Where the analyst's cultural background is very similar to that
of the patient, problems will arise with optimal distance. Where there
is great diversity, the problem will be around empathic immersion.

Roland (1989, 1996b) worked with Indian and Japanese patients in their respective countries and in New York. This afforded him the optimal distance required to question his previous assumptions about the nature of the self and led him to assert that psychoanalytic theories are biased by Western philosophies and values. In his view, Western psychoanalytic theory and practice are shaped by culturally derived philosophic assumptions concerning individualism. He traces the roots of this to the religious sphere of the Reformation, and to the thinking of Enlightenment philosophers such as Voltaire, Diderot, and Descartes, all of whom placed supreme value on the attributes of self-direction, self-reliance, self-sufficiency, and independence. In such a worldview the individual is taken out of the context of a hierarchical, social, collective, and cosmic order and given sole responsibility for matters of conscience and moral behavior. Roland (1988) concludes that the psychoanalytic schema of the self, which emphasizes development of autonomy, initiative, and self-reliance, cannot be applied to either the Indian or Japanese psyche.

Kakar (1985, 1989) also speaks from a bicultural perspective, having studied and worked in the United States and India. In his view the type of introspection that is a sine qua non of psychoanalysis in the West can be traced back to Greek thought. The Socratic "know thyself" involves sorting out and scrutinizing the events of one's own life. There is no Indian counterpart to this process. In contrast, the Indian *atamanam vidhi* (know thyself), refers to a self "uncontaminated by time and space and thus without the life historical dimension which is a focus of psychoanalysis and of Western romantic literature" (Kakar 1985, p. 443). Kakar does not question the developmental constants that derive from the shared, universal experience of infancy and childhood within a family structure. He urges thoughtful study of the "cultural guises, disguises, elaborations, and transformations of analytic concepts" (p. 444).

In his discussion of aspects of the Japanese separation–individuation experience, Freeman (see Chapter 2) notes the difficulties that arise when we attempt to explain the emotional phenomena of one culture in the linguistic and conceptual categories of another. The respectful interchange of observations among American and Japanese analysts, which Freeman has done much to facilitate, has enriched understanding of the ways in which cultural filters may narrow our view of the diversity of human experience and the development of intrapsychic structures of self and other.

PSYCHOANALYSIS IN THE INDIAN CONTEXT

Ramanujam (1992), who has worked and trained in both India and the United States, notes that Indian psychiatrists are very ambivalent about classical psychoanalytic theory and therapy. He traces the entry of psychoanalysis into India back to the 1920s with the correspondence between Girindrasekhar Bose, the founder and first president of the Indian Psychoanalytic Society, and Freud. Based on his observations of differences between Indian and Western patients, Bose commented on the Oedipus complex in the Indian male as follows.

> The real struggle lies between the desire to be a male and its opposite, the desire to be a female. I have already referred to the fact that castration threat is very common in Indian society but my Indian patients do not exhibit castration symptoms to such a marked degree as my European cases. The desire to be a female is more easily unearthed in Indian male patients than in European. . . . The Oedipus mother is very often a combined parental image and this is a fact of great importance. [quoted in Kakar 1989, p. 355]

Freud replied with respect: "I am fully impressed by the difference in the castration reaction between Indian and European patients and promise to keep my attention on the opposite wish you accentuate" (quoted in Kakar 1989, p. 355).

British contemporaries of Bose were ethnocentric in their application of psychoanalysis to clinical work with Indian patients and came to contemptuous and demeaning conclusions about the Hindu personality. The influence of the colonial presence is noted by Ramanujam (1992). "In some subtle ways and with some not so subtle methods, the British denigrated the Indians as superstitious, uncultured, and barbarian. To presume colonial legitimacy, they had to represent themselves as belonging to a superior race whose mission was to help Indians become more mature and cultured" (p. 126). To this day there are few practitioners of psychoanalysis in major urban centers of India and this early ethnocentric, prejudicial thinking is undoubtedly a contributing factor.

Kakar's (1985) commentary on the unsatisfactory relationship between psychoanalysis and non-Western cultures suggests that the early embattled pioneers of psychoanalysis were more concerned about protecting and gathering evidence for its key concepts than in considering the potential contribution of other cultures with their different worldviews, family structures, and relationships. Roland (1996a) considers that colonial attitudes continue to surface in the Western analyst who may view Asian norms of dependency and interdependence, deference to superiors, and communication by innuendo as inferior to psychoanalytic norms involved in separation–individuation, autonomy, self-assertiveness, and verbal articulateness. In his view, the Western middle-class ideal of rational man, and a correspondingly negative attitude toward the religious or spiritual self, are problematic. He points out that some leading figures in Indian psychiatry who most vociferously reject psychoanalysis are profoundly involved in the Indian spiritual tradition and their own meditation. Indian patients will not mention their concerns with the spiritual and cosmic unless they are sure that the analyst will be receptive and respectful.

Those who reject psychoanalysis in India also reject a developmental model that stresses the emergence of intrapsychic structures and a sense of self necessary to function independently in so-

cial groups and in situations apart from the family. These highly individuated perceptions and inner representations of self and other
are not applicable to understanding Indian psychological development and ongoing life within an extended family structure. Roland
(1989) describes an emphasis on

> the emotional bonding of kinship that enables the Indian person to
> live in emotionally close and interdependent relationships, where
> the sense of self is deeply involved with others, where relationships
> are governed by reciprocal hierarchical principles, and there is a
> constant need for approval to maintain and enhance self-regard.
> [p. 60]

This raises the question: If Mahler had emigrated to India rather
than the United States, what theory of separation–individuation
would she have woven from her observations of Indian mothers
and their babies? Naturally, in a country of more than 840 million
people she would have found many types of family organization,
and, with increasing industrialization, patterns of child rearing and
family relationships are changing. Khatri (1970) attempts to identify some common characteristics of the Hindu family. He describes
an extended family of patrilineally related males with their spouses
and their children who live under one roof and share common
property. The orientation is toward the fulfillment of goals with
the family as the indivisible unit rather than a focus on individuals
within the family.

Cultural provision for the lengthy dependency of the human
infant is universal, but there are wide variations in child care practices. Some of the variations stem from culturally determined views
of the nature and purpose of psychological development. In many
Eastern cultures, including India, families view children as needing
to be drawn into interdependence with members of the kinship
group (Applegate and Bonovitz 1995). Thus the Indian baby is
surrounded from birth by direct, sensual body contact and is constantly cuddled in the mother's arms or those of a close relative. At

a few months of age he is carried on the mother's hip or back—
not so for the Western baby who is transported in a stroller, usually
facing out to the world away from the mother. For many years the
Indian child will sleep in the mother's bed, shifting to the bed of
another family member only when the maternal bed becomes too
crowded—again a contrast to the Western infant who is placed alone
in a crib, often from birth onward.

Kakar (1985) describes the young Indian child's early sensory
experience as one of being enveloped by the mother's smell, warmth,
and skin texture. Patients who have slept in their mother's bed until
puberty are common in Indian analytic practice. Furthermore, since
in most homes parents and children sleep in the same room, the
opportunities for children to witness sexual intercourse are common. The sexual excitement generated is so much a part of everyday life that it becomes gradually integrated into the psyche. Thus
it is not usually a source of disturbance, as it is in cultures where the
parental bedroom and sexual activity are private. What might be
considered sexual overstimulation and disruptive to the developing ego of the child in a Western middle-class family may be simply a matter of adaptation to the average expectable environment
for an Indian child. Kakar (1978) outlines a model of the mind that
emphasizes the innate capacity of the baby to adapt to the cultural
environment into which it is born. Because of this ego capacity for
adaptation, culturally determined living conditions, eating and sleeping patterns, and prohibitions and prescriptions for behavior do not
necessarily become sources of intrapsychic conflict among the various agencies of the mind.

Gender differences in child-rearing patterns contribute significantly to the development of the sense of self. Khatri (1970) notes
that the birth of a male child is favored over that of a female in the
traditional Hindu family and open favoritism is shown to brothers
in very concrete ways such as better food, clothes, and educational
opportunities. "Because of these aspects of the child-rearing environment, the ground is laid for a negative self-image, envy, and jealousy
with regard to males, and a perception of the world as basically

unfair" (p. 395). From an ego adaptive perspective, the tradition of inculcating values that encourage lifelong self-sacrifice and subservience to the male prepare the female child for her adult role as wife and daughter-in-law in the hierarchical family of her in-laws. Families give girls little information about menstruation or sexual aspects of womanhood, and public demonstrations of affection between husband and wife are not favorably looked upon. Khatri describes the husband as more invested in his peers while the marital relationship is "formal, distant, and sex-centered" (p. 396). These are global descriptions, and increasing industrialization has led to changes that in themselves contribute to intergenerational and intrapsychic conflicts, often quite painful and difficult to resolve.

Based on his clinical experience and other observations (less rigorous than those afforded by Mahler's research design but nonetheless useful), Roland (1988) offers the concepts of the familial self, the individualized self, and the spiritual self, as more descriptive of the intrapsychic structures developed within the Indian family. The familial self is the dominant structure and evolves out of the experience of having the kinship system or extended family as the matrix within which social, psychological, spiritual, economic, and sexual needs are met throughout the life cycle. Preservation of the integrity of the family unit, and its reputation and rank within its own *jati* (caste, in the sense of communities traditionally sharing an occupation within which marriages are arranged), takes precedence over concern for any one individual in the family. The husband–wife relationship is not central and takes a subordinate position to that of adult child–parent, in particular mother–son.

Multiple hierarchical relationships are defined by kinship position, birth order, and gender. There are very specific expectations for deference and loyalty in subordinates and for nurturance and responsibility in superiors. Roland coins the term *symbiosis-reciprocity* to describe how the inner world of the Indian is organized around images of "we," "our," and "us," rather than "I" or "me." The sense of self is that of a "we-self," which is oriented to this multiplicity of hierarchical relationships. Ego boundaries are more permeable within the context of the extended family. Speaking of the essentially normal adult, Mahler (1975) notes, "Consciousness of self and absorption without awareness of the self are two polarities between which he moves with varying ease and with varying degrees of alternation or simultaneity" (p. 3). It may be that in Western cultures the separation–individuation process leads to a greater consciousness of the self, whereas in Asian cultures the emphasis is more toward the polarity of absorption without awareness of the self.

Roland (1988) observes, "The normal separation, privacy, and autonomy of Western style relationships and the psychological space around oneself disappear into the more symbiotic mode of giving and asking, of caring for and depending on, of influencing and being influenced, of close warm emotional connectedness and interdependence" (p. 226). There is an inner tension between wishing and expecting fulfillment of libidinal strivings and awareness of the same needs and expectations of others in the group. To experience a sense of mutual well-being within the extended family requires empathic attunement to others' feelings, moods, and needs for closeness, dependency, and esteem. In childhood constant physical closeness and mother's handling of frustrations and anxieties by gratification result in intense dependency, or perhaps more accurately described, interdependency. In later years shaming, scolding, and physical punishment are used to shape the child's behavior within hierarchical relationships, and anger toward superiors is not sanctioned. Autonomous strivings are not adaptive within the hierarchical structure of the extended family and are therefore not encouraged. Individuation from the family is most likely to take place within the spiritual self at the end of the life cycle when the ideal is a detachment from human ties and relationships and an absorption in the cosmic world. Preoccupation earlier in the life cycle with one's own needs and career, in opposition to the family's wishes and needs, may be viewed as a disorder requiring treatment (Kakar 1985).

Adolescence, as described by Roland (1988) and Ramanujam (1992), does not involve the process of individuation typical in urban North America. The we-self is further consolidated because young people continue to live with parents and other family members, and major decisions regarding education, vocation, and marriage are made by elders in the family. Continuity of a self subordinate to the family unit develops along with clearly defined role expectations according to one's place in the hierarchy. Infantile objects are relinquished very gradually, and this process does not take place to the degree necessary in cultures where the child is being prepared to live an adult life that is independent of the extended family. Indian immigrants to the United States are thus transplanted into a very different cultural milieu that emphasizes autonomy and self-sufficiency rather than interdependence. Internal upheaval and re-organization are inevitable.

INDIANS IN THE UNITED STATES: CULTURE SHOCK, LOSS, AND MOURNING

Indians who have chosen, or are forced, to leave their extended family structure and values to live in a host culture with dramatically different values, traditions, and child-rearing patterns face formidable challenges. Internalized representations of culturally derived prescriptions and prohibitions may be incompatible with the external demands for initiative, independent thinking, and decision making that are intrinsic to the role of immigrant. Multiple losses include extended family, friends, home, community, and social and religious institutions. Paramount in determining outcome are the capacities to mourn, as well as to rally adaptive defenses against depressive reactions, the pain of separation from loved ones, and the dysphoric, unsettling experience of not belonging in an environment foreign to all of the senses.

As Dr. Mehta's chapter graphically details, the confusion and vulnerability experienced by immigrant parents in a foreign culture create additional turmoil for their children. The greater the shift away from the familiar values, language, patterns of relating, ethnic dress, food, religion, and traditions, the greater the experience of loss and confusion. The stress on the adaptive and defensive capacities of the ego may be overwhelming, resulting in a state of collapsed self-esteem, helplessness, and depression. Perhaps only the language of poetry can fully capture the painful affects experienced. I quote from a poem entitled "A World Without Seasons," by Akhtar (1995, p. 1077).

> In the greedy flim-flam
> For two worlds, we have lost the one in hand.
> And now,
> Like the fish who chose to live on a tree,
> We writhe in foolish agony.
> Our gods reduced to gross exhibits.
> Our poets mute, pace in the empty halls of our conversation.
> The silk of our mother tongue banned from the fabric
> Of our dreams.

Grinberg's (1978) comments on change as a trigger for depressive reactions having to do with threatened loss of ego functions and of those parts of the self that were linked to lost objects are useful in understanding some painful aspects of the immigrant experience. In the course of ordinary living, growth and maturation involve minute losses that call upon the capacity of the ego to mourn aspects of the self that will never return. For example, a young patient wept as his fifth birthday approached because he would never be 4 again. Grinberg notes, "The developmental process, when it happens normally, allows the ego to have time to work through its experiences of loss and to reestablish itself from the temporary and tolerated moments of confusion of identity which, most times, go unnoticed" (p. 246). When a family emigrates the changes are abrupt, multiple, and extreme. At either end of the life cycle there may be special vulnerability—for children because of their immature state of their ego, and for old people because of a diminution of ego resiliency.

The family described by Dr. Mehta had experienced multiple losses inherent in the immigration process. The necessary mourning, which must take place before an integrated, stable identity can be established, was no doubt compromised by the parents' need for hypercathexis of their new medical careers at the same time that they were confronting the developmental challenge of parenthood. It may be that some of their daughter's misery and confusion in adolescence had its source in mother's depressive reaction to loss, and disruption of her sense of self in a new culture.

FAILURE TO INTEGRATE DISPARATE ASPECTS OF THE ETHNOCULTURAL SELF AND OBJECT REPRESENTATIONS

Levy-Warren (1996) considers maturation of ethnocultural identity to be a critical component of adolescent development and continuity of the individuation-separation process. The greater the discrepancy between the ethnocultural identity of the family and that of the world outside the family, the more difficult it will be at any point in the life cycle, but particularly in adolescence, to consolidate a comfortable sense of belonging. Dr. Mehta elaborates on the vicissitudes of this process in immigrant children. Abrupt shifts in ethnocultural experience affect the process of internalization and separation-individuation.

Blatt and Behrends (1987) view internalization as the basic process through which all psychological development takes place. The first step is the establishment of a gratifying experience in a primary relationship, followed by progressive, minute disruptions of this relationship. Where the disruptions are gradual, and not beyond the developmental capacities of the child, the losses are managed by taking into the self the attributes and psychological functions that were lost in the disruption. This ongoing sequencing of gratifying experiences in a libidinally invested relationship and tolerable, phase-appropriate losses promotes self-object differentiation, the development of psychic structure, and is essential for the process of separation-individuation throughout the life cycle.

If, as the child moves out into the world, there are too much incompatibility and intolerable loss, or if there are sudden disruptions within the family, defensive processes such as splitting, disavowal, passive withdrawal, or hypomanic activity may take over. Rather than growth and consolidation of psychic structures, regression, stagnation, or defensive flight into a hypercathected aspect of the self may occur.

The following clinical vignette illustrates how abrupt changes in family structure and ethnocultural identity during adolescence came to the foreground in the analysis of an adult. Although the patient is not from India, there is common ground in terms of the impact of immigration on his psychological development, issues of loss and mourning, and integration of disparate cultural representations into a unified sense of self.

Case 1

In our first meeting Mr. D., a 54-year-old highly successful attorney, described feeling empty and as though he didn't really belong anywhere. Despite having reached the pinnacle of his career in international law and acquiring material wealth beyond his wildest dreams, he felt deeply unhappy. He had recently divorced his wife of thirty years after realizing that they were "strangers who lived together." He felt at a loss to explain why he had married her since they had no interests in common. The prospect of living alone terrified him and he dreaded going home to his empty townhouse after a long day at work. His relationship with two adult married sons who lived in nearby cities was cordial but not close.

In his hierarchically structured German-Jewish family of origin, decisions were made by adult males in the older generation. His parents did not include him in the decision to send him to be educated in the United States at age 14. His parents and two older sisters remained in Argentina. The family had fled there from Germany a few years before his birth. Upon arrival in the United States he lived in a large city with an aunt, uncle, and three cousins until he went away to college at age 18. Both aunt and uncle worked long hours and the cousins were older and involved with friends. Mr. D. was expected to care for himself in a way that was in stark contrast to his world in Argentina where the household had consisted of the patient's immediate family, grandmother, and an uncle and aunt and their four children. Other relatives visited daily and the house was never empty. There was clear direction from adults in the family about how he should conduct every aspect of his day-to-day life. In the United States Mr. D. felt that he had "fallen into a void."

We had been meeting ten months in four times weekly analysis when Mr. D. commented on the trace of an accent in my voice and pondered about my country of origin. It surprised him to observe that he felt comforted to know that I had been an immigrant to the United States. I was perhaps more surprised than he. After 25 years in America I did not think of myself as an immigrant and in general was not recognized as one. His comments gave me a glimpse of myself that seldom came into my awareness. The patient next remarked that few people knew that he had not been born in the United States and that for many years after his arrival he worked hard to erase all traces of his immigrant identity: his accent, way of dressing, preferred foods, and tastes in music and art. Several days later he told me that it was the fortieth anniversary of his arrival at Ellis Island and went on to marvel at how far he had come in fulfilling the American dream—from the young boy struggling off the boat dragging his one large suitcase, to the affluent attorney who drove a Mercedes sports car.

As we talked about these disparate images of himself, Mr. D. experienced a flood of emotion and an impulse to speak to me in German, the language of his childhood. He lost his usual composure, his voice trembled, and tears streamed down his face as he told me that he just now realized how he had "turned my back on that young boy with the suitcase." From the day he stepped off the boat in New York, he had energetically tried to hide who he was as he tried to build an American self. In high school and college he strove to hide his cultural and ethnic origins. He felt ashamed of them, hence his choice of a wife, who although Jewish, came from a family that had successfully assimilated into the mainstream upper middle class of an urban community. Throughout all this he feared exposure as a "fake." The self he manufactured and presented to the outside world never felt authentic.

Mr. D.'s repudiation of his old culture and idealization of the new was complex and multidetermined. His enthusiastic embracing of the new way of life was reminiscent of what Akhtar (1996) describes as a "practicing subphase-like hypomania" (p. 1058), with both defensive and adaptive functions, characteristic of the early period of entry into a new culture. Counterphobic assimilation of the new ways of talking, dressing, and thinking served to defend against the multiple painful losses Mr. D. had sustained in what was essentially a forced immigration. Because the changes were cataclysmic, true growth-promoting internalization did not occur. The immature, beleaguered ego of the early adolescent resorted to defensive splitting and devaluation. Early inner representations of the boyhood self were split off and he felt a terrible discontinuity, or as he put it, "a big black hole inside." He threw himself into his studies and later his career at the expense of all other interests and of intimate relationships. A combination of hard work and prodigious talent led to phenomenal success in building a law firm, but inside he felt as though he was "half a person—something vital was always missing." Devaluation and rejection of the ways of his Argentinean family protected him from the pain of overwhelming losses and gave expression to the rage he felt about having been extruded from the family in such an abrupt manner. In a fit of anger he went home from an analytic session and ripped in two a photo of himself as a boy with his mother. Almost immediately he was stricken with remorse and taped the pieces back together.

In the next several months of the analysis we retrieved remnants of his ethnocultural self and object world. In a concerted effort to integrate the disparate images of past and present, he spent Passover with his mother and sisters in Argentina and renewed contact with cousins, nieces, and nephews whose existence he had barely acknowledged. There was a mixture of anger, sadness, and perplexity that his mother could not really appreciate his phenomenal success. "She can't see who I've become." Instead, she chided him for being "too Americanized" and for the infrequency of his visits over the years. He felt bitter disappointment that his mother could not reflect back pride and admiration for his American self. However, the pain was eased by the pleasure she took in his enjoyment of her Passover cooking. For the first time since his boyhood, he relished the ethnic dishes, eating them "like a man who had been starved." When Mr. D. returned to the United States, he brought some of his mother's recipes and cooked them for his secretary. In his fantasy I would be unappreciative if he brought me these foods. My tastes were probably more sophisticated, like those of his law firm colleagues with whom he dined at fancy French restaurants. He felt shame about his "peasant" beginnings and imagined that I looked down on him. One day he did bring me bread that he had baked, and in a departure from analytic neutrality, I ate it with gusto. For the next law firm party, Mr. D. hired a Latin-American chef and was delighted at the response of his colleagues.

It became his mission to bring the Argentinean and the American branches of the family together. The fervent cathexis of hitherto lost objects was accompanied by episodic devaluation of his American friends and criticisms of their "blandness." As we analyzed both stances, we came to understand how they served to protect him from grieving irretrievable losses. Renewed contact with old grade-school friends at first brought narcissistic gratification as he basked in their admiration of his great success. As this faded, he realized with sadness that he could never bridge the gulf between their world and his. The old camaraderie, rivalries, shared escapades, sorrows, laughter, and fun were of the past and, while pleasant to remember, could not be re-created in the present. They could not even be recaptured if he had grandchildren because they would grow up playing American games and singing different songs. Again in the transference he experienced pain, anger, and disappointment that I could not really understand or share what he was telling me. I had never lived in Argentina, I knew nothing of the buildings, the streets, the secret hiding places, and I spoke neither of his childhood languages (Spanish and German), so he was forced to stay within the confines of English. His frustration with my deficiencies and our lack of mutuality was palpable. The sense of comfort with our shared immigrant experience had shifted to an uncomfortable "me" versus "you" split. Mr. D. felt hampered in his efforts to find lost aspects of himself because I was too different. For several weeks he could not take in my words or my attempts to understand. At times even the sound of my voice or the very sight of me irritated him. In the countertransference I had a strong sense of dislocation and experienced a longing to hear the comforting voices of my family in Ireland.

For a time Mr. D. remained acutely disturbed by a growing awareness that "I haven't put together the bits and pieces of who I am." At a high-level professional meeting, he was disconcerted by a sudden image of himself as a young boy who didn't know the language. His time sense was distorted and he arrived late or on the wrong day for a couple of his analytic sessions. Confusion with international time zones led him to call a colleague in the middle of the night. He brought me faded grade-school report cards and childhood photos that his mother had given him on the visit home, as well as drafts of various business talks and recent newspaper clippings about him and about conditions in Argentina.

In a dream, he kept getting on and off a moving train amid great confusion of people, smells, and noises, alternately losing his footing and scrambling to his feet. For the first time in his adult life Mr. D. experienced a loss of drive and direction. He became fearful that his ambivalence about his time commitment to his professional life would result in his "being left in the dust" and losing everything.

Throughout the fitful ebb and flow of Mr. D.'s analysis I could discern a steady developmental process, picking up many of the threads that had been lost in the disruptive upheaval and multiple

losses of his adolescence. Within the safety and support of the analytic situation he could engage in the painful process of mourning.
While interpretation remained an important aspect of the work, at
times my holding and integrative functions took precedence. Akhtar
(1995) speaks of the relatively greater role of the analyst as a new
object in the treatment of immigrant patients and states, "The similarities between the developmental process and the analytic process
may be more marked in such analyses" (p. 1074).

Case 2

In the instance of another analytic patient, Ms. A., there were
marked ethnocultural incompatibilities, tinged with hostility, between her mother and father. She grew up in two separate worlds
that she was unable to integrate in her psyche. The resulting cleav-
ages and discontinuities contributed significantly to derailment of
the separation-individuation process. Again, I focus on ethnocultural
elements of the work, omitting much of the very complex understanding of the patient and the analytic work.

Ms. A. began analysis at age 36 complaining of overwhelming
anxiety in new situations, a "roller-coaster" emotional life, and a
pervasive sense that "I don't know who I am." She had not felt
comfortable with herself since the age of 5, when her beloved father,
a well-known entertainer who played music and sang songs from
his homeland, had separated from her mother and soon thereafter
returned to his homeland. There he remarried and had another family. Although she visited him every summer, and he visited her
during concert tours, Ms. A. never felt at home with him in either
country.

As a little girl Ms. A. accompanied him to ethnic bars and restaurants, delighting in the spicy food, lively music, and animated
conversations. Father loved to drink and to flirt. Mother, a Protestant from New England, disapproved of what she termed father's
"carousing" and refused to accompany him socially, or to the pro-

fessional concerts he gave when musically talented family members visited America. For his part father could not tolerate what he termed his wife's stiff and prudish ways.

The parents had many problems, but the emotionally charged cultural incompatibilities often took center stage during bitter fights. Unable to reconcile the differences between mother and father, Ms. A. allied herself with father and built her identity around him. "I felt strong and happy in his company." When he left the home she refused to eat anything but the blandest of foods, and after he left the United States she found it intolerable to listen not only to his music, but to any music from his country. She lost interest in the guitar, which her father had begun to teach her, and she stopped singing. From this time on it became increasingly difficult to take in anything from the outside, and indeed during early adolescence she had to be hospitalized for several months because she stopped taking in her mother's food. Ms. A. described feeling as though part of her "insides had been ripped out" and that she had "limped through life feeling crippled with no hope of being whole." Throughout her life, but especially in adolescence, she would stand for hours at a time before the mirror "trying to find myself."

One is reminded here of Grinberg's (1978) term *narcissistic collapse*, which he attributes not only to the loss of the loved object, but to loss of valued aspects of the self that were closely linked with the lost object. Mother's hostile and competitive attitudes toward father and his ethnocultural attributes deepened the narcissistic wound and reinforced Ms. A.'s pathological defenses including splitting and projective identification. Realignment of the self with mother would have constituted betrayal of positive inner representations of father and of those aspects of her self-representation formed by her identification with him. Self-object differentiation, and development of gender identity, came to a standstill. Feelings of helplessness, humiliation and persecution pervaded the patient's inner life. Repeatedly she started a creative project only to abandon it in response to internal criticism and what she termed "soul-destroying doubt." At times Ms. A. projected treasured aspects of her self onto external objects and then felt painful rage that she had been robbed. For example, when news came of a cousin's public performance of her father's songs, she went into a frenzy of envy, rage, and depression. She was enraged that the cousin was appropriating what was hers. In her mind's eye she saw her cousin singing to a rapt audience, something she longed to do. At the same time she wept because she felt "robbed" of the possibility of singing her father's songs—this part of herself was gone forever. Omnipotent defenses and a narcissistic sense of entitlement contributed to her inability to devote herself to the hard work entailed in becoming a successful professional singer. The fantasy that the idealized father would return and take care of her was deeply entrenched, preventing her from working on her own behalf.

In the analytic situation, Ms. A. had little tolerance for the inevitable frustrations, separations, and perceived differences between us. Minute changes disturbed her and each one precipitated a depressive reaction. Issues of loss and mourning were all-pervasive. She was preoccupied with the fear that I would move back to my country of origin, and she seemed surprised when I returned from summer vacations. For the first two years, she was resistant to any material to do with father or her ethnocultural background. I learned of father's visits and concerts from newspaper advertisements. It was not until she had developed some assurance of my constancy, that she could begin to tolerate the painful affects evoked when she thought of him. Slowly she forced herself to listen to his music and then to make visits to an ethnic bar that father frequented during his visits. Recognition as her father's daughter, along with the expectation from the bar's staff that she would like the ethnic food and music, helped Ms. A. to experience herself as "someone." She brought me tapes of songs father sang to her as a child and we listened to them together. Although she wept, she could also take in a feeling of comfort and pleasure from our shared enjoyment of the music. She described hearing a voice singing inside herself. At times in the countertransference I found myself thinking of the Irish music of my early childhood that I now seldom heard.

Describing their model of the nature of therapeutic action, Blatt and Behrends (1987) note that in the analytic relationship, the "degree and form of gratifying involvement and separation that fosters individuation depends upon the developmental level of the patient" (p. 288). In the case of Ms. A. one important aspect of the relationship early in the analysis was my interest, acceptance, and clearly expressed enjoyment of ethnocultural aspects of her self and object world. For the first two years she often sat using my face as a mirror to find reflections of the split-off parts of the self that had been so strongly associated with the lost father. Attunement to and appreciation of culture and ethnicity helped to establish a holding environment. This in turn facilitated internalization of me as an object to be used in moving toward more mature levels of object relatedness and self-definition.

Case 3

A child's efforts to deal with self-definition are discussed in the following material from the analysis of a 6-year-old boy. I focus on issues arising from differences in skin color. Both Drs. Mehta and Miles (Chapter 4) mention the important influence of the affective valence of adults in helping children to integrate skin color into their overall identity. Dr. Mehta identifies mastery of skin color anxiety as an important developmental task in the multiracial community of the United States.

Ken's birth mother is white (ethnic background German) and his birth father is of American-Indian and African-American descent. He was adopted by white parents and is the only brown-skinned child in his classroom. In many sessions Ken struggled to make sense of his complicated life, in this instance his skin color.

In one session, selecting a brown crayon he began to color a brass lamp in my office which he knew from previous inquiries had letters of the Chinese alphabet inscribed on its base. He noted that the lamp was Chinese but its color was gold. He then asked if the brown crayon would wash off. Next he scribbled with the brown crayon on white paper. After announcing "This won't come off," he took a pink crayon and tried to color over the brown. Frustrated by his efforts he threw the crayon on the floor. When I empathically noted his efforts to erase or cover over the brown he picked up a white crayon that he applied to his arm. "Yes," he lamented, "I want to change my skin color. It makes the children laugh at me." He didn't respond to my inquiry about this, but took another brown crayon and began to apply it to my arm. "It's going to take a long time to color you in. There's just too much of you." He noted some freckles on my arm and wondered why they didn't join up. I noted his wish that he and I had the same color skin. He acknowledged that this was true and wondered why we were different. This led him to tell me how painful it was for him that his mother had fair skin, and this caused the children at school to question whether she was really his mother. He knew that she was not his birth mother but she was his "real" mother, but he wasn't really sure what that meant. "I don't look like her, so I think I must have come from a different planet," he concluded sadly. He then recalled the story of the Ugly Duckling and asked if his skin would ever get lighter. I told him that people laughed at the Ugly Duckling because they saw that he was different and this made them worry. Like the kids at school, they didn't know that there was nothing wrong with being different. It didn't mean ugly. Ken then initiated a contest to see who could come up with the most ways in which he and I were different, and ways in which we were the same.

Ken's adoptive mother had avoided talking about skin color, and in the adoptive father's extended family the subject was never mentioned because of conflict over his multiethnic and cultural background. It took considerable work in the analysis to uncover Ken's fantasies about his skin-color difference before he could integrate this into a more positive sense of self. As the school year progressed, he brought me stories about Abraham Lincoln and the fight for freedom of the brown-skinned slaves in the South. For a time he talked about being dirty and wishing he had a special kind of soap. After a weekend at the shore his skin darkened considerably and he held his arm up to mine to show me "we're even more different." His tone, however, was more matter of fact. There was evidence of progress in his positive attitude toward his skin color when he told me before a summer vacation that he was going to have a great time at the shore. He cautioned that I would have to be careful if I went out in the sun on my vacation. "You better watch yourself. Your skin isn't made for hot sun like mine is. If you don't cover yourself with all that yucky sunscreen stuff you'll get all red and blotchy and ugly!"

This vignette illustrates the broader applicability of Dr. Mehta's observations about skin color, based on her work with South-Asian families. She emphasizes the importance of the skin as an organ that establishes body identity, and describes how adult responses can interfere with the child's spontaneous efforts to integrate this basic aspect of his identity. She places skin-color anxiety into the realm of normal development, something the child needs help to integrate, rather than to split off or deny.

CONCLUSION

Psychoanalytic theory has much to say about the mirroring functions of the analyst. Winnicott applies the mirroring role of the mother in early development to therapeutic work: "Psychotherapy is not making clever and apt interpretations; by and large it is a long-term giving back to the patient what the patient brings. It is a complex derivative of the face that reflects what is there to be seen" (Quoted in Abram 1997, p. 214). To engage effectively in this process, the analyst's vision must not be distorted by images and values derived from his or her own ethnocultural background. Just as the analyst is advised to have benevolent skepticism about the patient's perceptions of both inner and outer worlds, benevolent skepticism is also useful with regard to the analyst's understanding and interpretation of ethnocultural aspects of transference, countertransference, and resistance. Otherwise, the analyst may not be able to see what is there to be seen in the patient; instead, the image reflected back may be one that denies the reality of the patient's world.

Where there is great disparity between the patient and analyst's ethnocultural experience, it may be useful to consider the mirroring function of the patient for the analyst. Looking at the patient enables the analyst to find reflections of his or her ethnocultural self that ordinarily do not enter awareness. This in turn can facilitate the search for optimal distance that is required to understand the patient's psychic reality. The capacity to see, understand, and value aspects of the patient's self and object world that are culturally derived assumes greater significance when splitting, denial, and projection have interfered with identity formation.

Differences between analyst and patient in terms of skin color, linguistics, and values may require variations in analytic technique, especially in the early stages of the process of engagement. If the analyst's demeanor in the analytic situation is incompatible with that of the patient's ethnocultural expectations, the patient may not be able to form the gratifying relationship, which Blatt and Behrends (1987) consider essential to therapeutic action. In Kakar's (1985) view the cultural pattern in India

> requires that irrespective of the nature of the patient's psychopathology, the analyst be much more actively involved. . . . The analyst's humaneness, sympathy, and therapeutic intent cannot be subtly conveyed in an atmosphere of reserved formality but need a more active and open expression. [p. 443]

Mahler's adventurous spirit led her into a world previously unchartered—that of the preoedipal child and the beginnings of the separation-individuation journey. Psychoanalysis benefits greatly from Dr. Mehta's exploration of cultural and ethnic variations in the separation-individuation process and her model of the bicultural self. She elucidates the implications of these variations for the analytic process. Settlage (1985) observes, "Outside of its own field, psychoanalysis is all too often equated with the couch-bound image of its treatment method" (p. 322). We can take heart from the efforts of the 1997 Mahler symposium, the collected proceedings of which constitute this book, to change not only this image but the image of psychoanalysis as culture-bound.

REFERENCES

Abram, J. (1997). *The Language of Winnicott: A Dictionary and Guide to Understanding His Work*. Northvale, NJ: Jason Aronson.

Akhtar, S. (1995). A third individuation: immigration, identity and the psychoanalytic process. *Journal of the American Psychoanalytic Association* 43:1051–1084.

Applegate, J., and Bonovitz, J. (1995). *The Facilitating Partnership: A Winnicottian Approach for Social Workers and Other Helping Professionals*. Northvale, NJ: Jason Aronson.

Blatt, S. J., and Behrends, R. S. (1987). Internalization, separation-individuation, and the nature of therapeutic action. *International Journal of Psycho-Analysis* 68:279–297.

Grinberg, L. (1978). The razor's edge in depression and mourning. *International Journal of Psycho-Analysis* 59:245–254.

Hartmann, H., Kris, E., and Loewenstein, R. M. (1951). Some psychoanalytic comments on culture and personality. In *Psychoanalysis and Culture*, ed. G. B. Wilbur and W. Muensterberger, pp. 3–31. New York: International Universities Press.

Kakar, S. (1978). *The Inner World: A Psychoanalytic Study of Childhood and Society in India*. Delhi and New York: Oxford University Press.

——— (1985). Psychoanalysis and non-Western cultures. *International Review of Psycho-Analysis* 12:441–448.

——— (1989). The maternal-feminine in Indian psychoanalysis. *International Review of Psycho-Analysis* 16:355–362.

Khatri, A. (1970). Personality and mental health of Indians (Hindus) in the context of their changing family organization. In *The Child in His Family*, ed. E. J. Anthony, pp. 389–412. New York: Wiley.

Kirschner, S. (1996). *The Religious and Romantic Origins of Psychoanalysis: Individuation and Integration in Post-Freudian Theory*. New York: Cambridge University Press.

Levy-Warren, M. (1996). *The Adolescent Journey: Development, Identity Formation, and Psychotherapy*. Northvale, NJ: Jason Aronson.

Mahler, M. (1975). *The Psychological Birth of the Human Infant: Symbiosis and Individuation*. New York: Basic Books.

Ramanujam, B. (1992). The implications of some psychoanalytic concepts in the Indian context. In *Psychoanalytic Anthropology after Freud: Essays Marking the Fiftieth Anniversary of Freud's Death*, ed. D. Spain, pp. 122–133. New York: Psyche Press.

Roland, A. (1988). *In Search of Self in India and Japan: Toward a Cross-Cultural Psychology.* Princeton, NJ: Princeton University Press.

———— (1996a). *Cultural Pluralism and Psychoanalysis. The Asian and North American Experience.* New York: Routledge.

———— (1996b). How universal is the psychoanalytic self? In *Reaching Across Boundaries of Culture and Class: Widening the Scope of Psychotherapy,* ed. R. Perez-Foster, M. Moskowitz, and R. Javier, pp. 57–84. Northvale, NJ: Jason Aronson.

Settlage, C. (1985). Epilogue: psychoanalysis as a humanistic science. In *New Ideas in Psychoanalysis: The Process of Change in a Humanistic Science,* ed. C. Settlage and R. Brodbank, pp. 319–330. Hillsdale, NJ: Analytic Press.

8

THE IMPACT OF THE CULTURAL HOLDING ENVIRONMENT ON PSYCHIC DEVELOPMENT

Concluding Reflections

Henri Parens, M.D.

As psychoanalysis is entering its second century, it is timely for us to loosen our peremptory grip on the exclusionary supremacy we have given—and in many corners still maintain—to understanding our patients psychoanalytically solely from our findings in the clinical situation, and to allow explorations of the importance of personality formation and, on the one hand, psychopathology of biology, of genes, and biochemical physiology, and, on the other, of society, culture, and ethnicity. It is to the latter domain that this M. S. Mahler symposium has addressed itself.

Drs. Freeman, Mehta, and Miles have each opened a window on that vast domain of forces at play in identity formation, the domain of culture, race, and ethnicity. Dr. Carlotta Miles correctly lays out a panoramic view of the complex network of subcultures within what many of us too simplistically assume to be *the* African-American culture. It is not *a* culture in America, Dr. Miles tells us, but a *set of subcultures*. Dr. Purnima Mehta focuses her analytic microscope down and privileges us with the view of a developing, struggling adolescent girl of immigrant Indian parents. Here we get a glimpse of both the struggle experienced by her South-Asian parents transplanted into a culture meaningfully different than that which organized their primary identifications, as well as their daughter's normative adolescent tasks of development, focusing especially on the influence of two well-defined cultures on this adolescent's identity formation. Dr. Daniel M. A. Freeman brings his multidisciplinary expertise and erudition to bear on the view he opens to us of Japanese culture by looking at it from the lens of its residual essense, its mythology. Having long explored and studied his topic, Dr. Freeman brings unique knowledge to his detailing of a large piece of the separation-individuation process organized over millennia by Japanese culture.

As we consider Dr. Mehta's single case study, Dr. Miles's sociopsychological study, and Dr. Freeman's mythology-derived cultural study, the expanding panoramic view of the issue they address lends itself—without, however, promising an answer—to the central question: Do major tasks of development differ from culture to culture?

In *An Outline of Psycho-Analysis*, Freud (1940) said that in the rearing of the child, the parents are the representatives of society, that is, of culture, of race, and of ethnicity. Freud, the first object-relations theorist, spoke again and again of the influence of the parents on the developing child. From his defining object relatedness as either narcissistic or anaclitic (1914), to his embedding drive theory in object relations (e.g., a drive, to be considered an instinctual drive, requires an object; thus, the libido is anaclitic[1] [1915]),

---

[1]It seems insufficiently appreciated that when he defined what constituted an instinctual drive, Freud (1915) stated that it consisted of an aim, a force, a somatic source, and an object. Inherently, then, a drive is anaclitic; to be an instinctual drive it requires an object. In this, the libido drives and forges attachment (Parens and Saul 1971). I think it important that Anna Freud (1960) failed to insist on this assumption in drive theory in her caustic criticism of Bowlby, who before had unflatteringly criticized Anna Freud's explanation of the role of libido theory in the child's attachment to the mother (Bowlby 1958). I find it a regrettable dialogue because, I believe, Anna Freud's criticism—along with those of Rene Spitz (1960) and Max Schur (1960)—brought about the rift we have known for years now between psychoanalysis and attachment theory.

to mourning the loss of an object (1917) and that normal development brings about sequential object losses that yield component identifications (1923), to the process of identification itself (1921, 1923), to the structuring of the ego as "the precipitate of past object cathexes" (1923), and similarly so for the development of the superego (1923), to his proposing a separation–anxiety series (1926) in which he first centralized the child's relationship to the mother in early childhood, to his ground-breaking conceptualization of the central role in the genesis of neurotic conflict of the normative Oedipus complex, a triadic object relations complex [1900, 1913, 1923), Freud cast the seeds for our recognition and understanding of the role of the parents, and thus of culture, race, and ethnicity, in identity formation and in the development of the self. It was not, however, until the last year of his life, in 1939, that Freud wrote that the parents are the representatives of the society and the culture in which the child is reared, and that by means of rearing practices and identifications he or she becomes a member of that specific society/culture as if bearing the stamp "Made in U.S.A." or "Made in India."

IDENTITY FORMATION IN A DUAL-CULTURAL ENVIRONMENT: DR. MEHTA'S CONTRIBUTION

Dr. Purnima Mehta leads us, guided by key psychoanalytic theorists Erikson and Winnicott, to an exploration and conceptualization of what Dr. Mehta, following Rakoff, speaks of as one's cultural identity. Linking it to Winnicott's (1960) conceptualization of the multivariant power of the holding environment, Dr. Mehta turns her lens to the arena of cultural identity formation in adolescence:

> As long as cultural issues remain the same, an individual has a period of relative quiet to develop his or her identity. . . . The adolescent's cultural environment complicates an already difficult period of

disequilibrium related to identity development. . . . with cultural upheaval there is a potentially increased difficulty in adolescent identity formation."[2]

We know that many factors contribute to and influence the (structural) ego's developing abilities to cope and, therewith, critically contribute to the evolving sense of self, in terms of Erikson's (1959) ego-identity, Mahler and colleagues' (1975) separation-individuation, Mahler and McDevitt's (1989) emergence of the self, Kohut's (1977) evolving selfobject, and Stern's (1985) progressively evolving self. Among those factors that influence the development of self during adolescence is the larger vessel—society, culture— that dictates the mores and characteristics of the holding environment, including especially the ways these are represented to the child by the family (primary relationships), but also, in latency and adolescence, by peers and other significant adults (secondary relationships). Specific mores and generalizable attitudes of each given culture, society, and ethnic group have impact on the developing self in accord with the degree, nature, and the (often changing) meaning to the self of these attitudes and mores, and the ego's ways and means of coping with these various attitudes and mores. In addition to this complex interplay of forces coming from without and within the self are the specific mores and attitudes that come with specific generations, as each generation perforce seeks to distinguish itself from the parent generation in sufficiently defined forms to facilitate separation from the family of childhood and optimize the adolescent individuation process.

Dr. Mehta's effort is a model that can meaningfully widen the application of psychoanalytic thought to social questions. Her exploration of the Indian-American adolescent she analyzed, specifically in the stir created in this adolescent's identity formation by her living in a dual-culture environment, has large implications for

---

[2]Throughout this chapter unreferenced quotations will come from the author's chapter under discussion.

what it means to be American and for immigration concerns world-wide. Emigration and immigration have vastly increased during the twentieth century, and with this trend multicultural assimilations and accommodations (Piaget 1937) in adolescence must occur. Immigration into economically, politically, and educationally advantaged countries has dramatically increased. The coexistence of multiple cultures is of large concern in Third World countries where national-geographic boundaries have fluctuated. These modifications have an impact on adolescent development and identity formation.

Mehta is right in that we have not addressed sufficiently the effects of growing up in two cultures simultaneously. Yet, it is a phenomenon that has had impact on psychic development probably for millennia. It is especially remarkable that here in the American melting pot we have not sufficiently examined analytically first-generation adolescents reared in immigrant homes where mores and attitudes differ from American ones.

The United States has had immigrants from all corners of the globe. During its first century as a country, up to the early 1900s, the United States essentially consisted of European immigrants—Italians, French, Germans, Poles, and Russians—all molded by coexistence in a new land to assimilate American mores and attitudes. Another component was the enforced, enslaving migration of native Africans, whose tasks of adolescence were not only burdened by cultural differences but also by the ignominious traumatization of enslavement. A third component from the nineteenth century on, has been immigration from Asian cultures. In the twentieth century, there was a large wave of Europeans escaping Hitler in the 1930s and early 1940s, and in the last forty years there has been a dramatic influx from Asian and Central and South American cultures.

Much of the late nineteenth to early twentieth century immigration consisted of Jews. Jewish adolescents have struggled generation after generation to grow up, as Dr. Mehta says, 9 to 5 o'clock in their culture and from 5 to 9 o'clock in their parents' culture. Thus Dr. Mehta's challenge to herself and to us is of enormous dimensions and invites us to the study of this issue.

I disagree on the one hand with Erikson's view that we can't write as Americans, and on the other hand with Kohut that our self identity and representation is essentially constituted of selfobjects. Regarding Dr. Mehta's closing reference to Erikson (1950), yes, we can write about our comings and goings, about our having been and becoming, but we can also write about the *state of being who we are* even as we go from who we have been to who we will yet become. We can write about who we are, here and now (as Gill [1982] insisted in another context). And it is about who we are as individuals, evolving our singular identity formations, apart from as well as a part of those objects who, by means of internalizations and identifications, come to constitute our sense of self and our self representations. Dr. Mehta writes about who her adolescent patient was as well as about who she was becoming.

Dr. Mehta explores many questions in her chapter: (1) What is dual culture? That is, what is challenging to the adolescent's ego and therewith her identity formation that arises from disharmonious or outrightly conflicting attitudes among the two cultures? (2) What burdens does the adolescent experience because of what her immigrant parents feel is unacceptable or undesirable in American culture? The parents feel their Indian cultural identity is in jeopardy by their valuing of American culture. American culture understandably erects obstacles to the perpetuation of the Indian identity in their offspring's generation.[3] (3) What burden does it create for the adolescent that her parents at times experienced aspects of American culture as unacceptable and undesirable so as to explain troublesome but normal adolescent–parent conflicts, such as the adolescent battles of wills that are spinoffs from the adolescent development–syntonic continuing individuation (Blos 1967) and the shifting cathexes from the parents of childhood to the peer group (Parens and Saul 1971)?

---

[3]Elsewhere, following some of Freud's (1940) seminal thinking on this question, I have proposed what some of the factors are, as well as how and why specific cultural identifications occur and lead to healthy culture- and ethno-specific identifications (Parens 1996).

These three questions may not be easy to sort out. As Dr. Mehta readily recognized, it was essential to "disentangle Nina's symptoms as a troubled, unhappy youngster from any significant cultural influences and determinants." What in Nina caused her to be so troubled as to attempt suicide? Were there intrapsychic conflicts? Past troubled relationships with her parents, including the traumatic effects of having a narcissistic mother and unavailable father who rationalized their daughter's emotional problems as being caused by American mores and attitudes? Conflicting pressures coming from her parents on the one hand and her peer group on the other, which she could not comfortably mediate?

Dr. Mehta, as the analyst of this adolescent, had the opportunity to experience directly Nina's parents' cultural input. But was it a cultural expectation the parents had of Dr. Mehta when they hoped that an Indian psychiatrist would be more familiar and allow a friendlier interaction between them and her, and be less firm about time and money, as Dr. Mehta tells us? Are psychiatrists in India less formal than American psychiatrists? The data suggest that both Nina and her parents at times self-protectively rationalized their difficulties as arising from cultural disharmonies.

I am not unsympathetic to these parents. They had all the problems that come with rearing three average and demanding latency/adolescent children plus the problems of their both being responsibility-laden professionals. But in addition, it is they who especially felt the burden of being immigrants, as Akhtar (1995) has so elegantly conceptualized, of being a dyad of Indian parents, and of being the parents of an adolescent who after years of evidencing emotional problems attempted suicide. As Dr. Mehta recognized, the challenges to this family of changing and not changing, including modifying and resisting the modification of self representations, and of adapting to two well-defined and conflicting sets of mores and attitudes, superimpose a heavy burden on the normally difficult tasks of life facing both adolescent and parents. It is noteworthy that analysts living in this nation of immigrants have not addressed this subject more widely.

While recognizing that "the two cultures took on a variety of meanings for both parents [and adolescent patient] from the start," Dr. Mehta saw clearly that Nina's problems had intrapsychic and interpersonal dynamics only too well known to us in America. She feared her sexuality, she felt unloved and libidinally deprived, attaching "herself rapidly to me with an object hunger suggestive of preoedipal disruption." And, she suffered from "significant masochistic trends in order to deal with a narcissistically preoccupied mother and an invested, but busy father." Not distinctive Indian! Not distinctive American! These factors could be found anywhere in the world.

In addition to and as part of Nina's analysis, Dr. Mehta tried to focus on the effect of culture on identity formation. Dr. Mehta links the issue of dual/multiculturalism with the issue of prejudice, a long-term interest of mine (1996). Because Nina was disappointed at the slow pace of change brought about by her analytic treatment— a universal complaint—she perceived it emotionally to be due to Dr. Mehta's being Indian, just like her mother. The more or less split-off disappointing transference object, the bad mother, as Dr. Mehta rightly observes. It is because she is "Indian!" Antoine Hani (1995) has spoken of prejudice against the self, against one's own race or religion, as did Jean-Paul Sartre decades ago in his treatise on anti-Semitism. I have come across African-American patients who do not want to see a black doctor as well as women who do not want to see a woman doctor. The need to reject a denigrated component self representation played its part in Nina's struggle for identity formation, and it does so in prejudice as well.

Dr. Mehta tells us that Nina's not being a "real American" had impact on her self representation. She felt contempt for herself as well as for her analyst and her Indian parents, who insisted on this cultural split. Adding to Nina's intrapsychic dynamics is her parents' own deprecation of Indian families, who, in their efforts to cope, turn to each other for support. They feel interdependent in this foreign land where autonomy and self-reliance (independence) are prized. (See Akhtar [1995] for a detailed view of the complex fabric of intrapsychic challenges experienced by the immigrant self.)

Some prejudice is seen in both Nina and her parents feeling that anything Dr. Mehta did that disappointed or troubled them was "American." For instance, Dr. Mehta's "analytic neutrality . . . was viewed as too American and cold by both the patient and her parents." And adding to prejudice against the self, Nina's perceiving Dr. Mehta as "gratifying and indulging" caused Nina to view her "as soft, weak, and Indian." Nina had constructed internal representations of what is "Indian" and what is "American," and these served as symbols or explanatory paradigms for what she perceived as "good" and as "bad." For Nina and her parents, each symbol had the potential of being either good or bad, depending on the play of intrapsychic and interpersonal dynamics.

Nina's story reveals the confusing interplay of the three questions I posed above. Dr. Mehta teases them out quite well. For example, she proposes that the fact that Nina is an American child with an acquired Indian identity, and that her parents are Indians with an acquired American identity, creates a "primarily derived child–parent developmental conflict, which can, depending on the parent's responses to the child's birth in America, become neurotic if not addressed." No doubt factual cultural differences did create a burden on Nina, but good use was made of these differences to protect against intrapsychic and interpersonal problems. For instance, Nina chose an Indian boyfriend as a solution to her own pubertal-age "danger situation," her sexual anxiety (A. Freud 1958). As Dr. Mehta puts it, Nina made it a "cultural conflict," converted by externalization from an intrapsychic conflict. Here we see the defensive use of her Indian versus American culture choice to fend off id versus ego–superego conflict-derived overwhelming anxiety.

Dr. Mehta does not just speak of Nina, the adolescent. She touches also on the preadolescent's experience of being an American child of South-Asian parental origins, including the critical issue of skin-color differences and skin-color anxiety, a point also touched on by Dr. Miles. Dr. Mehta is also very engaged by and concerned with Nina's immigrant parents, and in a professional manner sympathizes with the dilemmas facing them as Indian parents of their American-born child. In addition, Dr. Mehta draws on her own experience as the analyst of Nina, some of it as an actual Indian transference object, and some of it from her countertransference, with a "core identity [that is] Indian, [and an] acquired identity [that] is American." This fact has impact on her treatment of Nina, who, on the other hand, has a core identity that is American, and an acquired identity that is Indian. There are consequences, as Dr. Mehta suggests, of this dissimilarity between her and Nina that helped shape Nina's transference.

SOCIOPSYCHOLOGICAL VIEW OF A CULTURE: DR. MILES'S CONTRIBUTION

Dr. Carlotta Miles has opened our eyes to yet another insufficiently explored domain of human experience that is relevant to our understanding the influences that forge psychic development and to our clinical work. It is especially relevant to the goal of problem prevention and to the application of psychiatric and psychoanalytic knowledge to the rearing of the next generation. Freud (1933) wrote that the application of what we learn in the psychoanalytic clinical situation to the rearing of our children would be the avenue by which psychoanalysis would make its greatest contribution to society. The same holds for psychiatry in general (Parens 1988, 1993a,b, Parens et al. 1997).

Dr. Miles shows what mental health professionals can do to have impact on society in general and specifically on the African-American community. The frame of her thesis is that, based on socioeconomic class parameters, the African-American population consists of three subcultures. Relevant to development-forging influences and development-promoting strategies, Dr. Miles discusses "the child-rearing practices of three distinct African-American cultures: the lower/underclass; the middle-middle class; and the upper-middle and upper class, or 'elite blacks.'"

Dr. Miles profiles key characteristics among these three groups. Regarding child-rearing practices, she poignantly experiences the underclass child asking, "Are you my mother?" For these children, healthy attachment and basic trust, the keystones of emotional-adaptive development, are jeopardized. Basic to this inference and all that rests on it, including healthy/unhealthy separation-individuation, Oedipus complex experiencing, the development of adaptive capabilities (ego functions), and of conscience formation, is Dr. Miles's observation that "bonds are made and broken randomly and little attention is paid to separation anxiety." And this occurs where there are "multiple siblings and therefore large, extended families idealizing, but not practicing, the 'village concept' of child-rearing."

In the lower/underclass, given that infants "may show little or no evidence of [attachment] to the mother . . . or in the worst cases may simply be depersonalized . . . many babies have the initial attachment phase interrupted." From here, they do not form an age-appropriate positive sense of self or of object relations, nor do they go through an age-appropriate normal-enough separation-individuation. It is not their biogenetic potentials that fail them; it is their experiences.

Where there is some degree of attachment—commonly a D-type attachment[4] (Crittenden 1988)—another jeopardizing experience occurs: a too-early displacement by a new baby, along with the mother's inability to adequately care for the older child who then "develops a negative association with separation and [intensification] . . . of ambivalence" toward self and relationships. I too have documented research findings and impressions (Parens 1970), as Dr. Miles says, that in this population "there is [insufficient] basic understanding of parenting . . . skills or of child development, [and that commonly] discipline is punitive. . . . Children are not pro-

---

[4]A D-type attachment refers to a child who has a troubled, disorganized attachment to the mother.

tected, and . . . are typically traumatized to the point of *lowering their cognitive abilities*" (italics added).

Dr. Miles asks, rhetorically I think, whether exposure to much violence "with little apparent value of the lives of others and little ability to . . . mourn losses . . . is because there has been so little cathexis of early objects?" I agree with her, on this and on the assumption that there is a consequent pathological limitation and restriction of intellectual functions of the ego. The study we reported in 1970 that thrust us into formal parenting work and research was especially determined by our finding compromised adaptive—including cognitive—functioning and development based on poor attachment and object relations associated with excessive traumatization in children reared in dysfunctional families, as described by Dr. Miles.

Dr. Miles's thoughts about why our therapeutic efforts with this population have such a high failure rate as well as the finding that many from this population do not avail themselves of the services in their neighborhoods are right on the mark: "There is little basis for trust" in the provider—that is, basic mistrust makes the object not trustworthy (Erikson 1959)—nor is the provider an object in whom and from whom emotional investment can be expected or counted on—that is, failure in object constancy as defined by Mahler. Indeed, ambivalence toward the mother is profound in many, and rage and hate fuel much of the violence.

The Middle and Upper Classes

The differences Dr. Miles describes between the experiences of the child in the lower/underclass who wonders "Are you my mother?" and the middle-class child's experience of giving his/her mother's life meaning—"My child is my life"—are great. In middle- and upper-class families the nuclear family is organized and has integrity and relative stability, even with and in spite of the fact that 46.5 percent of these black families in 1994 had "a single female householder." (While the single-parent family is at serious disadvantage on a number of major parameters—aloneness-loneliness, sole-solitary responsibility for child rearing, single income for the parent, and single parent and object hunger for missing father or missing mother—it is well established that many single parents do a remarkably good job of child rearing and homemaking, providing in ample measure a child's basic emotional and physical needs.)

I was puzzled by Dr. Miles's finding a dilution of attachment to the mother when an African-American infant from a middle-class family is cared for by a caregiver of a different skin color. I agree that, beyond 3 or 4 years of age, it can engender conflicted feelings about the child's own skin color, as is the case with any child of any ethnic-racial group who becomes attached to a substitute caregiver (at a secondary level[5]) from another ethnic or racial group. However, that this attachment to a substitute caregiver can bring about a dilution of the child's emotional investment in the well-enough bonded mother[6] I find puzzling. I would have expected a broadening of acceptance of a secondary object with a different skin color without a dilution in a primary object attachment, or even

---

[5]Object relatedness can be classified according to the level of emotional "energy" (cathexis) invested in the object. Thus, as was proposed elsewhere (Parens et al. 1997), we invest in objects so as to form with them primary, secondary, and tertiary relationships. We form primary relationships with our mothers, fathers, children, mates, and possibly grandparents, a favorite aunt or uncle, or a rare other object who comes to mean that much to us. The loss of any one of these objects leads to and requires a full mourning process to resolve the pain induced by that loss. We form secondary relationships with good friends, favored cousins, aunts, and uncles, favored teachers, and specially valued neighbors. The loss of such an object causes us some distress, leads us to empathize with and feel sympathy for those for whom this person is a primary object, but it does not lead to a mourning process in us. The loss of a tertiary relationship—formed with objects we cathect modestly—causes us no personal distress, though we can empathize and sympathize with those for whom this is a meaningful loss. In this sense, the attachment an infant makes to the stable substitute caregiver usually leads to its evolving into a secondary relationship.

[6]I use the concept *attachment* (as used in the psychoanalytic and attachment literature) strictly to refer to the child's tie to her/his mother, and the concept *bonding* (Klaus and Kennell 1976) to mean the mother's tie to her child. I do this within the context that what happens between child and mother (and father, too) to effect both attachment and bonding is absolutely interactive and reciprocal.

in some circumstances the formation of two primary object relationships.

I believe that infants are well capable of forming several primary attachments without dilution of any one of these primary love objects. These attachments differ along parameters I shall describe below, but they do not lessen or dilute the eventual emotional investment the infant makes in each one. I base this view on the assumption that quality—age-appropriate intensity and goodness—of attachment is most determined by the qualitaty of the parent–child relationship. The structuring of the libidinal object (Spitz 1946, 1965) is gradual during the first year of life, and its stability is profoundly influenced by the quality of parent–child interaction, a point on which child analytic researchers agree (A. Freud, Spitz, Bowlby, Winnicott, Mahler, Provence, Sander, Stern, Greenspan, Parens, and others). Voluminous work by attachment researchers, starting with Mary Ainsworth's pioneering efforts (Ainsworth et al. 1978, Ainsworth and Wittig 1969), categorize attachment by its qualitative interactional parameters and imply that the stability and degree of attachment is embedded in these qualitative interactional parameters.

Why did Dr. Miles find such dilution of attachment? Were these mothers in some way insufficiently emotionally available to their infants? If not qualitatively so, perhaps in the amount of time spent with their babies? I do agree with what Margaret Mahler (1969) said to Barbara Walters in a television interview, that a somewhat variable but minimum amount of good quality time must be spent with the infant for a healthy attachment to develop. Although the infant is primed biogenetically to attach to (an) object(s), there are qualitative and quantitative requirements of the object to give to attachment its potentially variable (phenotypic) but positive characteristics. This point is agreed upon by many infant researchers and is the focus of the debate on whether or not it is harmful for infants less than 1 year of age to be in day care—to be separated from their mothers—for more than twenty hours a week (Parens et al. 1988). The Scandinavian countries, way ahead of other countries in the implementation and study of day-care effects, have for years discouraged day care for children under 18 months of age, accommo-dating the financial strain this imposes on young families by paying stay-at-home mothers a substantial part of the salary they were earn-ing in the workplace.

But this issue is complicated because children can form mul-tiple but different primary attachments with no difficulty. They form a specific and unique attachment to mother, and one to father, and one even to siblings. Of critical importance are the object's emo-tional investment in, responsiveness to, and expectations of the in-fants. And we see that infants turn to these objects on the basis of specific needs and functions they assign to each parent—mother for comforting, father for play and excitement. Even during the first year, infants can and do form multiple attachments usually in a hier-archical and function-dependent way without dilutions if object relatedness is good. If Dr. Miles proves to be right that "one sees a diluted attachment to mother" in middle-class African-American children when cared for by a caregiver of "radically different . . . color and features," further exploration of this finding is needed. In no way does my question take away from Dr. Miles's finding that such color differences lead to a "color tagging," and that color of skin does raise questions, can create doubts about self and object, and may in some facilitate self-hatred.

When the middle-class families Dr. Miles tells us about were compared to the lower/underclass parents, there was a "dramatic . . . superego development, with typical, traditional middle-class concern for reputation, reliability and accountability, and appro-priate behavior and respect for authority figures, especially parents and grandparents," and "there are very high expectations for edu-cational achievement." There are serious problems in child rear-ing, as I found, too (Parens 1988), based on misunderstandings of children's behaviors such as separation anxiety—one of the key indices of attachment (Parens 1972, Spitz 1965)—and based on believing that "the 'good' baby is the one who will go to anyone and the 'difficult' baby is the one who insists on choosing." We have found, in research and in the clinical setting, serious problems in child rearing based on such misunderstandings, due to lack of information and culture-specific traditional convictions, not only of normal child development but also of how to optimize normal development—our definition of parenting—across all socioeconomic strata and ethnic groups in American and European countries. This is true as well for the African-American upper-middle and upper classes Dr. Miles describes. This group, Dr. Miles tells us, "shares many characteristics with parallel Caucasian-American cultures, [although] there are significant differences, some of which relate to child rearing."

I would ask Dr. Miles what findings lead her to the view that, in contrast to the African-American middle class, in the upper-middle and upper class African-American families "while surrogates are important, *the mother is the primary maternal figure to whom the child is firmly bonded*" (italics added). One distinction is that the upper-middle and upper-class mother is not as oppressed as the middle-class single mother, due to the latter's economic strains and the lack of a mate. But the lack of a mate does not operate as an oppressive factor in the 48 percent of lower middle class mothers for whom the "diluted attachment" finding occurs too, according to Dr. Miles. It is clear that the stress of economic strains is a large, oppressive factor for the lower middle class families.

On the other hand, I am not convinced that the young children of the better-off black families being given more than they may need in material things is what secures the absolutely primary object relatedness their mothers enjoy. I do not believe that material indulgence is a strong factor in optimizing, in young children, libidinal investment in objects. While children need sufficient material gratification, and can be seduced by material offerings such as sweets and toys, this is not the stuff that gives the structuring of the libidinal object stability, nor that establishes basic trust; in other words, it is just not the stuff of which a B–type attachment[7] is made.

---

[7] A B–type attachment refers to a child who has a very secure attachment to the mother.

Where I think the "color tagging" matters in our African-American families, as Dr. Miles brings home to us so clearly, is that racism impacts powerfully on both perpetrators and victims, and leads to accommodations, or the lack thereof, aimed at securing safe and healthy survival. This occurs in child-rearing practices across ethnic and racial groups in all corners of the globe. It seems unavoidable, given that there are ethnic and racial majorities and minorities everywhere, and that many factors bring about human discontent, that minorities come to be blamed for all sorts of discontents as an outgrowth of normal identificatory self-organizing processes that miscarry (Parens 1996a).

CULTURE THROUGH THE PRISM OF ITS MYTHOLOGY: DR. FREEMAN'S CHAPTER

Dr. Daniel Freeman engages us in a comparative cross-cultural study not only to look at one of the oldest Far Eastern cultures, but also to be looked at by them at the same time. "We and they at times . . . see or experience phenomena from different perspectives," he says. He encourages us "to recognize ways in which our cultural filters are organizing our understanding of emotional data within culture-bound categories."

Dr. Freeman's many years of study of Japanese child development, specifically of separation–individuation and its clinical applications, his many interchanges with Japanese colleagues, and his notable knowledge of Japanese mythology make his work a valuable source of information. While the Japanese interest in psychoanalysis dates from the early 1900s and, as Freeman tells us, Freud's, Klein's, and Winnicott's writings are well known there, Freeman's own studies of separation–individuation as seen in Japanese mythology have significantly contributed to the recently growing Japanese interest in separation–individuation theory. In fact, Freeman was instrumental in the distribution of Margaret Mahler's films to five universities in Japan.

On the Separation-Individuation
Process in the Japanese Child

Dr. Freeman tells us that the Japanese mother, who especially "values intimate physical contact with her infant"—the infant sleeps with her in the same room as the rest of the family—has a much closer physical relationship with her infant than is the case in many other societies. Freeman finds that in general the Japanese mother "feels herself to be 'at one with' the baby," whereas the "American mother tends to perceive her infant as a separate individual with his or her own needs and feelings," and accommodates to her infant accordingly. The Japanese mother relies more on nonverbal communication, on touch and movement cues, whereas the American mother values reciprocal vocalization and encourages autonomy. Thus, Freeman tells us, the intimate experience of the Japanese infant "fosters a sense of trust, optimism, and shared omnipotence." In optimal circumstances he is surely right. Interestingly, under optimal circumstances, the American infant's experience with his mother, too, fosters good basic trust, optimism, and shared omnipotence. A similarly good degree of basic trust and optimism can be achieved in both ways of the mother being with her baby, because the common denominator is the qualitative libidinal investment made by the mother in her child, the normal child—of any culture—being, in turn, biogenetically primed to progressively invest emotionally in her/his mother in full measure.

It is regrettable that infants' and children's crying seems universally problematic. It is not just the Japanese mother who is made uncomfortable, even embarrassed when her baby cries. So is the American mother—and those around the baby. The reasons are multiple. My concern is that the outcome for the infant is troublesome. What is regrettable is that this negative parental reaction universally interferes with the mother's natural and powerful ability to soothe and comfort her unpleasure-experiencing child. Indeed as Spitz (1965) remarked, it is rather universal that our coenesthetic perception of affects, in ourselves and in others, which is essential for the capacity for empathy, is interfered with by parents' efforts to suppress some of their children's natural and desirable awareness and reasonable expression of feelings.

Freeman's study, by virtue of the valuable inroads it makes into a specific line of development and the child-rearing practices that influence it, raises our ability to propose prevention strategies. In this spirit, I want to develop a point that grows out of my reading of Dr. Freeman's thoughts and to address a critical assumption I believe he makes. He suggests that discontinuities in the mother's holding behaviors and ways of relating that facilitate and gratify the infant's symbiotic experiencing activate the process of differentiation and individuation in the infant. He refers to Mahler (Mahler et al. 1975) in support of this idea. In my reading of Mahler, I find her suggesting that where there are failures in the mother's providing a symbiosis-fostering milieu, differentiation and individuation may compensatorily be activated early or it may be delayed. Similarly, stranger reactions and separation anxiety may be intensified by maternal behaviors that do not optimize the infant's symbiosis, but this can in other infants lessen the intensity or frequency of these structuring-of-the-libidinal-object indices (Spitz 1946, 1965), or attachment indices (Parens 1972).

This is my concern: I do not believe that differentiation and individuation are inherently activated by default, by discontinuities in the mother's symbiosis-facilitating behaviors. Differentiation and individuation, which I assume to be universal, are activated by a powerful biogenetically preprogrammed thrust to autonomy that, especially during the practicing subphase, leads to battles of wills (and the first conflict of ambivalence) (Parens 1979a,b, 1989). In our observational experience we found that at about 6 months of age, with the psychobiologic differentiation Spitz (1965) spoke of as the era of "the second psychic organizer" (believed by him then to be 7- to 8-month anxiety), a noteworthy upsurge of aggression occurs that fuels the thrust to autonomy, as if it turns it on, and is soon followed by entry into the practicing subphase (Parens 1979a, 1980, 1989, Parens and Pollock 1978). This active biogenetically preprogrammed process, I believe, is what triggers differentiation and individuation.

It is this, I suggest, that the Japanese mother probably *feels* stirring in her 6-month-old that leads her to responsively reinforce "the tendency in her infant to look beyond the boundaries of [his] symbiosis"; and, again, this I would suggest is what makes Japanese mothers want "their sons to become as precocious and powerful as the fabled super-boy Kintaro [and] . . . their daughters to achieve . . . self control and etiquette at a very young age." However, side by side with encouraging her infant's looking beyond the symbiosis and wanting him to achieve, the Japanese mother tends to bring about controls much earlier in development than the American mother over what I consider to be autonomy behaviors. Freeman tells us that "systematic teaching of restraint, orderliness, propriety . . . begins in the second half of the first year, earlier than in many other cultures." In Japan, the infant's "mother begins to systematically shape his behavior, teaching control of posture and movement, respect behavior, control of affective expression, and cleanliness." This occurs, Freeman points out, "before practicing subphase behavioral issues concerning autonomy and motoric activity become prominent, [and that this then] tends to decrease subsequent negative struggles."

I have proposed that the upsurge of (nondestructive) aggression that inherently fuels the thrust to autonomy—the thrust to become an initiator, a generator of action—is what sets differentiation and individuation in motion. I wonder if this upsurge of aggression is what the Japanese mother responds to with the controlling, shaping, and guiding behaviors Freeman describes. Two culturally determined outcomes he reports may follow from this precocious structuring and containing tendency in the Japanese mother: (1) the tendency to fewer "negative struggles," and (2) the "relatively prolonged . . . process of separation-individuation that lasts considerably longer than in Western culture."

Regarding the tendency to fewer negative struggles, a number of Freeman's descriptions give me the impression that, on the one hand, the Japanese mother is much more patient and tolerant of her infant's "disruptive, assertive, and aggressive behavior," that she gives the child "the responsibility to figure things out . . . and to self-regulate [and that she] gently guides him, and quietly makes her expectations clear." On the other hand, though, she begins to regulate her infant's autonomy behaviors "systematically" as soon as they begin, from about 6 months of age on. Two questions follow from this: (1) Is the gain of fewer negative struggles, which we call "battles of wills," at the expense of overly containing the development of autonomy? Is this guiding of autonomy or is it overly controlling and therefore thwarting of autonomy? In my view the thrust to autonomy comes from the same nucleus of self that contains primary narcissism, and it is the most generative factor in the self, the factor that gives rise to initiative and creativity. (2) Is the Japanese mother overly idyllically portrayed by Freeman or is she in fact, as he describes, so patient and tolerant due to her own very early disciplined and very well contained affects and behaviors? To be sure, many American parents and their children would benefit greatly from better containment of their own affects, impulses, and behaviors.

Regarding the relatively prolonged separation-individuation, is the prolongation of this development influenced by the high valuing of *amae* in and of itself? Is it due to the fact that following millennia of child rearing the Japanese are culturally systematically regulating too early their children's thrust to autonomy, that thing in the infant that drives differentiation and individuation? Or is it due to an imbalance in favor of *amae* over autonomy and individuation? Does it create a problem for development to culturally prolong separation-individuation, or does it simply shape development differently with no cost to the individual or society?

On Emotional Refueling

Freeman's focus on emotional refueling touches on what I too, for thirty years, have found of substantial clinical and child-rearing concern in our American culture—the anxiety created in our autonomy-enhancing culture by the normal recurrent dependency needs for the libidinal, nonerotic, gratification people experience. Patients view themselves as immature because they need libidinal nonerotic (as well as erotic) gratification, or in other words, they need the emotional availability of an object. To an extent in our culture we have made pathogenic what is epigenetically age-appropriate, normal dependence. Parens and Saul (1971) detail this concern in an epigenetic conceptualization of dependence/self-reliance in humans. F. A. Johnson's *Dependency and Japanese Socialization* (1993), relying heavily on the work of Doi, addresses the problem of our cultural resistance to what the Japanese identify as *amae*. I regret that Doi's own treatise on *The Anatomy of Dependence* (1973) was not published before our own effort, because it would have given further weight to our own thesis that there is a then unexplained—I have since come to postulate a plausible cause (see below)—resistance to normal dependence in our culture.

I have wondered about the role of normal epigenetic dependence in humans and what Kohut conceptualized as selfobjects. Kohut's emphasis is on the development of self and narcissism. But he was also clearly cognizant of the powerful need for the object— as are all analysts since Freud (1915)—as attached to the self to give the sense of self-integrity. It seems to me, though, that in Kohut's emphasis on self structuralization, the dependence on the object was insufficiently profiled. Viewed from one of its facets, the *selfobject* concept envelops the self's dependence on the object by integrating the object into the self representation. However, the selfobject as a lifelong internal self representation does not account for two crucial aspects of self: (1) It does not account for the self as independent from the object, as an autonomous self, the self whose core is primary narcissism, as Freud defined it, and as it eventually evolves by the separation-individuation process. (2) It does not point to the continuing epigenetic dependence of the self on the extant object(s), that is, that we have recurrent needs for gratification by the object(s).

Returning to Freeman's considerations of emotional refueling in Japanese culture, he rightly points to the beneficial value in emotional development of *amae*. Recognizing, as Freeman emphasizes, the difficulty inherent in concept translation, be it from language to language or from model to model (Parens 1997), as Doi and Johnson have seen, there are significant similarities in *amae* and what we emphasized to be libidinal needs, especially the nonerotic libidinal needs humans experience epigenetically throughout life (Parens and Saul 1971).

In our autonomy-enhancing American culture, I wonder if dependence anxiety or perhaps, more correctly, loss of autonomy anxiety makes us repudiate normal dependency needs even to the point that, as Ribble said in 1943, parents in America cannot tolerate dependence even in their infants!

Freeman is addressing emotional refueling, that key concept from separation–individuation theory, not the question I am raising pertaining to the vicissitudes of autonomy and individuation. But his emphasis on the rich way the Japanese mother provides her child with *amae* leads me to ask whether there is any evidence that the culturalization of *amae* comes at the cost of thwarting the Japanese infant's normal thrust to autonomy. Is there a link between *amae* and holding on too tightly, not allowing individuation? Does culture urge the Japanese mother to coerce *amae*, to demand that the child indulge himself in *amae*? *Amae*, Freeman says, may be "implicitly offered." But Freeman also tells us that the child is gradually helped to not expect unreasonable gratifications of his wish for *amae*. This would speak against the assumption that she coerces or demands *amae* indulgence.

In my prevention and clinical work with parents (Parens 1988, 1993a, Parens et al. 1997) in the United States, recognizing its value to healthy development in children, I recommend that parents offer, but not coerce, their libidinal availability, that crucial component of what Mahler conceptualized as "emotional availability" (Mahler et al. 1975). By contrast to the Japanese parent's valuing *amae*, her gratifying her child's libidinal needs, making herself emotionally available to her infant for that sector of his needs, a major problem we have often encountered in America is the young mother who commonly worries that if she holds her baby, the baby will grow into an overly dependent person. Many a mother has told me, "My mother says that I'm spoiling my baby by holding him when he wants me to. I'm holding him too much she says; he'll never want to be on his own!" Many parents in our culture fail to recognize two points: (1) that being emotionally available and providing *amae* in reasonable doses when asked for by the child optimizes the development of the child's sense of self and self-reliance, whereas thwarting *amae* excessively intensifies libidinal need and the child's dependency—as withholding food from the hungry child intensifies hunger; and (2) that the thrust to autonomy is freed up and facilitated when the child's libidinal needs are sufficiently gratified.

Too many American parents do not recognize that there is a powerful thrust to autonomy, to asserting oneself on self and environment (Parens 1979a) in the normal child, and that it will be felt by the infant who indeed will *not* want to be held by mother or be on her lap. Just looking at their infants would inform them that there is a powerful thrust to get off that lap, out of those arms, explore, and do things. Many parents do not see this until they run into battles of wills with their young child when they set limits! Then, unfortunately, because of the negative reactions set into motion by the battles of wills, they experience the child's behavior as narcissistic orneriness and stubbornness. I think that most parents everywhere fail to recognize that the battle of wills is an interpersonal conflict caused by the parent's thwarting—often quite reasonably so—the child's thrust to autonomy, which is fueled by the child's nondestructive aggression and motivated by the need to master self and the new world into which the child was born. And in normal children, it has ample power, given that it serves self-preservation (Parens 1979a).

What Freeman's study shows us is, whether or not the Japanese mother values *amae* (possibly without being aware of its great value to the emotional health of the child), she knows that by her culturally advocated, early, overly disciplined control of her child's thrust to autonomy she is making the mirror error made by too many American parents, who value (probably without being aware of its inner strength) their child's thrust to autonomy and fear gratifying the child's normal libidinal dependency needs. If I am mistaken about this assumption about the Japanese mother, hurrah for Japanese mothers!

DO MAJOR TASKS OF DEVELOPMENT DIFFER FROM CULTURE TO CULTURE?

As I believe all psychoanalysts do, I assume universalities in psycho-biological differentiation development in humans, that across races and cultures psychic development is biogenetically preprogrammed in an epigenetic manner, much as is the case for embryologic differentiation development (Erikson 1950, 1959). But we have an opportunity to revisit this question here and to gain further insight into what factors may influence differences if not in essential developmental potential, then in its actual development, and in different races and cultures of our species.

From what I see in Dr. Mehta's study, I do not find evidence that the tasks of adolescent development inherently differed in her patient from that in the American adolescents I have analyzed. I infer from Dr. Mehta's remarks that she too does not find the normal tasks of development to differ in her Indian–American adolescent from that of American adolescents. Like her American counterparts, Dr. Mehta's patient had to deal with her burgeoning sexuality and sexual identity formation, with her continuing, now adolescent individuation, and with effecting the shift in the centrality of her object cathexes/relations from her family of childhood to the peer group. The tasks are the same; many ways of coping are the same. Take, for example, the devaluation of her parents by the adolescent, a clumsy effort to make them less valuable in order to make the task of separating and individuating from her parents less onerous. American adolescents have to do what Dr. Mehta's Indian-reared adolescent had to do. And like Indian adolescents, many American youngsters whose preadolescent psychic lives already are strained will be at risk for deterioration, if not a breakdown, in adaptive (ego) functioning.

But there are implications in Dr. Mehta's discussion of parametric differences within these tasks of development created by the specifically Indian mores and attitudes Nina's parents lived by. For instance, American parents would love their adolescents to respect them and comply with their wishes, but most know that these will be achieved only to a degree. American families do not expect the time-honored virtues of respect, compliance, and virtuosity in their teenagers as do Indian parents, such as Nina's parents. American families tend not to be so offended or troubled by a relative degree of uncooperativeness and even rebellion in their adolescents. But it is not just among Indian parents that offspring compliance is counted on. Lotte Koehler of Munich is convinced that one of the factors that led to the compliance among German military personel to carry out orders that ran counter to civilized conventions was the fact that compliance with authority among German youth and even adults is highly prized and vigorously inculcated (personal communication). (As I was about to cross a street on a red traffic light in Hamburg, one of my German colleagues gently held me back and, chuckling, told me, "We don't cross the street on a red light in Germany!")

I also infer from Dr. Miles's chapter that she does not hold to development being inherently, biogenetically programmed differently in the three subcultures of our African-American population, as she has conceptualized this group of Americans. I take it that she too makes the assumption I make, that the biogenetically preprogrammed developmental processes, be it the emergence and unfolding of separation-individuation, of attachment, of affects, of the Oedipus complex, or of conscience formation, are inherently the same in every corner of the globe. Every child's (1) biogenetic givens—strengths and vulnerabilities—side by side with (2) the culture, mores, and attitudes in which the child is reared, and (3) the variable individual conditions in every child's life, including (a) specific characteristics in the child–parent dyad as well as (b) the intensity and characteristics of the traumas they sustain, are the inter-active factors that make for the variations we see (Kendler 1996, Kendler and Eaves 1986, Parens 1993b, Parens and Shapiro 1997). That we do not cross the street on a red light in Hamburg is not biogenetically preprogrammed; it is the product of internalized, civilizing limit setting on a thrust to act autonomously, which could be hazardous to self and others. It is in the influence of child rear-ing that we find cross-cultural differences.

Dr. Freeman's chapter yields several conclusions. First, we can infer from it that he does not assume, and that there is no indica-tion that we need assume, an inherently different biogenetic pro-gramming in the Japanese child's separation–individuation than we have come to know in children of Western countries. Second, the Japanese child's separation–individuation is indeed made different from the Western child's by cultural dictates that have evolved over millennia. This is so along two parameters: (1) the Japanese child's separation–individuation stretches over a longer period of develop-mental time than the Western child's; and (2) that libidinal gratifi-cation is provided with greater comfort and positive regard, and it may be that the Japanese child's thrust to autonomy is possibly too vigorously contained in an effort to socialize the child, as compared to the American child. If these assumptions hold, we can hazard two suggestions for both Japanese and American and other parents: we all need ample doses of *amae* along an epigenetic profile, and we all need ample support and guidance in how to master our gen-erative thrust to autonomy.

REFERENCES

Ainsworth, M. D. S., Blehar, M. C., Waters, E., and Wall, S. (1978). *Patterns of Attach-ment: A Psychological Study of the Strange Situation.* Hillsdale, NJ: Lawrence Erlbaum.
Ainsworth, M. D. S., and Wittig, B. A. (1969). Attachment and the exploratory behavior of one-year-olds in a strange situation. In *Determinants of Infant Behavior,* vol. 4, ed. B. M. Foss, pp. 113–136. London: Methuen.

Akhtar, S. (1995). A third individuation: immigration, identity, and the psychoanalytic process. *Journal of the American Psychoanalytic Association* 43:1051–1084.

Blos, P. (1967). The second individuation process in adolescence. *Psychoanalytic Study of the Child* 22:162–186. New York: International Universities Press.

Bowlby, J. A. (1958). The nature of the child's tie to his mother. *International Journal of Psycho-Analysis* 39:350–373.

Crittenden, P. M. (1988). Distorted patterns of relationship in maltreating families: the role of internal representational models. *Journal of Reproductive and Infant Psychology* 6:183–199.

Doi, T. (1973). *The Anatomy of Dependence*. Tokyo: Kodansha International.

Erikson, E. H. (1950). The problem of ego identity. *Journal of the American Psychoanalytic Association* 9:50–121.

——— (1959). Identity and the life cycle. *Psychological Issues Monograph*, No. 1. New York: International Universities Press.

Freud, A. (1958). Adolescence. *Psychoanalytic Study of the Child* 13:255–278. New York: International Universities Press.

——— (1960). Discussion of Dr. John Bowlby's paper. *Psychoanalytic Study of the Child* 15:53–62. New York: International Universities Press.

Freud, S. (1914). On narcissism: an introduction. *Standard Edition* 14:69–102.

——— (1915). Instincts and their vicissitudes. *Standard Edition* 14:111–140.

——— (1917). Mourning and melancholia. *Standard Edition* 14:239–258.

——— (1921). Group psychology and the analysis of the ego. *Standard Edition* 18:67–143.

——— (1923). The ego and the id. *Standard Edition* 19:3–66.

——— (1926). Inhibitions, symptoms, and anxiety. *Standard Edition* 20:77–174.

——— (1933). New introductory lectures on psychoanalysis. *Standard Edition* 22:3–182.

——— (1940). An outline of psycho-analysis. *Standard Edition* 23:141–207.

Gill, M. M. (1982). *Analysis of Transference, Vol. I: Theory and Technique*. New York: International Universities Press.

Hani, A. (1995). *Self-prejudice*. Presented at the Meetings of the American Psychoanalytic Association workshop on prejudice. New York, NY, December.

Johnson, F. A. (1993). *Dependency and Japanese Socialization*. New York: New York University Press.

Kendler, K. S. (1996). Parenting: a genetic-epidemiologic perspective. *American Journal of Psychiatry* 153:11–20.

Kendler, K. S., and Eaves, L. J. (1986). Models for the joint effect of genotype and environment on liability to psychiatric illness. *American Journal of Psychiatry* 143:279–289.

Klaus, M. H., and Kennell, J. H. (1976). *Maternal–Infant Bonding*. St. Louis: C. V. Mosby.

Kohut, H. (1977). *The Restoration of the Self*. New York: International Universities Press.

Mahler, M. S. (1969). Interview with Barbara Walters, "Today Show," March 5.

Mahler, M. S., and McDevitt, J. B. (1989). The separation-individuation process and identity formation. In *The Course of Life, Vol. 1: Infancy and Early Childhood*, ed. S. I. Greenspan and G. H. Pollock, pp. 19–35. Madison, CT: International Universities Press.

Mahler, M. S., Pine, F., and Bergman, A. (1975). *Psychological Birth of the Human Infant*. New York: Basic Books.

Parens, H. (1970). *A preliminary report from the project: correlations of the "libidinal availability" of the mother with the development of psychic structure in the child*. Paper presented at the winter meetings of the American Psychoanalytic Association, New York, NY, December. (Abstract in *Summaries of Scientific Proceedings*.)

—— (1972). Indices of the child's earliest attachment to his mother, applicable in routine pediatric examination. *Pediatrics* 49:600–603.

—— (1979a). *The Development of Aggression in Early Childhood*. New York: Jason Aronson, 1994.

—— (1979b). Developmental considerations of ambivalence, part II of an exploration of the relations of instinctual drives and the symbiosis—separation-individuation process. *Psychoanalytic Study of the Child* 34:385–420. New Haven, CT: Yale University Press.

—— (1980). An exploration of the relations of instinctual drives and the symbiosis—separation-individuation process. Part I: Drive motivation and psychic development—with special reference to aggression and beginning separation-individuation. *Journal of the American Psychoanalytic Association* 28:89–114.

—— (1988). A psychoanalytic contribution toward rearing emotionally healthy children: education for parenting. In *New Concepts in Psychoanalytic Psychotherapy*, ed. J. M. Ross and W. A. Myers, pp. 120–138. Washington, DC: American Psychiatric Press.

—— (1989). Toward an epigenesis of aggression in early childhood. In *The Course of Life, Vol. 2, Early Childhood*, ed. S. I. Greenspan and G. H. Pollock, 2nd ed., pp. 689–721. New York: International Universities Press.

—— (1993a). Toward preventing experience-derived emotional disorders: education for parenting. In *Prevention in Mental Health*, ed. H. Parens and S. Kramer, pp. 121–148. Northvale, NJ: Jason Aronson.

—— (1993b). Does prevention in mental health make sense? An interface of psychoanalysis and neurobiology. In *Prevention in Mental Health*, ed. H. Parens and S. Kramer, pp. 103–120. Northvale, NJ: Jason Aronson.

—— (1996). *The origins of prejudice and of healthy distinctions in identity*. South Asia forum videotape, Philadelphia Psychoanalytic Institute and Society, S. Akhtar, Moderator, October. (Recorded for distribution.)

—— (1997). *Implications for the clinical situation of revisions of the psychoanalytic theory of aggression: Part 1: Theory reformulations, an update*. Presented at the Psychoanalytische Institut, Ulm, Germany, April.

Parens, H., and Pollock, L. (1978). *Toward an Epigenesis of Aggression in Early Childhood, No. 2: Aggression and Beginning Separation-Individuation*, revised. Audio-Visual Section, film #5a, Eastern Pennsylvania Psychiatric Institute, Philadelphia, PA.

Parens, H., and Saul, L.J. (1971). *Dependence in Man: A Psychoanalytic Study*. New York: International Universities Press.

Parens, H., Scattergood, E., Duff, S., and Singletary, W. (1997). *Parenting for Emotional Growth: A Curriculum for Students in Grades K Thru 12. A Textbook and Lesson Plans*. Bala Cynwyd, PA: Parenting for Emotional Growth.

Parens, H., and Shapiro, B. (1997). Expanding the horizon of prevention in mental health (work in progress).

Parens, H., Singletary, W., and Bridger, W. (1988). *Effects of day care on the very young.* Grant proposal for Request for Application–National Institute of Child Health and Human Development.

Piaget, J. (1937). *La Construction du Reel chez l'Enfant.* Neuchatel: Delachaux et Niestle, 1963.

Ribble, M. (1943). *Rights of Infants.* New York: Columbia University Press.

Schur, M. (1960). Discussion of Dr. John Bowlby's paper. *Psychoanalytic Study of the Child* 15:63–84. New York: International Universities Press.

Spitz, R. (1946). The smiling response: a contribution to the ontogenesis of social relations. *Genetic Psychology Monographs* 34:57–125.

———— (1960). Discussion of Dr. John Bowlby's paper. *Psychoanalytic Study of the Child* 15:85–94. New York: International Universities Press.

———— (1965). *The First Year of Life*, with W. G. Cobliner. New York: International Universities Press.

Stern, D. (1985). *The Interpersonal World of the Human Infant.* New York: Basic Books.

Winnicott, D. W. (1960). The theory of the parent–infant relationship. In *The Maturational Processes and the Facilitating Environment*, pp. 37–55. London: Hogarth.

Index